1/'08

For Roger Sc

with warm regards

Jean L Hanson

Love Thy Neighbor As Thyself

Love Thy Neighbor As Thyself

LENN E. GOODMAN

OXFORD
UNIVERSITY PRESS
2008

OXFORD
UNIVERSITY PRESS

Oxford University Press, Inc., publishes works that further
Oxford University's objective of excellence
in research, scholarship, and education.

Oxford New York
Auckland Cape Town Dar es Salaam Hong Kong Karachi
Kuala Lumpur Madrid Melbourne Mexico City Nairobi
New Delhi Shanghai Taipei Toronto

With offices in
Argentina Austria Brazil Chile Czech Republic France Greece
Guatemala Hungary Italy Japan Poland Portugal Singapore
South Korea Switzerland Thailand Turkey Ukraine Vietnam

Published by Oxford University Press, Inc.
198 Madison Avenue, New York, New York 10016

www.oup.com

Library of Congress Cataloging-in-Publication Data
Goodman, Lenn Evan, 1944–
Love thy neighbor as thyself / Lenn E. Goodman.
p. cm.
Includes bibliographical references and index.
ISBN 978-0-19-532882-0
1. Golden rule. 2. Altruism. 3. Brotherliness. 4. Equality—Religious aspects—Judaism. 5. Conduct of life. 6. Judaism—Doctrines.
7. Jewish ethics. I. Title.
BJ1286.G64G66 2007
296.3'6—dc22 2007024219

9 8 7 6 5 4 3 2 1

Printed in the United States of America
on acid-free paper

Preface

It was in my college years at Harvard that I first heard of the Gifford Lectures and dreamed that one day I would travel to Scotland to give lectures on natural theology under those famous auspices. I was reading the Gifford Lectures of William James, the lectures that became *Varieties of Religious Experience.* In graduate school at Oxford, I read other Gifford lectures, most notably C. F. von Weizsacker's series, published as *The Relevance of Science.* Later still, as a young philosophy professor in Hawaii, I read others, including John C. Eccles's series on the mind, published as *The Human Mystery.* But the dream remained just that, until the summer of 2003, when a letter arrived inviting me to deliver Gifford Lectures at the University of Glasgow in the fall of 2005.

I would join lecturers whose presentations went back to those of Max Müller in 1888–1892. Among the past lecturers were A. C. Bradley, Arthur Balfour, Samuel Alexander, J. B. S. Haldane, William Hocking, Ralph Barton Perry, Herbert Butterfield, Richard Southern, Basil Mitchell, Carl Sagan, Richard Dawkins, Anthony Kenny, George Steiner, Mary Warnock, Ralph McInerny, Simon Blackburn, and many more who had spoken at Glasgow about theism and reason.

The topic specified in my invitation was more than congenial: I was to work with three other thinkers, representing Christian, Muslim, and naturalist perspectives, and all of us were to speak on the biblical commandment "Thou shalt love thy neighbor as thyself." My fellow lecturers were John Hare, of Yale Divinity School; Abdulaziz Sachedina, of the University of Virginia; and A. C. Grayling, of the University of London. Each of us would give two lectures, and we would meet for a roundtable and exchange of views, under the chairmanship of Alexander Broadie, the learned occupant of the same chair at Glasgow once held by Adam Smith. A formidable scholar, Broadie trains his erudition on Scottish philosophy. But it extends to many another field, and to eras long before the time of John Scotus Eriugena (John the Irishman) and far beyond the Scottish Enlightenment, on which he has written with verve and insight. His conversation was one of the many unexpected rewards of the stay Roberta and I enjoyed in Glasgow.

The lectures that we four gave and the discussions that followed were irenic in spirit but candid. Few members of the lay and academic audience who attended were specialists in our own specific metiers. But all who came were engaged by the issues we had before us, and the debates that followed spilled over from the lectures and the roundtable, well beyond the usual postlecture queries, comments, and responses, into conversations and explorations that exceeded what the Gifford committee might have pictured—although probably not at all out of keeping with what the planners may have hoped.

My own lectures are presented here, in revised and expanded form, accompanied by a Q&A section that reflects those later conversations and interactions. I hope in this way to address at least some of the challenges posed in the work of my fellow lecturers, as well as the queries that came from the lecture audience and their counterparts among readers who were not present but have pondered the issues that the lectures address.

John Hare, son of the well-known British philosopher of law, had come to Glasgow with his family. Deeply immersed in a Christian Kantianism, his lectures struck sparks of light as well as heat with Anthony Grayling, a lively gadfly of religion, who reads Kant in a far more secular vein. Grayling spoke for a rather secular Aristotle, whom he defended against Hare's charge that Aristotle motivates no real theory of justice and lacks any notion of free will. Hare, for his part, noted that God is mentioned twice as often as *eudaimonia* in the surviving canon of Aristotle's works. He stressed that *eudaimonia* for Aristotle finds its peak in contemplation of the highest, that is, of God. Clearly, one issue between the two men was whether theism and humanism are compatible or inevitably at odds.

Grayling is well known for his distaste for religion. For him, religious ethics is something of an oxymoron. Religion, generically, in his view, bears the taint of the black crimes of the Crusades and the Inquisition. Human rights, by contrast, are the fair heritage of the Enlightenment. Ethics, in his perspective, when premised on theism, sacrifices sodality to piety, making obedience in the end the only virtue and alienating human beings ultimately, as Feuerbach claimed, not only from one another even but from ourselves—by undermining human pride and autonomy and sapping the very claim to human knowledge.

Grayling seemed to find it welcome and refreshing that my own philosophical approach did not fall squarely into the crosshairs of his sights. It does not predicate morals on arbitrary commands but sees an ongoing dialectic between ethics and religion, as our insights about value, including moral value, inform and are informed by our ideas about the divine. This is the dialectic I call chimneying, borrowing the image from the climbers who push off opposing rock faces as they work their way upward in a narrow defile. The facets of those two faces form the toeholds of argument in the present book.

Abdulaziz Sachedina is a friend of long standing. I had met him in the mid-'90s, when the Academy for Jewish Philosophy gathered in Charlottesville, on the beautiful campus that Thomas Jefferson laid out in the days of the American Enlightenment. That meeting was hosted by a friend of even longer standing, David Novak, for some years now a professor of Jewish thought and philosophy in Toronto. David had been eager, characteristically, for the Academy members to meet the Christian and Muslim colleagues with whom he so enjoyed fruitful exchanges of ideas.

I saw Abdulaziz again not long after the dreadful events of September 11, 2001, when he spoke at Vanderbilt. He stood out among the many who responded to those events, by voicing not only horror but opprobrium for the perpetrators, calling on his fellow Muslims to renounce the violence that their co-religionists had perpetrated in the name of their God. At the time of our Glasgow visit, Abdulaziz was on academic leave in Iran, promoting his visions of a democratic, constitutional, and pluralistic Islam, anchored in respect for civic equality and not mere tolerance of others. He was smarting from the sting of a fatwa barring Sunni Muslims from studying with him. But he was undeterred from urging Muslims and all others to give up their claims to a monopoly on truth and a single gateway to salvation. "How can you love a person whom you believe is damned?" he asked.

Reason and revelation, Sachedina argued, are rightly seen not as rivals but as partners. Religion will never be merely private or personal. It will always, and rightly, seek a voice in the conduct of public affairs. But, *pace* the Iranian mullahs, religion in general, and Islam in particular, Sachedina urged, does not rightly seek to govern but only to speak out in behalf of human dignity. Reading deeply into the founding sources of his faith, he pointed to the separate spheres of practice (*muʿāmalāt*) and guidance (*muʿ ābarāt*) that Sharia sets out. The state has the responsibility to implement justice in the former sphere; religion, to set out its ideals in the latter.

Although his family had not accompanied him to Glasgow, Sachedina spoke often of them as we guest lecturers shared meals with our academic hosts. It was clear that all of us had deep loyalties to our communities. None of us, of course, could speak for those communities. But all of us spoke not just as individuals but also as active participants in a tradition, be it Jewish, Christian, Muslim, or secular. Our work, in each case, aims to reach somewhat beyond the academy, and we write with a sense of responsibility to and for the traditions we had been called on to represent.

Sachedina's central theme was the need for interreligious understanding. The Qur'ān, he said, calls on all persons to know justice, but not necessarily to know God. Our human *fiṭra,* or natural endowment, grounds the ethical knowledge that we need. So confessional unanimity is not God's expectation, or even a desideratum for human relations. Accordingly, he urged, Islam needs to revisit its medieval laws about the *dhimmī*, or tolerated minority communities. Societies should be pluralistic, open, and secular in governance, pursuing justice for its own sake and finding peace and harmony, not hegemony, through that pursuit.

I have not a great deal to debate with him on this score. I would only encourage others, Muslim and non-Muslim, to follow up on his lead. Readers who wish to trace some of the rich veins that Islamic culture could pursue in that regard might like to read my own most recent book, *Islamic Humanism.* But, since both critics and exponents of religious ethics have often presumed that the idea of divine commands commits believers to subordinate their moral sense to arbitrary imperatives and indeed to shoulder as obligations prescriptions that we humans would otherwise regard as wrong or even evil, I have taken the opportunity, in the Q&A section here, to reflect on one rather interesting contribution from the Islamic tradition, al-Ghazālī's effort to steer Islam away from an extreme version of that view. And, in the same way, I have marshaled the Jewish texts that I think disarm similar claims about Judaism, by defusing them at the source.

John Hare, whose religious tradition shares a scriptural canon with my own, has worked out a theology of ethics that shows striking differences from much that I think the Jewish tradition stands for. And, since Jewish perspectives are so often less familiar, even to Jews, than Christian readings of the cognate themes, I've engaged in a pretty extensive dialogue with Hare's work and the related sources, secular and religious, in the Q&A.

My lectures themselves, as published here, are pretty straightforward. The first seeks to put some flesh on the bones of the biblical commandment "Love thy neighbor as thyself," that is, to explain just what that command expects of us, as made clear by its larger and its more immediate contexts in the Hebrew Bible and as elucidated in the rabbinic tradition that envelops Jewish readings of the Torah and activates them as a way of life. The second lecture seeks to answer the question as to the relations between ethics and God. My thesis, already adumbrated here, is that the two areas inform and enlarge each other: We learn about God through our ethical understanding, and we learn about ethics through our understanding of God.

The idea of covenant and the imagery of love between God and his creation bespeak an existential connection that grounds an intellectual and moral trust in God's goodness. The idea of God, spoken for by that trust, infuses every practical and intellectual aspect of the Judaic moral ideal, as will become very clear as the argument of this book unfolds.

Many of my friends who are scholars of Jewish thought expect a book of Jewish philosophy to be descriptive—although their own hermeneutic practice often commits them to very engaged descriptions of Jewish ideas. I should confess here that none of my writings in Jewish philosophy seek simply to describe the sources in which those ideas are voiced. My commitment is to pursue the argument where it leads. I cite the sources, canonical or philosophical, only to show that the destinations I have reached are not alien to or incongruent with the insights of others or the tenor of the tradition. For part of one's commitment to a tradition, if one is to be a philosopher committed to a tradition, is to see (and say) how and where the tradition makes sense—and, of course, to recognize and acknowledge where it may have failed to make sense or to make the best sense that it could and then seek to remedy the problem, using one's own resources and those that the tradition itself (in all its diversity) may afford. It's that kind of constructive work, the work of critical appropriation, that keeps a tradition alive and prevents it from becoming a mere shard turned up by an archeologist and preserved in a glass case in the museum—or (what's worse) turned into a mortmain of uncomprehending and uncomprehended constraint.

It's my pleasant duty now to thank the members of the Gifford committee and the faculty and administration of the University of Glasgow for my invitation to deliver the Gifford Lectures and for the warmth and genuine hospitality and interest they showed during our visit. To name the members of the committee: Alexander Broadie, Peter Bussey, David Jasper, George Newlands, Julie Clague, Mona Siddiqui, Andrew Nash, Tony Sanford, David Saxon, Perry Schmidt-Leukel, Richard Stalley, and Susan Stuart. My warm appreciation extends, as well, to the audience that came to the lectures and to the anonymous readers who evaluated the present volume for the Press. Special thanks to

Cynthia Read, who has now served as editor of four books of mine at Oxford University Press. Her thoughtful care and her confidence in my work have been sources of strength to me, and to the work, as well. James Grady and Greg Caramenico, my research assistants at Vanderbilt, lent me their learning, their patience, and their skill as this manuscript took shape.

Off in our American Cambridge with their spouses, building their families and working at their own careers, my two lovely daughters have lent me strength in other ways—Allegra, by spinning the voices that teem in her thought into fictions that carry both laughter and truth, and Paula, fighting cancer in her patients and, in her lab, piecing out the tesserae of light in the shiny bodies of her zebra fish, to help map the knowledge that will put disease increasingly on the defensive. It's a source of strength and faith to know that there are two such souls, and wives, and mothers in the world, worthy reminders of the beauty and wisdom of their own mother, Madeleine.

In Los Angeles, my father, Cal Goodman, now at the midpoint of his ninth decade, continues his marvelous work with artists and gallery owners, helping them to find their constituency, their image, their message, and their metier, lending spirit and ideas to everyone he touches from the rich wellsprings of his intellect. Here in Nashville, my friends Rabbi Saul Strosberg and his good wife, Daniella Pressner, have lent their sense of joy and love to our entire community. And my own dear spouse, Roberta Goodman, wise and insightful, solid in her judgments and steady in her love, has been a model of the kind of generosity and goodness that are the real focus of this book.

Readers of this text will find it saying more than once that we do not simply draw our moral knowledge from the record of God's commands. It's more natural for us (rather than trying to trapeze downward from such heights) to work upward, from what we know—from finite beauties, lasting truths, and human goodness, to the Infinite that is their source. Roberta's beauty of soul, love of truth, and goodness of heart, always focused on the character and interests of others and never merely on their uses or appearance, afford as clear a case as one could ask for of the soundness of that reasoning. It is to her, once again, that this book is dedicated.

Contents

Abbreviations

B.	Babylonian Talmud
ED	Saadiah Gaon, *Sefer ha-Nivhar ba-Emunot* v^{e}*-Deʿot*
J.	Jerusalem Talmud
JPS	Jewish Publication Society
M.	Mishnah
MT	Maimonides, *Mishneh Torah*
SUNY	State University of New York
YJS	Yale Judaica Series

In citations from multivolume works, volume numbers are separated from page numbers by a period. Thus Ginzburg 5.34 refers to page 34 in volume 5 of Louis Ginzburg's *Legends of the Jews.*

Maimonides' *Mishneh Torah* is cited as *MT*, by volume (Roman numeral) and tractate number (Roman numeral in small capitals), tractate title, chapter, and article. Thus, *MT* XIV v Laws of Kings and Wars, 6.8–10, refers to volume 14 of Maimonides' Code, Tractate 5, the Laws of Kings and Wars, chapter 6, articles 8–10.

Love Thy Neighbor As Thyself

I

Love and the Ethical

It takes more than mimicry to learn a language, or so the linguists tell us. Each of us constructs the language we will speak, building its rules of syntax and usage as we interact with parents and peers. Imitation plays a part, of course, as anyone knows who's watched a young mother vocalizing to her infant on the bus and heard the cooing responses. But the difference between mimicry and speech comes vividly into focus as language use advances. The child doesn't just make sounds but uses them as signs, voicing desires and expectations, discomforts, disappointments, and delight. Given meanings, the sounds become language, echoing, answering, or addressing the intentions of the interlocutor. So language is rooted in empathy. Empathy, then, should be natural, and I believe it is.

Empathy is active in art, and advertising. Coleridge and many critics in his wake may speak of the "willing suspension of disbelief," as though they were explaining and not just renaming our emotional engagement in a work of fiction or stagecraft. What actually explains that engagement, I think, is our recognition of objects and types. The sheer act of identifying what is portrayed attunes us to the interests and concerns we witness in representation, allowing identification in a different sense. Not that we've somehow left behind our good sense and entered a fantasy world, unable to distinguish reality from fiction. That would make art an illness and its enjoyment a pathology. Rather, we hope for a certain kind of resolution to the story as we watch or read, as though we were involved—although we know that the events we read of or see enacted are not actually unfolding, and although we never take the picture plane to open onto its own reality.

The representation itself draws us in, even as it is not taken for anything but a representation. Indeed, that's part of the magic and the charm of art—that we read the metaphor as a metaphor and see the picture as a picture, even as we relate to what it represents. A Vargas drawing does the work it was designed to do, because it is suggestive. A horror film can be frightening. The audience members know what they will see before they sit down. They know that they will witness fiction and illusion, yet they expect to be scared, not by the events but by the effects that can make hair stand on end, flesh quiver, hearts race. Nothing is more natural than empathy.

Old-line aesthetics often explained beauty and sublimity in terms of empathy.[1] The great mountain or the sea, the Grand Canyon, the desert or the sunset elicit emotion, it was said, because they overwhelm. No longer seen as an encounter with the numinous, the expected response was laid to a somatic reaction to the upthrust peak, or the weight that seemed to loom overhead, the night that seemed to lour, or the chasm gaping at our feet. We cringe or crumple, theorists conjectured, beneath the towering bulk. We tremble at the brink of the crevasse. Height or depth, actual or illusory, is transformed by physiology into a goad of emotion: We shrink, or lift our heads, strain our vision, cup our palms over our ears at the roar of Victoria Falls, or cover mouth and nose against the sulphurous vapors of Onsen. Part of the response is convention, to be sure, and part, perhaps, from a more general semiotic. But physiology no doubt does lie at the base. The Northern Lights still spur emotion, voiced now in a collective *Ooooh*, an expression impoverished of the words that secular awe once plucked from the religious idiom, today made pale by overuse or deveined perhaps by too physiological a reduction.

If empathy is so natural, why isn't ethics? Emotions of sympathy, love and hate, attraction and aversion—all the classic virtues and vices, Spinoza tells us, spring from associations of ideas.[2] I see your suffering, and I feel your pain—since you are like me, and I relate your feelings to my own, held in memory or at arm's distance, in virtuality. But the responses are not always kindly. I may covet your goods and envy you for them. Not so subliminally, I may link your having to my lack. Love turns quickly into hate, and Catullus will hate and love at once, when Lesbia is no longer his. Here's the stuff of stalkings, arson to the family home, immolation of the children.

Pity is roused at the sight or even thought of another's suffering, proportioned not just to the pain but to the notional likeness of ego to victim. But pity can breed cruelty, when we seek distance from sufferings observed or build a wall of coldness or derision against debilities we contemplate. The Epicureans knew this well and cultivated distance from human suffering: "How sweet it is," Lucretius wrote, "when storm winds roil the sea's smooth surface, to watch another's struggles from the shore."[3] Philosophically, these egoists made strategy from the tactics that every witness to a crime or accident has felt or felt tempted by: Struggling to efface the sense of likeness, one deepens the notional difference between self and sufferer, digging a trench against the pain. That's also the sick ploy of racism, torture, and humiliation, projecting on the other all that's hated in ourselves or feared toward ourselves, finding a whipping boy or scapegoat for the evils ego hopes to dodge.

Ambivalence is what sets empathy apart from ethics. The Stoics, like Spinoza, traced all of ethics to attraction and aversion.[4] And today's evolutionary ethics, willfully confounding ethical altruism with any behavior that's not immediately self-serving, deems ethics not just explained but brought to terms and given its marching orders once it finds a genetic pathway to the origins of any unselfish act. The Enlightenment philosophers of moral sentiment, in the same vein, sometimes thought they'd said it all once they'd found and catalogued the generous and ungenerous impulses of the psyche.

Hume, for one, places great stock in sympathy. His tale is prompted in large part by his suspicions of reason, which he deems powerless to move us to action.[5] Only emotion, he argues, can do that. Sympathy is crucial here, since it can move us to benevolent actions. I see two flaws in such accounts as this. First, as we have just suggested, the emotional lamp may sway and spread its light or warmth or heat in many directions. It seems imprudent at best to rest our moral responses on so flickering and guttering a flame. Second, Hume ascribes to sympathy "the great uniformity we may observe in the humours and turn of thinking of those of the same nation"—rather than, say, to "any influence of the soil and climate."[6] But that would suggest that some nations, by their very birth or climate, lack the makeup needed to be warmly moral or to be as ethical as one might wish them to be. And it seems to urge sympathy itself to lean quite differently toward some than toward others—an outcome Hume seems to welcome a bit too heartily when he seeks limits to benevolence.[7]

Hume grants that the sympathy he counts on might (or, as he insists, generally *would*) make us esteem the rich and powerful and scorn the poor and abased.[8] But that makes sympathy a sorry ground for ethics—or grounds for a sorry ethic. I suspect that Hume has drawn far too sharp a line between the cognitive and the affective. Such cuttings are characteristic of Hume's method in philosophy: *A* is not *B*, so *A* does not entail or warrant *B*. In this way, the causal nexus becomes a mystery; *is* does not entail *ought*—so facts cannot warrant moral judgments or prescriptions; the atomized data of perception include no impression of a mind—so minds are just bundles of impressions; the past does not include the future, and evidence is not the same as inference, so induction is impossible; and so on.[9] In the same way, we are asked to reason that thoughts do not motivate and therefore that ethics cannot be rational.

Hume does seek less craggy terrain when he argues for the general concurrence of reason and sentiment.[10] But he saps that effort when he surrenders moral judgments to "some internal sense or feeling, which nature has made universal in the whole species."[11] Assigning reason a merely calculative, instrumental role[12] overlooks or actively denies the powers of judgment that we use constantly in assaying our daily choices, the challenges we face and the problems we address. Construing reason so narrowly demands just the dismissive outcome Hume intends.

Instrumental or calculative reason is narrow. And the confinement of reason to an instrumental or calculative (rather than evaluative or deliberative) role is to compress it painfully and to the point of falsity. If it's true that reason and human emotions really do speak incompatible languages and address incommensurable values, it becomes problematic, on Hume's account, how we even know what our situations are. For, clearly, any notion of agency requires an ability to interpret experience in cognitive, conceptual terms and to gauge, assay, or appraise the significances (intentions, in medieval parlance) of the persons and other beings that we encounter. The human mind, I believe, integrates these functions. That is what it is equipped and evolved to do. For, as any good pragmatist would stress, few if any notions that we entertain are so neutral and colorless as to carry no value content.

Adam Smith offers a richer portrayal of the moral landscape than Hume does. Benevolence remains central on his account, and Smith, like Hume, rests benevolence on sympathy. But Smith grounds sympathy on the *thought* of another's situation, not an irreducible and unreflective bit of physiology or irrational psychology. Smith's more integrated story leaves more room than Hume's for modulation and modification of our response. And it allows for detachment, and thus for self-criticism and moral growth. Rules and a sense of duty may further modulate and guide our responses. These, for Smith, still depend ultimately on the sentiments evoked by our experiences. So Hume's problem rears its head again: Insistence on the primacy of sentiment too readily underrates the role of principle in informing sentiment.

For Hume, principles are always the product, never the source of sentiments. So appeals to principle, in his eyes, are always circular or suppositious, a charge that Hume gives color by subtly muddling his tale of origins with an analysis of real essences or warrants. The real relations between principles and passions seems in fact much more a two-way street.

The Stoic idea of moral takeoff seems to afford a more sensible account of the relations between sympathy and principle, since it allows moral judgments and intentions to disengage from their presumptive roots. Morals, on the Stoic account, outgrow the mere attraction and aversion from which they have arisen. Morals begin, the Stoics reason, when virtue and right detach themselves from any merely mechanical connection to the objects of animal avoidance and pursuit and are made goods in their own right.[13]

Darwin, unlike his more reduction-minded followers, knew that no evolutionary account of ethics could succeed by reducing what has emerged back to the very roots from which it was said to be derived.[14] After all, if the outcomes of evolution are identical to their origins, the evolutionary process would have gone nowhere, and the proposed evolutionary explanation of the presumptive products of that process would have nothing to explain. The evolutionary account of morals in terms of instinct, on that basis, would collapse into tautology.

Some Darwinians today, overeager to pin ethics to evolutionary imperatives, lose sight of that bit of Darwin's wisdom—as E. O. Wilson does, for example, when he writes: "Scientists and humanists should consider together the possibility that the time has come for ethics to be removed temporarily from the hands of the philosophers and biologicized." Wilson writes as though ethics has long been the object of a territorial dispute but tragically held in thrall by "the philosophers."[15] Philosophers, he holds, may differ superficially. But even the best of them seem to share a prevailing prejudice in behalf of intuitionism, "the belief that the mind has a direct awareness of true right and wrong that it can formalize by logic and translate into rules of social action."

Intuitionism, by this account—indeed, any claim that we can discriminate right from wrong—is a blind spot, a failure to acknowledge that the brain in which our moral choices get made is itself a product of evolution: "The purest guiding precept of secular Western thought," Wilson urges, "has been the theory of the social contract as formulated by Locke, Rousseau, and Kant. In our time the precept has been rewoven into a solid philosophical system by John Rawls (1971)." Having made out Rawls as an intuitionist, Wilson grips his pin firmly to transfix his latest specimen, but he does not strike for the thorax: "The Achilles heel of the intuitionist position is that it relies on the emotive judgment of the brain as though that organ must be treated as a black box. While few would disagree that justice as fairness is an ideal state for disembodied spirits, the conception is in no way explanatory or predictive with reference to human beings."[16]

Whew! Where does one start? Well, to begin at the end and work back: normative ethics is not meant to explain or predict behavior; its brief is prescriptive. Neither Rawls (who relies heavily on the models that economics and game theory propose as schematics of human choice) nor any other responsible philosopher ignores human nature and the human condition. It is both a strength and a weakness of Rawls's theory of justice that it weighs anchor in very concrete (even local or parochial) assumptions about the values and ideals of those expected to adopt it. And Rawls's version of the social contract idea and his claims about justice as fairness are anything but idealist. On the contrary, Rawls is militantly secular, and the social contract idea was generalized by many an exponent of ethics-by-convention in a conscious effort to ground ethics in human relations and institutions and not in any mandate from above—or even from within. Rawls's claims, moreover, have been anything but uncontroversial.

Philosophers today continue to differ widely, as they have ever done in the past, over core ethical principles and the particularities of their application. Perhaps these differences reflect divergences of interest or background. Perhaps they involve differences of emphasis or experience. But I think it would be about as likely and about as appropriate for a variety of philosophers to voice identical ethical visions as it would be for an art museum to fill its walls with identical oil paintings. Museums, after all, don't usually hang copies—except in the gift shop.

But Rawls's theory of justice is not a general ethical theory but an account of political legitimacy. It offers one philosopher's vision, worked out in careful detail and clearly representative of certain trends of thought that were quite fashionable (but hardly universal) in its moment and milieu. Despite the pretensions of its admirers, it cannot be said to stand alone as the great normative philosophy of its era. Indeed, in keeping with the positivist ambience of its original conception in the 1950s, it was carefully couched in descriptive language, as an account of what we (a telling word!) would or could be expected to call justice.

Even when read prescriptively, Rawls's theory, although widely admired, was also widely scouted. It was never universally accepted, even among Rawls's Harvard colleagues. In political philosophy, and in ethics proper, deontologists, utilitarians, virtue ethicists, feminists, perfectionists, pluralists, socialists, communitarians, and many others continue to argue, often persuasively, for rival views. A synthetic-minded thinker might readily extract more truth from the shimmering rainbow of their reflections than from any single wavelength in the array.

Nor is it fair to label Kant an intuitionist—or a social contract theorist! (Wilson would never have allowed his graduate students to tag his ant or termite specimens so cavalierly.) Kant's appeal, as he saw it, was to reason, not intuition. And even his ideas of the social contract were deeply imbued with his thoughts as to the moral demands of reason. Again, on a historical note, social contract theory is not the mere work of such men as Locke and Rousseau. Spinoza, Hobbes, and others played key roles. Locke, Rousseau, Hobbes, and Spinoza are among the godfathers rightly claimed by a secular tradition. But none of them was exactly a secularist. All made strong claims about the nexus of God to morality and polity. But none of them wrote for or about disembodied spirits.

The social contract idea has both Eastern and Western, ancient and modern, secular and scriptural roots. In the seventeenth and eighteenth centuries, it was an intellectual bulwark against the divine right of kings. But I find the notion puzzling that mere agreement (or virtual agreement, as in Rawls) makes a social or political arrangement just. Still less would I insist that common consent is sufficient to make a decision morally justified.

Wilson allows his readers to confuse questions of origin with questions of warrant. Asking where ethics comes from allows an easy, if deceptive, shift from matters of right and wrong to matters of history or evolution. Falling into a genetic fallacy, confusing the nature of a thing with its origin, eases a further slip into a naturalistic fallacy, equating a norm or value with some fact that we associate with it. The historical and biological questions are both interesting and pertinent. But they afford no sufficient guidance to moral inquiry.

Ethics, finally, has never been a philosophers' preserve. It belongs to all of us whenever we make a choice or reflect on choices that we face. But it will not be aided by being "turned over" to ethologists, nor will it be enriched by such durance. For descriptive narratives cannot displace (let alone answer) normative questions. When explanations from genetics, endocrinology, or neurophysiology are introduced in ethical discussions, the usual intent is to rationalize unfortunate patterns of behavior. Or, when the appeal is broader and less casuistic, the effect most often is to license a kind of wishful incoherence: trumpeting a moral imperative and call to arms, an urgent summons to combat and overcome what have only just been affirmed to be the determinants of our choices.

Clearly, no mere impulse is normative, no matter how deep rooted, just for being an impulse.[17] Much moral wisdom is captured in the idea voiced in

Mishnah *Avot*, the Ethics of the Fathers, echoed in the Muslim *ḥadīth* and reechoed by Jewish pietists and Muslim mystics, that the real hero is one who controls his impulse; the real battle is not for dominance over others or glory in their eyes but for the mastery of the ego.

The thought is traced to Ben-Zoma, whom the Mishnah quotes as saying: "*Eizehu gibbor? Ha-kovesh et yitzro*" "Who is a hero? He who subdues his bent"—more familiarly rendered: "Who is mighty? One who conquers his inclination"(M. Avot 4.1). Alī b. ʿUthmān al-Hujwīrī cites as a *ḥadīth* of Muḥammad a gloss on the Qur'ānic (29:69) call to *jihād*: "The holy warrior [*mujāhid*] is he who battles with all his might against himself [*jāhada nafsahu*]"—that is, who struggles against the ego. And again: "We have returned from the lesser battle [*al-jihād al-aṣghar*] to the greater [*al-jihād al-akbar*]. . . . It is the struggle against the self."[18] Hujwīrī backs up this familiar Sufi gloss, making the *jihād* against the ego a greater contest than that against "unbelievers," by explaining that the former is more painful. He treats asceticism as our chief weapon in this harder battle. Regrettably, militant Islam does not always shift its focus from the lesser to the greater battle.

Baḥya ibn Paquda, the great Jewish pietist philosopher, adapts these sources in his *Book of Guidance to the Duties of the Heart*. Well known by its shortened Hebrew title, *Ḥovot ha-Lᵉvavot*, and widely studied today, Baḥya's work was influenced by Sufi Muslims like Muḥāsibī and Makkī and parallels the work of his Muslim contemporary al-Ghazālī. But Baḥya downplays the ascetic thrust of his Sufi predecessors and transforms the holy warrior of the Muslim writers into a *ḥasīd*, a devout and devoted person whose piety is expressed most clearly in acts of loving kindness (*ḥesed*) toward others. As Baḥya explains, culling another phrase from the same series of reflections by Ben-Zoma: "*Eizehu mᵉkhubad? Ha-mᵉkhabed et ha-bᵉriot*"—"Who is honorable? One who honors God's creatures." That is, Who has real dignity in God's eyes? One who treats others with the respect they deserve as God's precious creatures.[19]

Biblically, we're commanded to test the dicta of a seeming prophet by asking what we must always ask about: the rightness or wrongness in what is being preached or proposed.[20] All the more must we test those whisperings (as the Qur'ān[21] calls them) that come from within. For the impetus toward wrongdoing, as Baḥya warns,

> is mingled with the powers of your soul and mixed in the temper of your spirit. It shares with you in governing your sensibilities, bodily and spiritual, and sets up its dominion at the heart of your deepest secrets and all that you hold at the inmost core of your being,

> insinuating its counsels into every movement, overt or inward, which you execute by your choice. It lies in wait for your forgetful moments. You may drowse and lose track of it, but it is never asleep to you. You may seem to toy with it carelessly, but its play is never idle; it is always intently focused on you. It may clothe itself in sunny guise, deck itself out in trappings of love of you, and so, by subtle deceptions, become your trusted advisor and seem to be your most faithful friend. It will fawn and wink and run to please you with false flattery, all the while firing its deadliest darts, aimed at your destruction.[22]

What Baḥya is teaching in this pietist reflection on the psychodynamics of motivation is how readily impulse can deceive us. If *ethical* altruism is our aim, the simple truth is that, just as language is not mere mimicry, ethics is not mere empathy. The image of another's face does not make that other a thou—or Margaret Keene's mawkish paintings with their big-eyed waifs, calculated to stimulate caring and concern, would be high art.[23] We might regret the fact that morals are not instinctual, but a fact it remains—and I for one do not regret it. For, if ethics were unthinking, there would be no sense in ethical admonition, advice, or reproof, no distinction between reflex and obligation, and no room for self-directed or inspired moral growth but only evolution, through the random variation of genes and environmental selection of useful heritable traits. Morally, by contrast, I must discriminate consciously and conscientiously among the impulses that crowd the mind when I contemplate another's joy or suffering, or my own—much as I need to get hold of myself and choose, in the case of vertigo, whether to pull back from the ledge or succumb to free fall.[24] Giddiness alone cannot advise me, and neither ego nor superego is a true enough friend to gauge the size and shape, tenor and direction of my ethical obligations. That's why, I think, the Torah tells us (Leviticus 19:18) not just to *empathize* but to love one another and stipulates further: *as thyself.*

This command, recorded in Leviticus: *Love thy neighbor as thyself,* forms the subject of this book. The words, I think, deserve a little parsing, as does their counterpart, the demand for equality that underlies all liberal constitutions and undergirds the very idea of law—for justice, as the Torah insists, rejects favoritism and makes all persons equal before the law. In Deuteronomy (1:17) we read: *Ye shall not recognize faces in judgment; great and small shall you hear, and fear no one. For judgment is God's.* Translating a bit more idiomatically: *You must be impartial in meting out justice. Hear out the high and low alike, fearing no one. For justice belongs to God.* And further on: *Thou shalt not bias justice by recognizing a face or taking a bribe. For bribery blinds the wise and distorts the pleas of the just* (Deuteronomy 16:19). Favor and favoritism compromise even an honest cause. So it is with similar intent that Exodus warns against following the crowd into wrongdoing and balances that caution with a warning against allowing pity for the underdog to embellish his case (*tehdar b^{e}-rivo*) and pervert justice (23:2). For that is just as unfair as favoring the powerful over the powerless (Exodus 23:6).

Equality before the law is not a function of power and still less of our capacity for harm to one another, as Hobbes would have it. Consider his words:

> The cause of mutual fear consists partly in the natural equality of men. . . . For if we look on men full grown, and consider how brittle the frame of our human body is . . . and how easy a matter it is, even for the weakest man to kill the strongest: there is no reason why any man, trusting to his own strength, should conceive himself made by nature above others. They are equals who can do equal things one against the other; but they who can do the greatest things, (namely kill) can do equal things. All men therefore among themselves are by nature equal; the inequality we now discern, hath its spring from the civil law. (*De Cive*, Chapter 1, § 3)

Hobbes measures power by the potential for violence. His aim is to quiet the pretensions of vainglory, his deeper foe. But what a nasty sense of equality his mating of power with violence breeds, and how revealing is his vision of law as the source not of equity but of inequality—a thought still echoed when Rousseau writes, "Man is born free but everywhere he is in chains." Hegel does little better when he identifies as Master and Slave those who are less and more afraid to die. That grounds political relations not on our moral recognition of one another's personhood or even on our capacity to aid and befriend one another but on mutual threats of death.

But, in the Mosaic tradition, equality is a matter of right and thus of law. And it extends beyond the law of the courts. For the Torah makes moral equality both a premise and a product of its legislation. As the Talmud admonishes: "One who exalts himself at his fellow's expense has no share in the World to Come."[25] Ethics cannot give us all equal skill or power, stature, wealth, or fame. But it does demand recognition of existential desert, the bare desert of personhood, a dignity that does not utterly vanish while we live, or in some ways even after death.[26]

As Thyself specifies a degree. It means, for instance, as the Jewish codes inform us: give up your own life rather than commit murder.[27] But it also specifies a quality. We are not asked to dissolve, to fuse or mingle personalities, or routinely immolate our interests for others' sake. Individual interests are presumed. Without them, the biblical imperative becomes empty rhetoric. Mutuality is a moral implication of equality, treating the other as another self. But mutuality melts into sentiment and equality collapses into formalism when stripped of positive regard and active caring. And the Torah's gauge and model for that caring is self-regard. Naḥmanides saw that point clearly when he acknowledged an element of hyperbole in the biblical *as thyself*: "A human heart cannot undertake to love one's fellow as oneself. Didn't Rabbi Akiva himself teach us 'Your own life takes precedence to that of another' (B. Bava M^{e}tzia 62a)? What the *mitzvah* ordains is that one deem all of another's concerns as weighty as one's own."[28]

The point is not to displace self-interest but to hold the interests of others in the same regard that we would hope for in our own case. The Hebrew, Naḥmanides notes, does not say simply "love thy fellow," making *re'akha* the direct object, but *give* (or *extend*) *love* toward *thy fellow*. . . . The goal, Naḥmanides suggests, is aspirational,[29] aiming not to eliminate self-regard but to overcome its invidiousness. We are urged, therefore, not to single out some one area (say, judicial or civil) in which to treat others as equals, while reserving other realms (perhaps intellectual or spiritual) as our more private preserve. Rather, what is called for is complete openness, treatment of others as our moral equals in *all* regards, just as we would wish to be treated by others. We owe each other respect in every area of concern. Our own desires for such regard give us a ready yardstick for gauging the deference that is the due every human being.

The *Ḥinnukh*, ascribed to Aaron Halevi of Barcelona,[30] a pedagogical and generally Maimonidean homiletical recasting of the reasoning that supports the biblical commandments, offers a prudential rationale for the mandate to love our neighbor: Our love will be reciprocated if we heed these words, and a society where love is the rule will be pacific. Good advice, of course. But such instrumental readings of an obligation fail adequately to anchor its normativity: We can see why one might wish to live in peace or even harmony with others. But that does not explain why it is worthwhile that we, or anyone, *should* do so. That peace and harmony are preferable to strife and aggression *assumes* that human lives have worth, a worth, indeed, that is enhanced by the fruitfulness of human lives when peace and harmony prevail.

The prudential reasoning of the *Ḥinnukh*, in other words, is dialectical: It rests on widely shared assumptions but proves nothing to those who fail to share those assumptions. It does not discover and make clear what it is that makes peace preferable, say, to the strife, emulous, aggression, and quest for dominance that many a romantic idealizes and that many a would-be realist presumes to be dictates of reason and self-interest. Leviticus, by contrast, calls on us to focus our concerns and direct our actions toward the interest of our fellow human beings, not merely as useful allies or potential enemies to be won over but as moral counterparts, deserving a regard commensurate with all that we ask or aspire to. It thus far outreaches prudential concerns. The issue is not just that you get what you send, that your karma might be back to bite you—you scratch my back and I'll scratch yours, and, if not, I'll scratch your eyes out. Rather, what is commanded rests on properly moral grounds: Each human self has real worth and dignity of just the sort that we would rightly claim in our own behalf. The command, then, is not mere bombast or hyperbole. It invites us to find worth in our own interests, goals we cherish, values that build our personhood and give content to our claims to liberty. And, building on that foundation, it urges us to see and act on the recognition that others too have goals, needs, hopes, fears that matter *not just to them but objectively* in the same ways ours do. Love grounded in this way does not mean serving every caprice that might dart across another's fancy. Nor does it mean wanting for others just what we want for ourselves. Still less is it wanting others to be just like us. That bit of moral triumphalism or spiritual colonialism is a seduction to be shunned, a temptation subtly traced by Spinoza when he draws his critical line between piety or humaneness and overbearing ambition.[31]

The love that the Torah commends and commands means accepting the sanctity of each person's capacity to choose and cherish. We need not share each person's goals, and it's morally dubious to expect all human hopes to be alike. But our first obligation to one another is respect for subjecthood. Recognition of that obligation is no merely modern demand. At Numbers (27:16), when Moses asks God to find a successor to his leadership, he calls on God as the *God of the spirits of all flesh*. The Midrash spells out what it takes this striking form of address to mean: that God knows every person's mind. He knows that no two are alike, and Moses acknowledges that fact and sets into high relief the need for a leader who will treat with each individual *as an individual*—"according to his mind" (Numbers Rabbah 21.15, cited by Rashi ad loc.).

Even to begin to implement the ethical desideratum suggested in that characterization of God and the resultant qualifications of the good leader presumes a social setting. And it is in the light of that presumption that the Torah works to harrow a channel for the social roots that will anchor and nourish sure expectations as to the consideration we owe one another, guiding our responses to one another's needs, desires, and deserts. The seedbed the

Law seeks to cultivate is an ethos in which ego is presumed but egoism rejected. Hence the language of love in Leviticus, modulating the delicate nexus between self and self.

Textually in Leviticus the other is called *re'a*. William Tyndale, the great English translator martyred by Henry VIII for translating much of the Bible, followed a line of English readings running back at least to 1301 and was followed in turn by the King James version, in translating *re'a* as "neighbor."[32] The word does not just mean 'one who lives nearby.' Rather, as James Murray explains in the *OED*, in contexts "inculcating men's duties towards each other" the word 'neighbor' takes on "a widely extended sense." Chaucer, in the Parson's Tale, spells it out: "In the name of thy neighbor thou shalt understonde the name of thy brother."[33]

Commonly *re'a* means a counterpart;[34] but, etymologically, it bears connotations of care, perhaps taken up from the pastoral life of its first users.[35] Hence its core meaning: friend or fellow.[36] Ethically, as Hermann Cohen showed, the Torah's usage frames the category of the fellow human being.[37] For the *other* does not remain fixedly other and is not deemed an outsider or alien (*zar, nokhri*)[38] but is brought into the sodality as a *ger*, technically a guest or client. Thus biblical fellowship, Cohen finds, is "elucidated" and "made intelligible" when Leviticus lays out the scope of its ethical demand: "And if a stranger sojourn with thee [*yagur 'itkha ger*] in your land, ye shall not wrong him. The stranger that sojourneth with you shall be unto you as the homeborn among you, and thou shalt love him as thyself; for ye were strangers in the land of Egypt; I am the Eternal your God."[39]

The fellow man whom God enjoins all Israelites[40] to love is not just a neighbor, then, in some merely neutral sense. Inclusion of the stranger in the biblical injunction as one whom we must love as we love ourselves shows that even anonymity does not arrest the demands of personhood at some static minimum.[41] Rather, the concept of the other expands, through the biblical usage, to evoke the idea of a *moral* counterpart: Strangers are comrades and companions. Accordingly, the idea that what's mine is mine and what's thine is thine (verbally, the nub of Justinian's imperative, *suum cuique*, to each his own[42]) is decried rabbinically, as *middat S^edom*, the ethos of Sodom, sordid selfishness, which love finds wanting and which the Law, as a living tissue, ceaselessly seeks to heal, by enlivening our sensibilities and ordaining practices that will make the recognition of personhood ever more active in our lives.

Ḥesed is what is missing in the ethos of Sodom, a divine attribute, beneficence, that we are called upon to cherish when Micah (6:8) sums up God's expectations: *He hath told thee, O man, what is good, and what the Lord requireth of thee—Just this: To do justice, to love kindness* [ḥesed], *and humbly to walk with thy God.* Humility and decency before God, justice and generosity toward one another, as Micah reminds all who will hear him, is the pith of what God requires. *Imitatio Dei* crystalizes in a life of *ḥesed,* lovingkindness. Thus, the Rabbis' ethical reading of the commands to emulate God's holiness (Leviticus 19:2; Deuteronomy 28:9): "As God is merciful and compassionate, so too must you be merciful and compassionate" (B. Shabbat 133b). Spiritual perfection means nothing and ritual scrupulosity is empty without this. Why, asks the Ḥafetz Ḥayyim, does God command us not only to love God and keep his commandments but also *to walk in his ways and cleave to Him* (Deuteronomy 11:22; cf. 19:9, 28:9)? Because mere study and devotion, prayer and meditation, are unfulfilled and unfulfilling without active engagement in behalf of our fellow human beings.[43] Thus, the Rabbis see a model for human generosity in the stunning image of God's fashioning clothes for Adam and Eve (Genesis 3:21): We too must clothe the naked (B. Soṭah 14a)—and that in the best we have, as Maimonides explains:

> It is said in the Torah: *Abel, for his part, brought the choice firstlings of his flock and their fat, and the Lord esteemed Abel and his offering* (Genesis 4:4). That is the rule with anything done for the good Lord's sake—it should be the finest and best. If you build a house of prayer, it should be finer than your private dwelling.[44] If you feed the hungry, you should provide the best and sweetest of your table. If you clothe the naked, it should be from your finest garments. And if you consecrate something, it should be taken from the best you have. As it says: *all the fat is the Lord's* (Leviticus 3:16).[45]

Charity, rabbinically, is of a piece with justice. And the justice whose rules are circumscribed by the commandment *Love thy neighbor as thyself* (Leviticus 19:18) embraces all of civil and criminal law, from the statutes regarding tort and negligence[46] to those that regulate return of lost objects.[47] Justice, as understood in the Jewish legal tradition, includes charity, which finds its highest phase in aiding the helpless to self-sufficiency.[48] But *ḥesed* goes further. Charity is *owed* to the poor. They can sue for their entitlements. But charity can be seen to with cash. *Ḥesed* is everyone's desert, in all one's actions (B. Sukkah 49b). *He who mocks the poor cuts his Maker,* we read in Proverbs (17:5), *He who exploits the helpless cuts his Maker; one honors Him by kindness to the needy* (Proverbs 14:31).

At the thin, minimal edge of its demands, *ḥesed* calls on us to look after another's person and property as if it were our own—a fortiori the other's dignity and honor. Thus, Rabbi Eliezer says, "Let the honor of thy fellow be as dear to thee as thine own" (M. Avot 2.15).[49] And Rabbi José, similarly, "Let the goods of thy fellow be as dear to thee as thine own" (M. Avot 2.17).[50] Beyond that, when asked for help, one must respond as one would hope to be answered if making the request in one's own behalf. These counsels simply spell out the spirit of the biblical text: *If thou lendest money to My people, to the poor that is with thee, thou shalt not be as a creditor to him or charge him interest* (Exodus 22:24). What follows is a ban on keeping a debtor's pawned cloak overnight: *it is his only clothing, the sole covering of his skin. In what else shall he sleep?* (Exodus 22:25–26; cf. Habakkuk 2:6). Rashi glosses the force of the phrase *the poor that is with thee* as a reminder that one must treat those in need as though one were oneself in their place, without arrogance or condescension. The same holds true halakhically with any request—whether for advice, information, or material help. Persons are precious. Creditors may not dun or nag or even hint at the need for repayment of a debt. Not only may one not take in pawn necessities of daily life, but a creditor is forbidden biblically from even entering a debtor's home or seizing property from it as collateral (Exodus 22:24; Deuteronomy 24:10–13). And Halakha prohibits making use of any object held as security for a loan.

One's actions must be not just civil but gentle and generous, sensitive, aware, responsive to need before any favor has been asked.[51] Such actions are meant to spill over into attitudes and become facets of our character: We must meet others with a cheerful, smiling face, praise their virtues, rejoice in their good fortune, share their sorrow,[52] console their grief,[53] conciliate their quarrels. We must school ourselves in avoiding jealousy,[54] interruptions,[55] put-downs, invidious comparisons. Derogatory nicknames fall under the same ban.[56] Nor may one refer a question to one who does not know how to answer. Jesting does not mitigate the offense, since the joke was at another's expense.

Current fashion in standup comedy promotes the wholesale belittling of ethnic groups, genders, or nationalities with "equal-opportunity insults." But inclusion of one's own group does not lessen the offense or the offensiveness of this kind of substitution of vulgarity for honest humor and shock effect for wit. The Talmud remarks that to call someone ugly is not only to hurt that person's feelings but also to insult the Creator (B. Taʿanit 20b). Again, when teaching, we must not just lay things out but ensure that our students understand.[57]

Although generally characterized as more stringent in his rulings than Hillel, his contemporary, Shammai taught: "Greet everyone with a cheerful countenance" (M. Avot 1.15). Spelling out this precept, later ethicists say that one should face one's interlocutor, showing not just a profile or a blank, poker face but a responsive, expressive face, evincing warmth and interest. The

Talmud glosses Judah's milk-white teeth in Jacob's blessing (Genesis 49:12 cited at B. K^e^tuvot 111b) as a hint that a smile is the milk of human kindness. It takes the biblical prohibition against giving injury to others (Leviticus 25:17) as prohibiting even words that would cause pain (B. Bava M^e^tzia 58b). And, taking up this point, the *Ḥoshen Mishpat* (228:1) deems insults a more grievous affront than fraud. For money can be returned, but hard words are not erased.

Ḥesed, then, fleshes out the obligation laid upon us by the biblical command *Love thy neighbor as thyself.* It gives the love that the *mitzvah* calls for a broad range of practical expressions. Acts of virtue, the Ḥafetz Ḥayyim observes, inspire emulation.[58] But that means that more than material benefits flow from the practices of love. *Ḥesed* becomes a heritage,[59] allowing God's commandments to be seen not as chores but as privileges embraced with joy. Their valence is never neutral, their authority never alien. They are freely accepted as one's own will.[60] Their best reward is the strength and merit to fulfill yet further charges. As Ben-Azzai put it: "*Mitzvah goreret mitzvah*"—One *mitzvah* draws another in its train (M. Avot 4.2).

Biblically, *Love thy neighbor as thyself* is nested in a catena of *mitzvot* that inform its meaning (Leviticus 18–21). Many of these are ritual in nature, aiming to bar a culture of cruelty that reached its grotesque extreme in the sacrifice of children in the cult of Moloch (Leviticus 20:1–7). These rituals articulate the Torah's mission of aligning holiness with love. They seek to sunder the pagan linkage of divine power with violence[61] and to define and safeguard privacy[62] and dignity. They forbid incest and other sexual invasions that would violate intimacy by making the erotic public or transforming it into a commercial or even cultic commodity.[63] But, central to the goals these laws pursue as vehicles of holiness (Leviticus 19:2) are a group of *mitzvot* of more immediate ethical content: forbidding lying,[64] stealing, cheating, and deceit (Leviticus 19:11; cf. 19:35–36, 25:14; Exodus 23:7; Deuteronomy 25:13–16), favoritism in the law courts (19:15), vengeance, harboring a grudge (19:18), and rumor mongering (19:16). They forbid withholding a day laborer's wage overnight (19:13; cf. Jeremiah 22:13–17) and condemn cursing the deaf[65] and placing a stumbling block in the path of the blind (19:14).

Those last two *mitzvot* are traditionally read broadly, as the context suggests. That is, they are taken as bans against tempting or misleading those who are morally at risk. J. H. Hertz, the former Chief Rabbi of Great Britain, sums up the rabbinic reading:

> "Deaf" and "blind" are typical features of all misfortune, inexperience, and moral weakness. This verse is a warning against leading the young and morally weak into sin, or provoking them to commit

> irretrievable mistakes. The following are typical violations of this ethical precept: he who gives disingenuous advice to the inexperienced; he who tempts the Nazirite [–or the alcoholic!] to break his oath not to drink wine; he who sells lethal weapons to weak or dangerous characters—all these transgress the command "Thou shalt not put a stumbling block before the blind." Equally so does the man who administers corporal punishment to a grown-up son: it may make that son forgetful of filial duty and commit an unpardonable offense.[66]

The Jewish codes treat as a stumbling block the tender of a loan without an i.o.u., since this might tempt even an honest debtor to repudiate his loan by denying it. They hold the lender at fault, even if the loan is duly paid—for creating the temptation.[67] Arrogant behavior, too, is a temptation, if not to violence then to hatred, which is itself forbidden (Leviticus 19:16).[68] But even more blameworthy under this statute is one who sells a weapon to a dangerous person.[69]

All these specifics are corollaries of *Love thy neighbor as thyself.* The *mitzvah* is introduced, in fact, to support the ban on grudges, vengeance, tale bearing—and, pointedly, the positive obligation to reprove wrongdoers and the prohibition against refusing to render aid: *Thou shalt not stand idly by at thy neighbor's blood* (19:16)—a clear entailment of the practical demands of the obligation to love others as we love ourselves.[70]

Mere convenience, embarrassment, even risk do not trump another's danger or disgrace.[71] Rabbinically, the obligation to render aid is understood to include a duty to testify in criminal or civil proceedings.[72] Its demands are typified in the duty of a good swimmer to save a drowning person and of bystanders to halt a crime of violence, taking necessary risks and even using force against the aggressor—albeit only in due measure. A would-be murderer or rapist may be slain, but not a robber, or even a murderer if lesser force would suffice to block his crime.[73] For the assailant, too, is a fellow human.

The duty of reproof traces the contours of the love we owe one another against a more everyday backdrop: We are not to let our individuality spawn a sense of alienation. If we see another doing wrong, we must speak with him—privately, gently, tactfully,[74] lest his attitude grow entrenched. We are forbidden to shame him,[75] but tact is not silence. Love means overcoming reticence and, here, too, not standing idly by to watch another stumble.[76] Silence would make us complicit. It would almost be gloating. Love creates a positive obligation and demands the moral tact to offer correction and advice to our fellows—a fortiori to our children!—and not allow barriers to grow between us that would stop our being heard. This is the Enron obligation. It's not trivial, romantic, or utopian.

When the Torah offers *Love thy neighbor as thyself* to warrant the duty of reproof, the application shapes the generality. For morals, like the sciences, can work inductively. And induction is just as able to show off the middle terms on which an inference hinges as it is to vault from cases to the universal rule that links them or rappel back again to further cases. The middle term here, connecting the particular to the universal, is our common, yet unique personhood, whose boundaries are illuminated morally by the bans that hedge it about. Biblically, human subjecthood is defined in this way: not conceptually but operationally.

Reproof has a public as well as a personal side, clearest in the work of prophets as admonishers. For biblical prophets, as Morris Jastrow taught, are not foretellers but forthtellers.[77] Nathan goads David's conscience for sending Uriah to the front and taking Bathsheba as his own. Elijah confronts Ahab: *It is not I who have troubled Israel but thou and thy father's house!* (1 Kings 18:18). Moses, as Maimonides writes, had the courage and the conscience to come boldly before a Pharaoh "with nothing but his staff, to save a nation from the yoke of slavery, because he had been told, *I surely shall be with you*" (Exodus 3:12, cited at *Guide* II 38).

The duty to speak out is not confined to the inspired. It touches anyone with a moral compass.[78] Yet, its efficacy in the public square depends on civil institutions, just as its impact in private or communal relations depends on social tact. Communities must safeguard the "monisher" but also school him in the responsible exercise of his mandate—and educate his public in receptive listening and critical, uncanted hearing.[79] The law must protect (and guide) the whistleblower, just as it must protect the good samaritan, and provide some assurance of the adequacy of his skills and the parameters of their proper uses. For any good constitution will safeguard and foster free expression and its vehicles in the service of human dignity and other precious goods.

The ancient prophets took up their poesy, as they called it,[80] when moral outrage broke the silence and demanded ordered speech—visions, parables, promises, and warnings.[81] Poets may still feel that thrumming when the call to artistry for its own sake does not still it.

So Richard Wilbur, not the least artful of our American poets, invokes the memory of those

> Whose minds went dark at the edge of a field,
> In the muck of a trench, on the beachhead sand,
> In a blast amidships, a burst in the air.

And then utters the severe imperative:

> Grieve for the ways in which we betrayed them,
> How we robbed their graves of a reason to die:
> The tribes pushed west, and the treaties broken,
> The image of God on the auction block,
> The immigrant scorned, and the striker beaten,
> The vote denied to liberty's daughters.

To which he responds:

> From all that has shamed us, what can we salvage?
> Be proud at least that we know we were wrong,
> That we need not lie, that our books are open,
> Praise to this land for our power to change it,
> To confess our misdoings, to mend what we can,
> To learn what we mean and make it the law,
> To become what we said we were going to be.[82]

The journalist too is a monisher, when not simply saying what his readers want to hear. So is the teacher, when not simply informing students of what they already think they know—that is, massaging their prejudices. Likewise, the critic and social reformer, especially when they serve no parti pris and are not just plumping for a favored cause. The artist gives of his finest when the image projected is not lightly chosen but worthy of dignity, like the flesh defended by reproof in Thomas Hart Benton's *Susannah* against the prying eyes of the elders, or the nude in Thomas Eakins's late work *William Rush and His Model*, where the painter, casting himself as the sculptor, turns the model toward us frontally and asks her innocent face to answer the charges of prurience that dogged his career. The artist's demeanor as he gently hands her down from the plinth affirms her dignity and protests that of his art.[83]

The sanctity of free expression is sullied when put in service to a merely leering gaze. And the gold of free speech turns brass when all it frames is a sales pitch. In a commercial society, the huckster always finds advocates.[84] But able philosophers are all too ready, in the name of freedom, to bar prophetic voices from the public square.[85] Such bans were bruited long before Ahab's reign. And the noise is kept up by writers from Hobbes[86] to Rawls[87] and beyond. Happily, the censures are somewhat wishful. Unhappily, abuses continue to arouse prophetic voices and do not allow them to keep still. Such voices may be muffled from Beijing to Kinshasa, and even in the halls of the United Nations, where issues of slavery and polygamy, for example, are kept off the agenda. But voices of conscience cannot be silenced indefinitely. As

Amos says (7:14), when arraigned for treason before Jeroboam: *I am not a prophet or a prophet's son but a husbandman, a dresser of sycamore figs. Yet the Lord took me from behind my flock and told me "Go, prophesy to My people Israel."* Did Amos really prophesy that the king would be slain and Israel exiled, as the priest Amaziah charged (7:10–11)? He did picture Amaziah's wife reduced to whoredom and his children murdered (7:17). But his message was not his to modulate: *Does a lion roar in the forest when it has no prey?... Does a trap spring up from the ground when it has caught nothing?... The lion hath roared. Who can but fear? My Lord God hath spoken. Who can but prophesy?* (3:4–8).

Amos's burden is the Darfur of his day: atrocities perpetrated by Syria, Philistia, Moab, Tyre, and others (1:2—2:2) who *threshed Gilead on boards spiked with iron* (1:3). Alongside these evil doers, he condemns the complacent luxury of his own people: how they exploit[88] the poor (3:13–15, 4:1–4, 5:11–12, 6:4–6, 8:4–7), *scorn the public admonisher (san'u va-sha'ar mokhi'aḥ), and despise the just cause* (5:10). Conscience will not be silenced. Its mandate, as Amos has heard it, despite all the claims of constituted authority and vested interest, *is* God's roaring command.

The public obligation not to stand idly by at scenes of bloodshed has its core civil impact in the imperative to establish courts of law and a system of justice: *Judges and officers shalt thou appoint in all thy gates*[89] (Deuteronomy 16:18)—the one affirmative among the seven *mitzvot* that the Rabbis hold were given to all the seed of Noah.[90] In biblical Israel, the cities of refuge (Numbers 35:6–29) and the symbolic assumption of public responsibility for unrequited bloodshed (Deuteronomy 21:1–9) mark the moral and ritual poles of this command. But the obligation to love one another as we love ourselves finds its generic juridical expression in the prohibitions of bribery and favoritism (Deuteronomy 16:19),[91] capped by the emphatic *Justice, justice shalt thou pursue* (Deuteronomy 16:20): Just means to just ends—with no caviling over which to prefer when right and expedience seem to diverge.[92]

Today the obligation not to stand idly by at another's injury applies internationally, as a duty to intervene against famine, drought, earthquake, tsunami—and, yes, genocide, torture, disappearance, slavery, human trafficking, and oppression. Expedience counsels prudence, and prudence cautions expedience. Diplomacy is the tact of the international sphere. But even here the gap that realpolitik paints between the prudential and the moral proves illusory. For yesterday's ally of convenience is tomorrow's political pariah, and tyranny reads acquiescence as appeasement.[93] The moral caution regarding intervention is the demand that, before intervening in another's affairs, public or private, one had better be right[94]—in aims and means. Justice, and again justice, must we pursue.

Consider another corollary to *Love thy neighbor as thyself,* the obverse: *Thou shalt not hate thy brother in thy heart* (Leviticus 19:17). *Brothers* is the language now, not just neighbors or fellows, stressing the existential bonds among human beings. The Or ha-Ḥayyim, Ḥayyim ben Moses Attar, saw here an exhortation to see that our fellow man *is* our brother—and to treat him as such, quelling any animosity between us. The Rabbis saw an answer and an antidote to spite: Lend your things to others, even if they have refused the loan of theirs. Forget the slight.[95] Abraham Ibn Ezra, following the Talmud (B. Arakhin 16b; cf. Sifra to Leviticus 19) underscores *in thy heart,* reading the verse as a warning against harboring any secret hatred—nursing one's wrath to keep it warm, as Bobby Burns put it; but what the Torah warns against is a rancor borne with more malign intent than Tam O'Shanter's good wife held toward her poor husband. Candor is the remedy that Reb Ḥayyim points to and that Ibn Ezra calls for. So Naḥmanides explains: *If we tell our fellow how he has wronged us, he can admit his fault; we can purge our spleen and clear the air. Besides, in the light of day, some faults look nugatory.*[96] But rancor only festers when pent.

If candor builds the tact that strengthens trust, and trust builds tact in turn, I see virtuous as well as vicious circles here, turning in opposite directions: Failure of tact piles up walls between us; thoughtful candor can break down those walls. Hence Robert Frost's irony, subject to so much misprision: "Good fences make good neighbors" is the misanthrope's motto, a cynic's throwaway. Frost's own burden is this: "Something there is that doesn't love a wall, that wants it down." And this: "Before I built a wall I'd ask to know / What I was walling in or walling out." Frost's care is with our walling in or walling out our fellow human beings, despising or ignoring their personhood. The Torah raises that concern vividly: *u-mi-b^e^sarkha lo' tit'alem—Do not make yourself invisible to your own flesh* (Isaiah 58:7). What crystallizes from that command are concrete obligations: *to strike the wicked fetters, loose the yoke's cords, free the oppressed, and snap every yoke! . . . Share your bread with the hungry, take home the homeless poor, clothe the naked when you see him.* (Isaiah 58:6–7)—and, summing up: *do not make yourself invisible to your own flesh!*

One difficulty we face in reading the laws of the Torah stems from its mingling the work of a moral and a legal code, a constitution and an invocation to ethical and spiritual perfection. The agendas are distinct but not discrete, never wholly sundered from one another. The constant pressure, welling up from the sanctity of persons, is to ethicize the civil and sacralize the ethical. We are called on not just to avoid harming our fellow human beings[97] but to love them—just as we are called on not just to obey God's laws but to love him (Deuteronomy 6:4) and emulate his holiness (Leviticus 19:2). How can love be commanded? How can the maximal demands of moral perfectionism bed down comfortably with the minimalism rightly expected in a code of law?

Kant writes in the *Groundwork of the Metaphysic of Morals* that only the love that is an act of duty can be commanded:

> . . . love out of inclination can never be commanded; but kindness done from duty—although no inclination impels us, and even although natural and unconquerable disinclination stands in our way—is *practical* and not *pathological* love, residing in the will and not in the propensities of feeling, in the principles of action and not of tender sympathy. This love alone can be commanded.[98]

Kant's thesis, as he spells it out:

> To help others where one can is a duty. But beyond this there are many spirits of so sympathetic a temperament that without any further motive of vanity or self-interest, they find an inner satisfaction in spreading joy around them and take delight in the happiness of others, which they have made possible. But I say that however right and amiable it may be, such an action has no real moral worth. It stands on the same footing as other inclinations—the inclination toward honor, for example, which, if fortunate enough to hit on what accords with duty and is beneficial on the whole and thus honorable, deserves praise and encouragement, but not esteem. For its maxim lacks moral content, namely, of an action performed not from inclination but out of duty.[99]

Kant underscores his point by imagining a benevolent spirit reduced to despondency by sorrows of his own. If, in such a torpor, one rouses himself from self-pity, determined to aid others no longer from any emotion of compassion but "for the sake of duty alone," only then "for the first time has his action genuine moral worth."[100] Even a coldhearted, if honest person, "indifferent to the sufferings of others," would have genuine merit in his actions if he responded to the call of duty and helped them, despite lacking any inclination to do so or any joy in so doing.[101]

One can certainly see Kant's point. Moral worth should not depend on anything so fickle and contingent as inclination or the accidents of temperament. Coldness that can rouse itself to action is indeed commendable, and impressive, just because and insofar as it overcomes disinclination. But surely Kant has drawn too fine a line between actions in conformance to duty and those done (solely) from a sense of duty. Often an action will not be virtuous at all unless imbued with warmth or zeal or the vigor, thoroughness, elan, or follow-through that only genuine caring, zest, or joy imparts. A sense of duty may prove bootless and fruitless unless enlivened by human warmth. Help rendered indifferently may often be unwelcome. If cloaked in superficial bonhomie, it may lose its Kantian claim to good intentions. Besides, a physician, say, perhaps a medical resident whose long hours routinely demand heroic extensions of patience, endurance, concentration, expertise and care, can hardly perform even adequately, let alone admirably, without the firing up of will and lighting up of intellect that are needed to probe the literature, conceptualize the diagnosis, devise the treatment, and doggedly pursue its implementation, on which the saving of lives will depend.

By sundering moral worth from inclination and esteem from approbation, Kant has in fact barred virtue ethics by a stipulative fiat. For the agent virtue ethics speaks to is the integrated person whose thoughts and inclinations are attuned to principle (right rule, *logos*, nobility or fairness, as Aristotle calls it), not at odds with it—still less fixated on an ideal of duty abstracted from all concrete goods and inner promptings. And it is only the integrated person who is capable of regarding and optimizing the relevant congeries of goods, foregrounding those that matter most in a given situation and backgrounding or relegating to irrelevance those that do not, ordering motives, values, and inner promptings in the varied public and private circumstances of real life. To abstract from that motivational arena is to set duty, and action in the light of duty, quite apart not just from inclination and delight but from the very basis of our capacity to choose and act thoughtfully, graciously, compassionately, generously, or courageously.

Consider love, since Kant, like the Torah, raises a question about love and duty. My student Kevin Cutright tells the members of my ethics seminar that the love he holds for his wife would seem remiss were it not grounded in the qualities he holds precious in her but affirmed and lived by just from a sense of duty. Likewise, his love of God, he argues. Shouldn't that be captivated by God's perfection? And isn't piety of such sort as much an act of love as a bond of duty? Again, I would say, the same is true with the love one owes one's fellow human beings. This is not as lofty as the love of God or as intense as the love of a spouse or a dear friend. Yet, it can be as ennobling as the former, and it demands as much sensitivity and care as the latter. Doesn't duty in this love we owe one another rest in part on some measure of admiration for the human person and respect, if not esteem, for the varied individuals toward whom it is directed? How could it be effectual or sincere if it did not?

We have an obligation to acknowledge a truth, I think, just because it's true. There is no further duty from which this needs to be suspended—and there shouldn't be, lest we find ourselves launched into an infinite regress or forced to predicate our commitment to the truth on some ulterior or extraneous concern, which we would then have to warrant, since we had not yet agreed, as they say, to face facts, that is, to accept them as such. (And wouldn't the worry then arise, as it does for pragmatists, that the ulterior concerns meant to motivate our commitment to truth, might conflict with that commitment?) Truth, I believe, should stand on its own axiological feet.

But, by the same token, I would argue, just as we should recognize truths just because they are true, we ought to love what is good and perfect just because it is such, and we ought to do justice, to pursue justice, as the Torah puts it, just because it is justice. There is no question, then, 'Why should I be moral?' The right act simply is what we should do, and any line between the right and our best choice is falsely drawn, pretending that what is right is somehow usefully distinguished from what we ought to do.

The commandment to love God and follow His laws, in the same way, spells out in the language of law the content of our recognition of God's perfection. And, in the same way, the commandment to love our fellows is, I believe, no more nor less than a call to the recognition of their deserts: Persons must be treated as persons. *Love thy neighbor* makes explicit the obligation that the life of another person sets before us; the measure *as thyself* spotlights the existential equality of persons—lest we lose sight of the precious dignity of the other while yet preserving at least some fragment of a presumption of the dignity that is our own.

Just as we should love God for what He is, so should we love human beings for what they are: beings whose subjecthood places them on a plateau of moral worth.[102] The biblical imperative is a pithy way of saying that, without heavy reliance on abstract language. The call it voices will not mean much to those inclined to stifle a sense of moral obligation, but it issues a resounding call to almost anyone who values much of anything at all.

How, it might be asked, can there be an imperative not just on the order of *Thou shalt not steal* or *Thou shalt do no murder* but, reaching past behavior to our motives, like *Thou shalt not covet* (Exodus 20:14) or *Thou shalt not hate thy brother in thy heart* (Leviticus 19:17)? The parallel is not lost sight of in the biblical text. For *Love thy neighbor as thyself* comes directly on the heels of that last, as the alternative commanded in the next verse. Bans on covetous thoughts and the harboring of hatred forbid an attitude. So we must ask, Can laws regulate our thoughts? What does it mean when a law asks that of us? Clearly, laws like these intend to operate not merely in the public sphere but at the intimate nexus of thought and action. Their target is the mind or heart's intention. For even theft and murder are defined and differentiated from acts that might too readily be mistaken for them only by an agent's intent.

The Rabbis, like the Torah that is their text, are carefully and critically watchful of the borderlands between attitude and action. For it is here that an ethos unfolds, in individuals and in a community. They see vengeance as one thing and bearing a grudge as quite another. If your neighbor asks to borrow a tool and you refuse because he declined to lend you one of his, that is vengeance, the Rabbis say. But if you tell the would-be borrower 'Here. I'm not like you,' that's bearing a grudge (Sifra *K^{e}doshim* 4.10–11). The Law prohibits both. It forbids both getting even and harboring a grudge.

That reach of the Torah's ethical concern confirms Maimonides' case that its *mitzvot* subtend a virtue ethic. Its aim is to foster specific virtues and displace the corresponding vices. Thus, the Torah commands us to help our enemy reload his fallen ass and to return it to him when it has strayed (Exodus 23:4–5)—to help him change a tire, one might say. Maimonides explains that the specifying of an *enemy's* pack animal here makes it clear that the Law's intent is to quell and overcome our penchant for irascibility;[103] the command to return lost property (Exodus 22:1) aims not just at restoring what was lost (for everyone will lose things from time to time; that's just a part of life) but rather aims squarely at avarice, giving us the practice we need to overcome that kind of vice.

Other biblical commands function in the same way: *Rise up before a hoary head* (Leviticus 19:32), *Honor thy father and thy mother* (Exodus 20:12), and even *Thou shalt act in accordance with the law that they* [the duly appointed magistrates] *propound and on the verdict that they lay down for you, not deviating left or right from the sentence they pronounce* (Deuteronomy 17:11). Such laws are aimed at quelling excess and instilling modesty—and respect for the rule of law.[104]

The Torah, then, is not just a collection of positive laws. The commandments that ordain love and forbid hatred thematize concrete obligations, specify the aims and purposes of the acts the Law commands, and guide us in the modalities of their fulfillment and contextual elaboration. The *mitzvah* to help reload our enemy's ass covers fire damage as well as highway accidents. Its subject is love, not animal husbandry.[105] The charge is not an algorithm to be programmed in an automaton but an exhortation to a moral subject, the only sort of agent that can regulate not just its own behavior but its own intentions.

As an integrated code, the Torah ordains love and the eschewing of hatred, and it specifies means by which these aims are to be sought. It powerfully backs its negative commandments with affirmative counterparts: We are to love and not just tolerate the stranger (Leviticus 19:30). We are commanded not just to avoid cheating a widow or an orphan (Exodus 22:21–22; cf. Deuteronomy 27:19) but to sustain them (Deuteronomy 14:29, 16:11, 26:12–13; cf. 10:18). The movement from the negative to the positive is also an advance from abstract to concrete. But the Torah becomes radical not in pursuing extremes (as the word 'radical' sometimes seems to suggest) but in tracing actions to their roots in attitudes and seeking to reform those attitudes through the actions it commands. Hence Maimonides' reading of the Nineteenth Psalm: *The Lord's Law, which is perfect, reformeth the soul.*[106]

It is in this sense that the Torah forbids covetous thoughts and complements that command with material claims in behalf of generosity: One may not reap the corners of one's field or harvest fallen ears or pick fruit missed on the tree (Deuteronomy 24:19–21).[107] These must be left for the poor and landless—the stranger, the widow, the orphan.[108] No limit, as the Mishnah notes, is set to the dimensions of the corner. Indeed, the Rabbis gloss the obligation (Deuteronomy 15:7–8) to make up what the impoverished lack, as a duty to restore them to the life they once enjoyed[109]—although, of course, their own help is needed here, since real restoration means helping the helpless back to self-sufficiency.

Collating the *mitzvot* that set no upper limit, the Mishnah cites not just the corner of the field but also gifts to the Temple of first fruits and pilgrimage offerings—and it adds acts of kindness and study of the Torah (M. Pe'ah 1.1). The Talmud fills out the list by specifying such *mitzvot* as visiting the sick, welcoming and seeking out guests, comforting mourners, attending and burying the dead, and cheering and sustaining brides and bridegrooms. Taking up the biblical image of walking, when Micah (6:8) reminds his people that among God's simplest expectations is that they will *walk humbly* with their God, the Talmud sees a duty to accompany the bride and the funeral cortege (B. Makkot 23b–24a). As is typical in halakhic exegeses of this kind, the prooftext is a pretext, and the real nexus is thematic and ethical. Thus, the Rabbis derive the obligation to visit the sick from God's appearance to Abraham on the third day after his circumcision (B. Soṭah 14a, glossing Genesis 18:1 and 17:27). The Ḥafetz Ḥayyim underscored the general obligation by arguing that visits to the ill can be a matter of life and death—in part because the visitor may bring medicine or vital advice about which physicians to consult. Obliquely, but clearly, the argument specifies a more concrete component to the obligation than the unadorned notion of a sick call might have suggested: Moral support is itself precious, but our obligation toward the ill does not stop there.

In Genesis (18:1), when God appeared to Abraham, the patriarch, old and convalescent as he was, is pictured as seated at the entrance to his tent—inviting the midrashic inference that he was eagerly awaiting an opportunity to offer hospitality to passers by. And God's blessing of Isaac, reported in the same verse as the mention of Abraham's death (Genesis 25:11), is read by the Rabbis as exemplary of the obligation to comfort the bereaved.

God himself sees to the burial of Moses (Deuteronomy 34:6). Biblically, the reason is that no man is meant to know where Moses is buried—lest his grave site be made a shrine, diluting the purity of Mosaic monotheism. But the Rabbis see a powerful exemplar in God's undertaking this humble duty. Underscoring the rabbinic interest is Jacob's deathbed adjuration of Joseph to perform a true favor (*ḥesed v*ᵉ*-'emet*) for him, by burying him in his own land and not in Egypt (Genesis 47:29). As Rashi explains (ad loc.), obsequies for the dead are a true favor, for those whose dignity is most affected will be in no position to requite the honor given their bodies or their memory. Samson Raphael Hirsch elaborates (in his commentary, ad loc.): Jacob knew that Joseph would, of course, bury him with all due pomp. But true kindness would heed his wish and respect his sense of exile, even though the elderly patriarch had lived in Egypt seventeen years.

All these expressions of comity and recognitions of dignity in our fellows—all the open-ended duties, like the duty to rejoice the bride and groom and provide for their needs—Maimonides teaches—are rabbinically derived from *Love thy neighbor as thyself.*[110] Such concrete applications rescue that *mitzvah* from vacuity and make it operational. The obligations they lay before us are at once material and emotional. The actions impart an outlook, which in turn imparts a tone to life that befits the Torah's goal: that those who receive the Law make of themselves *a holy nation* (Exodus 19:6) where holiness reaches beyond justice and charity, expressing itself in an ethos of kindness, a way of life based on love. In that spirit, the Rabbis press the emulation of God to include the ideal of returning good for ill.[111]

What, then, can we say of maximalism? Laws that bear a penalty are and should be minimalist. But, when no limit is set to an obligation's scope, we're working, clearly, with imperfect obligations—a very different realm from that of civil or criminal laws.[112] Positive laws, as Plato explains, have sanctions, but rational laws are warranted not by sanctions or even appeals to authority or prudence but by reasons.[113] And reason, as Kant insists, is freedom's domain. We cannot be commanded to do or be everything. That role is reserved for God alone. But the exercise of our liberties mandated by the very idea of an imperfect obligation gives freedom its highest calling. Its charge is not to frame capricious choices but creatively to allocate our energies and resources, to forge a life for ourselves, our families, and our communities, and to build an environment worthy of our standing and that of our fellow creatures in God's image. In the exercise of our liberties, we shape and choose ourselves and make our lives and the lives of those around us.

In calling us to perfection and emulation of God's holiness, the Torah asks us not to do the impossible, to become infinite or disembodied, but to perfect our humanity, which scripture calls God's image. This we do by seeking out and cultivating what is best in ourselves, morally, spiritually, intellectually, socially, artistically, and, indeed, physically, since our embodiment, and that of others, is the locus of that image, the silvered glass in which God's face shines.[114]

2

Whose Commandment Is It?

The Talmud records a snatch of dialogue between Rabbi Akiva and Ben-Azzai.[1] Akiva called *Love thy neighbor as thyself* the great general principle (*k^e^lal gadol*) of the Torah; all its other norms were corollaries. But Ben-Azzai, the same who said, "One *mitzvah* draws another in its train," saw a logically prior principle in the Torah's premise that mankind was created in God's image. Singling out a text not framed in the imperative at all, he cited Torah's prefatory note to its calendar of Adam and Eve's descendants after Cain: *This is the book of the generations of Adam: When God created man, He made him in his own image: Male and female did He create them, blessing them and giving them the name Adam on the day of their creation* (Genesis 5:1).

The normative wealth Ben-Azzai found in this passage shows what he found missing in the *mitzvah* Akiva privileged: Our creation in God's image teaches us not to retaliate, even when another shames us. Simple reciprocity does not say that. It might even seem to invite us to answer in kind!

The fact is, one might not expect much love from others and so might gladly forgo their aid or favor, disclaiming all special regard for oneself. But mankind's creation in God's image together with the blessing that follows on its heels changes everything. For the immediate sequel of that blessing is that Adam begets Seth, *in his own image and likeness* (Genesis 5:2–3). The blessing, then, as the Rabbis read the text, was God's gift of the power to transmit the divine image to his offspring.[2] It is that divine image, transmitted to all humanity from generation to generation, that gives *Love thy neighbor as thyself* the positive content that we have seen implicit in the *mitzvah* from the start. Ben-Azzai finds it spoken for directly in Genesis, and the text bears him out when it cites mankind's creation in God's image to warrant its ban on bloodshed (Genesis 9:5–6).

God's words *Let us make man in Our own image* (Genesis 1:26) tell us that while we humans are not divine, our very existence, as Nahum Sarna puts it, "bears witness to the activity of God in the life of the world."[3] Humanity, by the nature of its being, is a portent, a book we can learn to read. As the Baal Shem Tov put it, "The ideal of man is to be a revelation himself—clearly to recognize himself as a manifestation of God." Akiva does not part company with Ben-Azzai on this point. For he was fond of saying: "Beloved is man to be created in God's image—but all the more beloved in being given to know of his creation in God's image" (M. Avot 3.18). "This awareness," Sarna writes, "inevitably entails an awesome responsibility and imposes a code of living that conforms with consciousness of that fact."[4] Egyptian and Mesopotamian court usage, he notes, hailed the *ruler* as God's image. Genesis has democratized the trope. And humans, unlike God's other creatures, are not said here to be created of divers kinds: There is just one human species.[5] Our common ancestry, as the Rabbis stress, belies all pretenses of nobler or baser birth—or destiny.[6]

All human beings are ennobled by our creation in God's image, Naḥmanides writes.[7] The Rabbis gloss the point in terms of the uniqueness of the individual.[8] In the book of Job, we read *It changes like sealing clay* (38:14). What changes here appears to be the earth, which shows new forms and colors with the rising sun—*tinted like a garment*.[9] But the Rabbis see an allusion in the image to the special molding of each human being: Within the human race, we vary. *We* are the variegated clay—unique exemplars of God's image.

In the Torah's highly historical vision, uniqueness means irreplaceability. Each human individual is a universe of possibilities, and actualities, never to be seen again. Baḥya thus finds a moral meaning in the biblical vision of creation:

> How varied are the marks we can study of God's wisdom in his creatures! We might say, with all the many sorts we find, that there are seven pillars of wisdom (cf. Proverbs 9:1) that anchor creation. First come the clear effects of God's wisdom in founding and plumbing the laws of nature—the earth anchored fast at the center, water above and around it, air above that, and fire beyond, all in

> divinely ordained and invariant equipoise and equilibrium, each keeping its properly defined place, the sea itself at rest, its waters pent in its bed, not trespassing its bounds, though waves may rage and winds may storm, as it is written: *I placed my laws on it and set bars and doors upon it, saying "Thus far shalt thou come and no further. Here thy surging waves shall halt!"* (Job 38:10–11). Or, of the stability of earth and sky: *Eternal, O Lord, doth thy word stand fast in the heavens. From generation to generation is thy trust. Thou didst found the earth, and it endures. At thine ordinance all stand to this day. For all are thy servants* (Psalms 119:89–91). The inspired psalmist writes in the same vein: *Bless the Lord, O my soul* (*... You spread out the heavens like a curtain,* and thus to the end of Psalm 104). The second pillar is the manifest expression of God's wisdom in the human species. For a human being is a little world, epitomizing the entire order and beauty of the cosmos, all its loveliness and perfection, as the inspired author explains in the psalm that opens *O Lord, how splendid is thy name throughout the earth* (*... When I behold thy heavens, the work of thy fingers, the moon and stars that Thou didst set in place, what is man that Thou art mindful of him, mortal man that Thou takest note of him. Yet Thou didst make him but little less than divine, and didst adorn him with glory and majesty, gavest him charge of the work of thy hands and laid all things at his feet*). (Psalms 8:4–7)[10]

Baḥya's cosmos is antique. Yet his wisdom resounds timelessly when he declines to set scripture against nature or God against science but treats causal law and nature's constancy as emblems and instruments of God's rule, wisdom, and love. Baḥya finds in the natural order a setting for human caring and freedom, not their antithesis. Compare what Nietzsche finds in the regularities of nature when he recycles the Epicurean idea of eternal recurrence. The intent, in that case, was to scotch the seeming dullness and rigidity of a rule-based morality so as to intensify and localize our moral sensibilities, sharpening to a keen edge our sense of moral freedom, by substituting for Kant's test of universalizability the idea of choosing *personally* once again (and ever again) as one chose before. Yet, the cosmology driven by Nietzsche's moralism vitiates the moral creativity it was meant to liberate. It dissipates the zest of active agency by robbing of uniqueness each moment of joy or loss, choice, or opportunity. The vista of old choices ever re-chosen bespeaks world-weariness: *The sun rises, the sun sets, and back it tramps to its place, where it rises yet again. Passing south, turning north, round and round the wind goes, circling back to where it began. All rivers flow to the sea, but the sea does not fill up. The streams return to where they flowed before—All tedious beyond words, beyond what any eye would care to see or ear could bear to hear. What has been will be, what has been done is what will be done. Nothing is new under the sun* (Ecclesiastes 1:5–9).

The sense of recurrence spreads a pall, biblically dispelled only by thoughts of new creation, by humans in God's creative image—new births, new starts, free choices initiating a new course, an open future. Heideggerians, sensing the dreariness of recurrence, make death the whetstone that will sharpen human sensibilities, the only whetstone, as they see it. But the common effect, when that blunt tool is frontally applied and death is made the ultimate, is too often only further moral dullness, coarsening, not keenness. Death stuns, and thoughts of death do not revive the spirit but deaden it. Witness of life, holding a human infant in one's arms, revives and sends a frisson of joy and affirmation through the body—electrical or biochemical in its roots, perhaps, but a frisson that flowers into an ethic and an ethos.

The Mishnah reports that judges in a capital case used to caution witnesses by appealing to the uniqueness of each human person:

> Capital cases are not like others. In the rest a party may pay money and requite a wrong, but in a capital case the witness must answer for the blood of the one convicted and for the blood of all his posterity to the end of time. For we find that when Cain slew his brother, it is written, *The bloods of thy brother cry out* (Genesis 4:10)—not "the blood of thy brother," *the bloods of thy brother*—his blood and that of all the offspring he might have had. Why was just one man created at the start? To teach that anyone responsible for a single death is biblically regarded as though he had caused a world to perish; and anyone who saves a single life, as though he had saved a world . . . and to proclaim the greatness of the Holy One, blessed be He. For a mortal stamps many coins from a single die, and they are all alike. But the King of kings, the Holy One blessed be He, stamped every man with the seal of the first, yet not one is the same as another. So each one must say: For my sake was the world created. (M. Sanhedrin 4.5)

Rabbi Meir, addressing this passage (B. Sanhedrin 38a), finds human uniqueness in the voice, mien, and mind of each of us: We are known by our voice and appearance; that protects our physical privacy. But we are also distinguished by our discrete minds, which give privacy to our thoughts.[11] Dignity, then, is wrapped up in human uniqueness: The personality objectified in our appearance and demeanor but resident in our thoughts and plans is precious, godlike, worthy of respect. Hence Ben-Azzai's inference: It's not just your person that I must love as if it were my own, and not just your property that I must respect as I would wish mine to be respected, but your dignity. Not just your good name, as though the Law banned only libel, but your self-respect, your individuality, social role, and place. I am not to shame or embarrass you, just as I would hope not to be embarrassed. And should I chance to be thick-skinned and impervious to shame (or so flatter myself), that fact or supposition is utterly beside the point. I owe you (and myself as well!) the respect that befits God's image. You are a unique work of art, an original, not a copy of any other being—and so is every other human individual—fresh molded, as it were, from God's own hand,[12] bearing the image not of some natural counterpart but of the highest and most holy.

Why all this talk about God? Does ethics need a God? Can't a person be perfectly moral without facing constant challenges to personal integrity spurred by credal questions and sectarian allegiances? That's the question I want to address here, starting, perhaps, from the recognition that in Judaism religion is never purely credal. For our religion is not just a faith but a way of life. Where faith does come into play, it's far more centrally and normatively construed as faithfulness. It means walking in God's ways, trusting in God's truth and justice, not merely—never mainly—holding certain views, let alone promulgating, inculcating, or actually seeking to enforce a set of dogmas! The enforcement of dogma is alien to the core norms of Jewish practice.[13]

Nor are the ethical norms that concern us here sectarian. They touch on what we owe one another as human beings. Every culture has its own ways of construing such obligations, and we all can learn from the varied ways in which human obligations are articulated. Familiarity, areas of harmony and similarity, may lull us in our penchant to leave unexamined lives unexamined. But differences can spark critical thinking, first about what we see or miss in another tradition and then about what we took for granted or left unquestioned in the accustomed or familiar. It's with this in mind that I pursue the conceptual roots and practical branchings of Jewish thoughts about *Love thy neighbor as thyself*—not because I expect others to water my tree but because I find philosophical profit in dialogue and the reflections it prompts.

If Judaism is a way of life, we need to ask whether practice is enough. Was Hermann Cohen right in pressing toward a Kant-inspired reduction of the divine to the ethical?[14] That kind of chemistry can damage and dissolve some of the deepest roots and highest reaches of a religious ideal. When a religion, as a way of life, frames its norms and mores as demands of the Transcendent, that invites inquiry as to what, if anything, religion adds—or, put another way, what God expects of us, what kind of life God would have us live and share with one another. Would our lives be different, ethically, without any thought of God?

Baḥya argues (as Kant will argue centuries later) that in ethics, intentions are of the essence. Mere "service of the limbs,"[15] as he calls it, mechanical conformity to a rule, can never be enough. But Baḥya's idea of devotion of the heart goes well beyond Kant's claim that moral worth must spring from self-legislation. His reasoning is that sound intent in adhering to the *mitzvot* demands intellectual commitment—rational devotion.[16] The Torah does, after all, urge us to love God with all our heart, and soul, and might—and in biblical language *heart* means mind. But how exactly does such commitment affect our ethical lives? How, if at all, is morality fulfilled religiously?

I see seven areas where monotheism enriches ethics, and I want to survey them here. Polemics readily point to crimes committed in the name of religious ideas, or with the sanction of religious authorities. Genocide and torture, crusades and jihads, acts of terrorism, persecution, and oppression are readily assigned religious motives. Gordon Kaufman argued years ago that the Absolute too readily eclipses other values or shrinks them to relativity, planting a kind of nihilism, vicious pragmatism, or opportunism in the bosom of theism.[17] I think that's true. It helps explain a lot. And it warns theists of the need for moral steadiness when they seek spiritual heights. It warns us too not to look too directly into the sun, lest dazzlement wash out or silhouette the softer, moral lights among which we humans make our lives and by which we find our way.

Religious notions and emotions can inspire fanaticism—although I think the Sincere Brethren of Basra (tenth century) were right in ascribing religious triumphalism less to piety than to politics.[18] Yet religions are repositories of much that we humans hold sacred, and we do get touchy about such things. People do hope to see their children raised to treasure what they hold most precious, and excessive zeal and spiritual chauvinism are real risks when emotions of this kind run high.

The safeguard lies in caution about what we hold sacred. The idea of God and God's will must be disciplined and guided by our moral insights if those insights in turn are ever to be guarded or informed by our idea of God.[19] Not that God is a projection of other values, any more than objective values are mere arbitrary commands of a capricious God. As I see it, the relationship between our idea of God and our conception of other value laden ideas is properly dialectical, a matter of chimneying. We push off from the sheer rock face of our moral (or aesthetic, or cognitive) values, and back again from our idea of the Absolute, gaining height and a clearer view, if we can, at each pendulum swing between the opposing faces. The vista, if we gain the height to glimpse the monotheist's idea of God as the Source of all good—of light and life, wisdom and forgiveness—changes the air. It will strip pious calls to violence, tyranny, or fanaticism of all pretense to legitimacy. When their charge goes off as a result, they leave behind only the tinsel wrap and ashes of their imposture. The robust core of God's identity with love and justice, beauty and truth, remains untouched.

The Difference Monotheism Makes

Here are the seven areas where I think the idea of God adds value to our ethical pursuit: They involve (1) positive content, as already suggested, that is, the shift from mere formal equity (or hierarchy!) to actual love, care, and concern; (2) absoluteness, at times a bête noire for critics of theistic ethics but at times cherished as their special pet, as, for example, when the talk turns to inviolable principles and rights; (3) stability, which is not mere resistance to change over time but a recognition of the sorts of change in circumstance that demand moral changes and the sorts that do not; (4) universality, that is, scope that applies to all things by virtue of what they are and not just by reference to the perception of shared interests or shared identity; (5) height, the reach of the ethical beyond the minimal demands of a statute; (6) inwardness, bringing conscientiousness into play; and (7) *imitatio Dei*, which returns us to our creation in God's image, now seen not just as a given but dynamically, as a challenge to be risen to.

1. *Love, Care, and Concern*

Start with positive content. That, I think, was the heart of Ben-Azzai's concern—not a real disagreement with Akiva but a supplement to his claim, aiming to ensure that the love ordained in *Love thy neighbor as thyself* is not lost behind the *mitzvah*'s formal structure or collapsed into a sheer tit-for-tat. *Ḥesed* was the issue. That means generosity. Thus the Ḥafetz Ḥayyim, elaborating on God's command to love *ḥesed* (Micah 6:8), urged that we must actively seek out ways of helping others and contributing to their well-being.[20]

The word *ḥesed* appears 245 times in the Hebrew Bible, applied most often to God's love. It occurs twenty-six times in Psalm 136 alone, celebrating the phases of the world's creation and the formative events of Israel's history, all ascribed to God's love, the recurrent focus of the refrain: *Ki l^e-'olam ḥasdo.* That line is often rendered "For his lovingkindness endureth forever." But I take the sense to be a bit stronger and more pointed: *Indeed his love is infinite!* Monotheism sees all goodness in the world as a determinate expression of God's boundless love. We reason from finite but manifest goods to the infinite goodness of their Source—much as induction reasons from finite, but thematized, experience to a universal conclusion. Genesis thus punctuates each stage of creation with God's judgment *that it was good,* culminating, on the creation of human beings, as if in a final inspection, with the climactic: *God saw all that He had made, and lo, it was very good.*

The world is full of goodness. The point is not that we call things good because God called them such but that we recognize God's goodness in the being He gave each creature.[21] As Isaiah (6:3) has it, *The fill of all the earth, is His glory.* That is, God reveals himself in the goodness found in nature. Safeguarding that goodness, the Torah commands one to dismiss the mother bird (Deuteronomy 22:6), forbids yoking an ass with an ox (Deuteronomy 22:10) or muzzling the ox when it threshes grain (Deuteronomy 25:4).[22] It bans felling fruit trees, even in a siege (Deuteronomy 20:19–20). The Rabbis, characteristically, generalize that last: The underlying commandment is a general prohibition of destructiveness.[23]

Core values stand out vividly against the backdrop of exigency, making time of war a crucial test of their limits: Jewish law requires besiegers not to invest a city wholly but to leave one side unencumbered, for escape by those who wish to flee.[24] The Torah expects kings to join their forces in battle (Numbers 27:16–17).[25] But it defers military service for the newly married, along with those who have planted a new vineyard or built a new house (Deuteronomy 20:6–7). It sends home the faint of heart (Deuteronomy 20:8, 24:5). Troops are to be exhorted with the hope that God is with them (20:1–4), premised on the further hope that their cause is righteous. But the fearful recruit is sent home, *lest his brother's heart quail, as his did* (20:8). The Mishnah calls for noncombatant duty by those who declare themselves afraid, and Maimonides counts the exhortation against fear (20:3) as one of the Torah's 365 negative *mitzvot*—violated if one succumbs to such fears. If comrades die because a soldier has let himself become distracted by thoughts of home or safety, it is as if he shed their blood.[26] That's a strong way of saying 'United we stand, divided we fall'—vividly underscored by the inestimable worth of each human life.

The Sabbath offers a more pacific expression of the Law's regard for the human person. Sabbath rest is mandated for the whole household, servants included. Sabbath prohibitions are set aside to save a life or to prevent human injury or animal suffering. But the halt to toil and commerce means more than a respite from physical labors. The day is meant to open doors to spiritual and intellectual growth. Symbolism, rather than dogma, becomes the vehicle by which higher ideas are conveyed and paths are illuminated toward values that transcend the quotidian. Sabbath observance reenacts the liberation from Egyptian bondage (see Deuteronomy 5:12–15). But, at the same time, Sabbaths celebrate the creation (Exodus 20:11, 31:17), when God himself (no mere servant of his role) is said biblically to have ceased his labors and to have imparted, beyond the first breath of life, an added spirit, emblematic of mankind's linkage to the Divine.[27]

Tacitus found it bizarre that every Jewish household was freed from labor every seventh day. Leisure, by his lights, was the privilege of a leisured class. The idea that everyone needs and deserves an enforceable respite was utterly alien. So he ascribed to "the charm of indolence" both the Sabbath and the corresponding respite of *sh^emiṭṭah*, granted by the Torah to the land each seventh year—with the produce of the fallow land reserved to the poor and to wildlife, "the beasts of the field" (Exodus 23:10–11).[28] The law that made Sabbath rest both universal and obligatory and the idea embedded in that law, of a temporal window onto eternity, did not arise without reference to the God idea. And, even now, when sharing in God's rest is freely chosen or casually ignored and Mammon speaks in softer (if still insistent) tones, the sanctification of Sabbath rest and the sanctity of the individual that it bespeaks would not be preserved without recourse to the God idea.

Is human dignity safe without the sacredness of selves? Yes and no. Personhood can surely be protected with legal, moral, and customary norms. One can certainly say that human beings are special. But norms change, and 'special' is a vague and slippery word.'Holy' is quite another matter. The demands go further and grow richer. The territory may be disputed at times, but the claims verge insistently toward the absolute. That's where the links between humanity and divinity do the heavy lifting. Torture and mutilation can be banned. It does not require reference to a God to forbid incest, rape, and other invasive disruptions of personal space or public commons. But, historically, those boundaries were not plainly marked without such reference. Conceptually, they can be very permeable without it. The idea of the inviolate gives footing in the here and now to the idea of the holy. And that idea in turn is sheltered and stabilized by the higher ideal that rises out of it and arches over it.

Notice the analogy here between two biblical prohibitions: *Thou shalt not shift thy neighbor's landmark (lo' tasig g^evul re'akha) which your forebears posted on the allotments assigned you in the land the Lord thy God giveth you as your inheritance* (Deuteronomy 19:14; cf. 27:17; Proverbs 22:28, 23:10), and, as if to generalize on that theme: *And now, Israel, heed the laws and rules that I teach you. Practice them, that ye may live—that ye may enter and own the land which the Lord, God of your fathers giveth you. Do not increase or diminish the matter (davar) I command you but preserve the commandments of the Lord thy God* (Deuteronomy 4:2). The boundaries of property are sanctified by God's ordinance; the permanence of those boundaries carries moral weight. But the larger boundaries of the Law itself are also inviolate. The fixity here is not that of a conservative or progressive, radical or reactionary politics. Nor is it a matter of strict construction versus ampliative interpretation. For the latter is itself a well-trodden rabbinic path. Rather, what Deuteronomy demands is recognition that laws and policies, like boundary markers, are not to be shifted at will.

That, of course, is the point of having a written law, its ordinances inscribed on stone (Deuteronomy 27:2–3), published and taught to the people (Exodus 24:7; Deuteronomy 31:11–13), its moral admonitions and the rituals that scribe them in the communal ethos passed on from generation to generation, studied and reflected on continually (Deuteronomy 6:6–9). It is why, even today, we symbolically hold aloft the carefully copied scroll of the Law in the synagogue for all to see. And it is why the Torah itself, anticipating the secular, self-serving motives of a ruler, requires even the king, like a schoolboy, to write out his own copy of the Law, under supervision by the levitical priests, who will oversee the accuracy of his text, and his understanding. For even a monarch is subject to the law (Deuteronomy 17:17–20). The core idea, so graphically enacted here: No one may rewrite the laws around personal desires, factional preferences, sectional agendas, or special interests. A just law does not change from case to case, and its core principles do not change from age to age.

But that is just a formal principle about laws in general. What is there materially in biblical law that would warrant such claims to invariance? The Law itself, any law that is implemented and practiced, is a living, growing thing. We can see biblical law itself in transition, for example, when we observe the shift in norms surrounding levirate marriage, from the ritualized shaming of a surviving brother who refuses to marry his widowed sister-in-law to a broad expectation that such a right or obligation will be renounced.[29] But the life-affirming principles of the law and the institutions that uphold those principles are inviolate. Even when their applications and interpretations shift, the changes are dictated *by* those principles—or, to put the general case more pointedly and concretely, by the sanctity of persons.

Consider the matter of self-incrimination. Jewish law in a capital case does not just exempt the accused from giving evidence against himself. It bans such testimony, arguing (with a keen awareness of human emotions) that a confession may aim at self-destruction. Simeon ben Shetaḥ is quoted in the Talmud as swearing that he saw a man chase another into a ruin:

> I ran after him and saw a sword in his hand, blood dripping and the slain still twitching. I said, "Villain! Who killed this man? Either you

> or I! But what am I to do? Your blood is not given into my hands. For the Torah says: *On the testimony of two witnesses or more is one put to death* (Deuteronomy 17:6).[30] May He who knows men's thoughts undo the man who slew his fellow!" (B. Sanhedrin 37b)

How does a rule of evidence become inviolable? How does a day or a year become sacred? Clearly, the appeal to God's law helps. But the moral foundation is human worth. That points us toward God and toward an adequate idea of God as the guarantor of the sanctity of personhood.

2. *Absoluteness*

Perhaps the salient role for the idea of the absolute in ethics is in defense of human rights. Jeremy Bentham calls rights nonsense, and absolute, imprescriptible or inalienable rights "nonsense upon stilts."[31] Bentham himself employed the idea of rights in some of his writings, but his witness of the French Revolution led him to deem all rights not actually laid down by laws hopeful wishes at best. At worst, in his view, claims to rights were anarchical, in effect a call for the violent overthrow of all civil authority. Granted, rights not recognized in law are difficult, if not impossible, to enforce. And revolutions fought in the name of rights mix the blood of good men and bad with the goods they seek and win, or betray, as the French Revolution, among many others, surely did.

Still whistling something like Bentham's tune, we must also recognize that civil societies vastly expand the scope and effectual exercise of rights through the institutions they create. They transform privileges into opportunities and realizable entitlements. Laws and institutions can turn vague hopes and expectations into actionable, achievable, normative, even normal practices. But, just as Bentham's experience of history cautioned him against the unbridled rhetoric of rights, so must we heed our own historical experience—and not least the witness of holocaust and genocide that have so scarred the twentieth century and bled into the twenty-first. Just as we recognize that rights would be largely ineffectual or inoperative on the civil, public plane without their positive delineation and demarcation in a body of law, so must we acknowledge that without the idea of natural rights, an idea whose very name Bentham branded a "perversion of language," legislators and the public who create legislators would all too readily deem themselves free to act with no color of moral restraint (since only their own laws and policies would govern their behavior).

Unless some way is found to mark off a category of deserts that *warrant* being held inviolable (even over and against the law!), none are adequately protected.[32] Reasons of state or force majeure—public policy or private interest—are always at hand to override mere "claims." And to the Utilitarian, as to the ancient Sophist, there are only claims—old conventions, time-worn practices, vested interests, and new or rival interests—to contest among themselves. Right and wrong, then, collapse into issues of perspective and wrangling over whose ox is gored and who bears the burden of evidence. Such disputes may afford good training opportunities for advocates to spar with. But make a metaphysic of the denial of rights, as utilitarianism and pragmatism often do, openly or covertly, wittingly or unwittingly,[33] and principle lies unprotected, subject to caprice, self-help, market forces, public inroads, and private assault.

Monotheism assigns absolute rights to persons, making subjecthood *by right* inviolable. The advocates of animals, or of the natural or even built environment, may offer to enlarge that franchise. But the net effect is less to expand the scope of rights than it is to debase the language in which rights are spoken of or claimed. That may not faze polemicists like Peter Singer, who use the rhetoric of rights in the public forum but vehemently reject the concept and any metaphysic that would support it. One does better, I have argued, to uphold the *relative* deserts of all beings, while setting apart, on a moral plateau, the special deserts of persons.[34]

Blurring the penumbra of personhood does not push animals to a higher plane than they live on. It only demotes the claims of persons, making it an open question, say, whether to save a stranger's infant from a house fire or one's own beloved pet.[35] That outcome, I think, is a fair *reductio ad absurdum* of the professed extension. But, as they say, one philosopher's *modus tollens* is another's *modus ponens*. One philosopher welcomes as a corollary of his view what another shuns or scorns as a damning consequence of a dangerous or unstable position. Suffice it here to say that monotheism defines and defends human rights because it holds the human person sacred.

Secular traditions have some trouble doing that. Pinning moral deference to sentience or pain alone sinks the effort. Contract theory cannot protect persons without becoming suppositious. For it assumes a social contract that we have all signed on to, or should, or would, if we but could. And then, in picturing that document (whose stoutest advocates proclaim it to be a myth), it presumes that, even prior to its drafting, we all have a right to expect others to keep their word—*although* there are no obligations prior to that free and explicit (or tacit?) agreement.[36]

Nor can the traditionalism of a Burke or Oakeshott—or Rawls—adequately protect personhood. We do not know that traditions, as such, are legitimately prescriptive, any more than we know that change as such is for the better. But the alliance of rights with deontology is both old and natural. For deontology shuns reduction of what is right to any other terms. Indeed, it refuses to derive right and wrong from any extrinsic source. Existential rights, as I would call them, are similarly unconditioned. That's just what absolute means: no strings, no ifs or buts.

Both deontology and rights have long and solid histories with monotheism.[37] For monotheism, like deontology, takes matters of right to be inherent in the way things are, as the laws of logic are embedded in arithmetic and as the identity principle is embedded in the nature of being: Just as a thing is what it is, so does it have the worth it has, and so do its activities and capacities affirm and express its nature and pursue its claims, insofar as it is able. Moral obligation is the demand, to which all aware and active beings are subject, to recognize and respect, foster and preserve those claims, insofar as they can be served without the immolation of higher claims.

Absoluteness in morals does not (or should not) mean rigidity. Circumstances matter, and the most plausible arguments for relativism typically assume altered circumstances and appeal to shared or stable intuitions about fixed reference points of right and wrong. That is, they appeal to a presumed or presumptive sense of objective right and wrong even as they urge the nonexistence of any such standard. Granted that rightness and wrongness will and should vary with circumstances, they are not a function of mere preferences or opinions. Nor, in many a case, do they vary with the identity of an agent or that of those who are affected by that agent's choices.

The shibboleth of relativists is that there is no value without a valuer. The analogous subjectivism about the senses has long been exposed as specious: Tyros in philosophy like to play with questions about a tree that falls in the forest and whether its fall makes any sound. The sophomore's conundrum here is based on an equivocation on the word "sound": Of course the tree disturbs the air around it and sends off waves of vibration that rumble through the soil. Whether anything is *heard* is quite another matter. But few would doubt that a falling tree breaks smaller plants as it falls, even if no one is there to see that happen. Of course there's no sight without a seer. But that does not mean that there's no bird without a birdwatcher. Why should any form of life, on earth or elsewhere, have its worth negated simply because no human has observed—or prized or collected—it? Is all value mere market value, and none of it intrinsic? If so, on what basis should one value market value?

Monotheists do appeal to God. Often they think of God as an objectifier, the ultimate judge. In so doing, they are invoking a moral standard, defrocked and secularized in modern times under the name of the ideal observer. In its more ancient garb, we have the admonition of Judah the Prince, the sage often cited simply as Rabbi, in view of his work as the compiler of the

Mishnah: "Know what is above thee: A seeing eye, a hearing ear, and all thy deeds written in a book" (M. Avot 2.1). God here is invoked as the conscience beyond conscience. But, even within the idea of God as judge, there is room and need for a moral dialectic, as is made clear in the Torah's narrative of Abraham's brave dialogue with God and against long established notions of corporate responsibility:

> *Wilt Thou sweep away the righteous with the wicked? Perhaps there are fifty innocents in the city? Wilt Thou destroy the place and not spare it for the sake of the fifty innocents within? Far be it from Thee to do such a thing, to slay the innocent with the guilty, so the righteous and the wicked fare alike! Far be it from Thee! Will not the judge of all the earth do justice?* (Genesis 18:23–25)

Abraham's exchange with God gives dramatic salience to moral principle. It rights the very idea of God, just as the idea of a commandment mandated by God's perfection can help us steady our moral line of sight. Abraham's plea for the Cities of the Plain dramatically enacts the dialectic between moral consciousness and God's judgment. For Abraham speaks deferentially to God, but with all due tact he presses a point of principle—a principle, we might add, that *could not* be pressed, say, by Odysseus to Poseidon or Aphrodite. Our apprehensions of God's will are not infallible, and neither are our moral judgments. But Abraham shows his moral and intellectual courage in holding God himself to what he feels confident must be God's own standard of justice.

Appeals to the idea of God as judge can be misleading if they suggest theistic subjectivism—as if the God of monotheism might be exchanged for some arbitrary godlet whose will could just as readily deviate from what is right or redefine the very notion. God, on an objectivist account, will no more make wrong actions right or right actions wrong than make what is false true. The realities don't depend on opinions. Genocide is always wrong, regardless of what we or our fellow Germans, Cambodians, Serbs, Croats, or Hutus may suppose. So is rape. So is all racial prejudice, taking up an attitude toward another solely on the basis of ethnicity. It's always wrong to sacrifice your daughter to your deity.[38] It's always good and right to aid others harmlessly and helpfully and to comfort innocent and hapless persons. Feeling otherwise or living among others who think otherwise or who have an interest in acting otherwise does not change the moral facts.

What does God contribute here? An objectifying lens, to be sure—if that speculum itself is not twisted, hijacked, or disabled. If we know that God is merciful, we should not imagine that his mercy means forgiving our sins provided only that we take enough infidels with us to the grave. Nor should we imagine that divine mercy would send anyone to eternal torture for failing to accept *our* offers of salvation or mouth the words of our favorite creed.[39] Asperity is not a mark of mercy and is not the hallmark of divine commands. On the contrary, it's clear evidence of counterfeiting—alienation and resentment passed off as God's by human pretenders, that is, religious impostors.[40]

But God for the monotheist is not just a judge but an *ontic* principle, the greatest reality, highest good and source of all goods, which are conceived as God's work, expressions of his generosity and wisdom. Looking at creation, then, we say that what is good is good intrinsically or instrumentally, and not just because God ordains it. We know what is right not simply by inspection of God's presumed commands but by the understanding we may have of nature itself. Our access to divine commands, like our knowledge of nature, relies on human wisdom and is constrained by the limits of our knowledge and at risk of deflection by our personal and communal biases and failings. Our very idea of God, as we've stressed, will reflect our moral and other values.

But God does orient the ontic hierarchy. Our knowledge of God is mediated by our knowledge of nature. Our human appreciation of values is more immediate and direct than our vision of the Summit. To be sure, our vista will be colored by our notions of our interests and deformed, to one degree or another, by the limits of our understanding. The idea of God's perfection can help us orient and stabilize the axes of our value judgments. It can help us in some measure to correct their tilt.

It is with such thoughts in mind that Plato argues that only the wise are fit to rule. For the capacity for rule, in the inner counsels of the soul or in public deliberations, demands choices among incommensurables. By their very nature, these cannot be weighed against each other—although they will often be measured by our willful preferences. What our valuations need, as a check on their subjectivity, is testing at the touchstone of the Absolute, the pure idea of the Good—that is, the idea of God.

Applying that touchstone in a very practical way, Jewish moralists will call refusal of charity a kind of idolatry. For the Decalogue forbids making gods of silver and gold (Exodus 20:20), and our lives give us ample occasion, as the Ḥafetz Ḥayyim playfully remarks, to see whether we've made gods of silver and gold, setting these metals above regard for persons, who are, in real terms—in the eyes of God, that is—no less precious than ourselves.[41]

Some might object that we have no ready test for moral judgments. I think that's mistaken. The *mitzvah* of love is itself a moral instrument. Granted, if we assume no knowledge of any values at all, there are none by which to gauge the relative worth of each choice we make against the seemingly remote standard of the Absolute. God is infinite, and the universal good God represents is of a wholly different order (or so the case might seem) from the daily choices we face.[42] But the Infinite does not shrink with distance, and God is no less immanent for being transcendent. Creation imparts value, and revelation attests to that value and commands its recognition. The commandment of love stands firm at the center of our obligations to one another. It charges us to calibrate the love we owe one another against the valuation we place on our own worth and dignity. So we're not quite so naked and without device as a merely sensuous epistemology might suggest. We have a moral guidepost, and our ability and responsibility to test any guidepost we are given (just as in the sciences we test all knowledge claims against all that we know) is no mark of deficiency but a sign of life and a source of strength and understanding.

When we judge, say, that slavery is wrong, we know that the comfort a master might derive from owning and using—even using up—another human being is incommensurate with the indignity to the slave, denied control over his or her own destiny. But we do not lack a measure against which to calibrate our choices. Mere common opinion, of course, yields no conclusive answers. Opinions over time have varied on this subject, and those whom we consult might well harbor a bias, conscious or unself-conscious. Contract here is mute, if not cacophonous.[43] For it tends to silence mere bystanders and ignore mere victims and outsiders. Besides, some men may sell themselves, or their children or their wives. Utility too readily offers an invidious answer in defense of slavery if it expects the harm of exploiting some to be outweighed by the benefits to them or others—for many of the harms of slavery are intangible. Even conscience might be lulled into complacency by convention, habit, familiarity, and tradition or seduced into self-deception by concupiscence or triumphalism.

But if we ask ourselves whether enslaving another is a good way, the best way, of showing that other love of the same kind and in the same measure as we would hope to be shown ourselves, slavery would rarely pass the test, and then only by very special pleading as to the circumstances—or by postulating attitudes readily exposed as vicious or perverse. Slavery, as a practice, fails the test if we take seriously the commandment *Love thy neighbor as thyself* and see the love it calls for as embracing every person. It fails miserably, abysmally, by failing to hold sacred the dignity of each person as a unique expression of God's infinite goodness.

Rhetorically, the shift from self to other is mediated in the mirror of God's gaze. So Malachi says (2:10), *Have we not all one Father? Did not one God create us?* But, morally, the spring is recognition of the existential worth of every subject. That hinges in turn on ideas of desert vested in the recognition of the worth of being. Such ideas need not directly or explicitly invoke divinity. But they point decisively toward God's absoluteness. So, here, instead of seeing the other in the mirror of God's eye, we see God mirrored in the eye of the other.

Consider another case where the claims of human dignity stand out in stark relief. There may be circumstances where polygamy or polyandry makes prudential sense. Historically and anthropologically, such practices can be explained and understood—although we must always be chary of apologetics disguised as explanations and chary, too, of the level of abstraction that explanations demand, cutting away from the painful realities of the particular. But, despite the open-mindedness of anthropologists and the broadly benign tolerance of social relativists (at least when contemplating societies they do not happen to live in and practices they do not have to live under), I can't think of any circumstance in which a human being is accorded the full dignity of personhood by being expected to share with another the love and devotion, intimacy, and trust that a spouse deserves. Nor can I think of any social setting in which the dignity of either sex is enhanced by such arrangements.

I instance slavery and polygamy advisedly. For, in both these areas, the Torah did compromise its values. Genesis (2:24) expects a man to *cleave unto his wife.*[44] Deuteronomy, as we've seen, expects even the needs of war to yield to the pleasure and duty of a bridegroom to rejoice his bride (Deuteronomy 20:6–7 with 24:5). Ecclesiastes (9:9) counsels a man: *See life with a woman you love all the fleeting days of the life you are given under the sun.* Proverbs (30:19) finds marvelous beyond words *the way of a man with a maid.* The Talmud's marital ideal is monogamous, and hardly any of the many rabbis cited there is known to have had more than one wife.[45] Yet both the Pentateuch and the Talmud countenance polygamy.

As for slavery, Leviticus (25:10) commands: *proclaim liberty throughout the land, to all the inhabitants thereof*; and Deuteronomy (23:16–17) ordains: *Thou shalt not deliver unto his master a bondman who seeketh refuge with thee from his master. He shall live among you where he chooseth, in one of thy gates, and thou shalt not mistreat him.* That prompts Hertz to say (ad Lev. 25:46), "A Fugitive Slave Law, such as existed in America, with the tracking of runaway slaves by blood hounds, would have been unthinkable to the Israelite of old." Such regulations as this and the compulsory manumission of slaves injured by their masters (Exodus 21:26–27) greatly mitigated biblical slavery, Hertz argues.[46] He quotes John Edgar McFayden (at Deuteronomy 23:16–17)[47] on the contrast with Hammurabi's code, which made it a capital crime to aid a fugitive slave. Clearly, the ideal of freedom is itself struggling here to get free.

But neither strict monogamy nor complete abolition is reached in biblical law—or throughout the world even today.

Biblical law allows a bound servant to reject the normal mandate of his liberation in the seventh year (Exodus 21:2–6). The proviso probably reflects the asperities of a harsh economy, where manumission might mean exile or isolation and could, in some cases, be more cruel than continued service. For it is not just clearer moral vision that frames today's ideas about freedom but also better conditions of life. Ethics is idle if it ignores what is feasible—as we see today in the realm of health care, where technique races ahead of means and need outpaces technique. We may call health and health care basic rights, but implementation of those rights depends on the technical, economic, and social resources deployed and deployable in their service. In this respect, Bentham was right about rights. We cannot prescribe what we cannot perform. But he was wrong in supposing that we have no obligations beyond those that we (acting as a society) have already enshrined in law or custom. That said, we can see a slope along which moral attitudes and standards grow, enlarging the scope of human dignity and the practicalities of its recognition. We do not restore the standards of the Mosaic code by seeking to reinvent its somewhat mitigated version of slavery but by recognizing its nisus and expanding the reach of the core values that inspired that mitigation.

The work of ethics is open-ended. As Rabbi Tarfon puts it: "It is not your charge to complete the task, but you are not free to give it up" (M. Avot 2.21). That dictum paves a third way, beyond Stoic *apatheia*, where outcomes, in the end, do not count, and Epicurean *ataraxia*, where not only exertion but even concern is relinquished. Rabbi Tarfon's view is strikingly progressive: Results do matter, but incomplete results do not excuse defeatism or lassitude. Rabbi Tarfon's admonition applies at the personal level, of course, where each of us must act and choose. But it also applies publicly—societally and communally—to the God-given task of *tikkun ʿolam*, mending and bettering the world. We enter history *in medias res*, with every human institution entwined around us and evolving along with us. So any effort we make to realize the good in our own lives or in the world will be halting in execution and partial in outcome. But that does not nullify the goal. The very idea of moral improvement, which is part of our task as individuals and as communities, presupposes corrigibility and thus the reality of moral truth and the possibility of moral knowledge.[48]

The Torah voices moral truths as divine imperatives. But that does not make them arbitrary dicta, as if they were the commands of some morally weak and insecure potentate. For the standard of God's Law is justice: *Right and just acts are more favored by God than sacrifices*, as the Book of Proverbs puts it (31:3). The nations of the world will admire God's laws for their wisdom, Moses urges in God's name (Deuteronomy 4:5–6). Fallible those nations may be, but their testimony is corroborative. It will be confirmed in turn, Moses says, as he rises into song, by the witness of heaven and earth (Deuteronomy 32:1)—as it should be, since God's laws are laws of life (Deuteronomy 4:1, 4:40, 5:30, 6:2, 6:24, 8:1), in tune with the laws God has engraved in nature. In the poetry of scripture, the fabric of the Torah thus becomes a signal instance of God's care (Psalms 98:9; Isaiah 26:8–9), an echoing special case of the laws of nature.

Biblically, the act of creation and the bounties found in nature manifest God's goodness. His justice, as Saadiah Gaon argues, is clearly implied by his generosity and grace.[49] And it is because the work of creation attests God's generosity and love that heaven and earth are called to witness to the justice of his Laws:

> Give ear, O heavens, as I speak.
> Hear, O earth, the words I utter,
> As my teaching falleth like the rain,
> My speech distilled like the dew,
> Like showers on the green,
> Droplets on the grass.
> For I proclaim the name of the Lord.[50]
> Give witness to the greatness of our God,
> The Rock whose work is perfect.
> For all his ways are just,
> A faithful God, never false
> But true and upright! (Deuteronomy 32:1–4)

The imperative *Give witness* addresses those called to testify: Heaven and earth will testify to God's justice, through the goodness manifest in their creation. So the same theme that opens the Book of Genesis is called to give evidence at the Pentateuch's close, after the Decalogue has been restated, many more laws have been reviewed, the consequences of adherence and disloyalty have been spelled out, and the people have been exhorted to follow and contemplate, teach and perpetuate God's Law: Heaven and earth argue for God's goodness and hence the justice of his Law, which Moses enjoins his people to cherish and live by. The falling rain and the dew distilled from the air each morning are paradigms of God's grace.[51] The concrete bounties of nature precipitate from God's transcendent goodness, manifested in the wisdom implicit in creation. That same goodness takes form explicitly, as well, distilled in the laws and norms of the Torah.

The same argument, moving from nature at large to human norms, structures Psalm 19, where the beauty and bounty of creation silently offer up their testimony in behalf of God's law:

The heavens recount the glory of God,
  The sky relates his handiwork.
Each day passes the message to the next,
  And night after night proclaims the thought.
Without speech or word,
  Their soundless voice
Spreads their sense through all the earth,
  Its tidings to the world's ends.
For the sun He hath pitched a tent there,
  And it issueth like a bridegroom from his pavilion,
Joyous, like an athlete to run its course,
  Starting at one end of the sky,
Round it passeth to the other,
  With nothing hidden from its warmth:
The Law of the Lord is perfect,
  Restoring the soul.
The witness of the Lord is sure,
  Making wise the simple.
The orders of the Lord are just,
  Delighting the heart.
The commandment of the Lord is fair,
  Enlightening the eyes.
The awe of the Lord is pure,
  Enduring forever.[52]
The rulings of the Lord are truth,
  And altogether just,
Lovelier than gold, than much pure gold,
  And sweeter than honey
Dripping liquid from the comb.

Thy servant too is cautioned by them—
  For in keeping them there is great import.
Yet who can discern his own flaws?
  Cleanse me, then, of hidden faults,
And restrain me from acts of arrogance.
  Let them not gain mastery over me.
Then shall I be innocent,

And clear of grave misdoing.
May the words of my mouth
And the thoughts in my heart
Be pleasing to Thee, O Lord,
My Rock and my Redeemer. (Psalm 19:2–15)

The monotheist's moral system, then, is not simply a top-down affair. God *is* the author of all value.[53] But all our sound apprehensions of value, for that very reason, lead back to God: It's not just that we know the right because we know God's will. We also know God's will because we know what is right. So we encounter God when we learn that He loves Noah for his justice (Genesis 6:9). Again, we learn about God and not just about morals when the Law propounds that God demands just weights and measures (Leviticus 19:36; Deuteronomy 25:15; Proverbs 11:1, 16:11). We learn about God when we understand that He expects justice of his people (Deuteronomy 16:20; Amos 5:15; Proverbs 21:3) and his rulers (2 Samuel 23:3). Perhaps most tellingly, we learn from God's self-revelation (Genesis 22:14) at Mount Moriah, where Abraham's encounter with God leads him (and us, as his trial unfolds) to see that it is not the immolation of love but the life of love and the love of life that God requires of us.

Both the name of the *parashah* that includes the binding of Isaac, that is, *Va-yera'*, and the name given the mountain on which that portentous event took place, Moriah, call attention to the play on words in which the Torah declares that God's true nature was revealed: *'Elohim yir'eh-lo ha-seh* (God will see to the lamb; Genesis 22:8); and at the denoument, *va-yiqra' Avraham shem ha-maqom ha-hu'* YHWH *yir'eh, asher ye'amer ha-yom: b^e-har* YHWH *yera'eh* (So Abraham named that place "God-will-see"—as it said today: "On the mountain is God revealed" (Genesis 22:14).

Dramatically, God's test of Abraham and his son climaxes with Abraham's evasive *God will see to the lamb* and its fraught counterpart in the same verse: *And the two of them walked on together*, marking Isaac's acquiescence and Abraham's pregnant awareness that Isaac knew what his father intended. But the narrative strikes its theme when Abraham discovers that his own words have proved prophetic, albeit with the sense he had intended reversed: *God will see* is everted to yield "God is seen." God is the agent here, not the passive object. And that is the sense of the opening lines of the story, announcing that Abraham was tested. But the outcome of the test is not a discovery about Abraham but a discovery about God: God is revealed on the mountain, not physically but morally. Opening up that theme, the Mosaic Torah will paint God's portrait in its laws and, more concretely still, sculpt God's lineaments not in stone but in the sight before us daily of the human face, created in his image.

We see the congruence of theism with morals and the spirit morals takes from theism in the obligation of truth telling. The Torah, as perhaps not everyone knows, forbids lying, not least when harm to another or illicit gain is the aim (Exodus 23:7; Leviticus 19:11–12).[54] Saadiah Gaon finds the obligation to truthfulness biblically underscored when personified Wisdom declares: *Truth is the study of my tongue; evil do my lips abhor. Every word my mouth uttereth is in justice, with never a twist or turn* (Proverbs 8:7–8).[55] The prescription of truth telling is readily taken as a corollary of *Love thy neighbor as thyself.* Kant, the staunchest philosophical adversary of lying, sees lies as manipulative. They deny the personhood of interlocutors by withholding the candor that dignity deserves.[56] But Saadiah takes a parallel tack when he lists lying, along with bloodshed, theft, and fornication, as a biblical concern directly accessible to human reason.[57] Bloodshed, he argues, thwarts the fulfillment God intends for his creatures. Fornication harms the family, robbing parents of the chance to care for their own children, children of the chance to honor their parents, and kin of the chance to lend affection and support to their relations. Theft subverts and supplants the work ethic, on which any society depends. But lies distort reality.[58]

In all four cases, Saadiah argues, human wisdom (*ḥikma,* echoing the language of Proverbs) sees the grounds for the biblical prohibition. Scripture need not have tabled the issue. Reason sees not just the harm of lies, their impudence or plain imprudence, but also sees lying as an affront to God, tantamount, as the Talmud teaches, to idolatry.[59] A lie, of course, is not just an untrue sentence; not every falsehood is mendacious. Both play acting and protection of innocents must be considered. But when a lie is wrong, it's not just that someone has been had. Saadiah's norm here, like Kant's, is deontological. Consequences matter, but harm is not all that is at stake.[60]

Saadiah's epistemology lays bare his rabbinic rationale: The liar, like a sophist—or a paranoid, we might say—seems to want to make the world over to fit his preferences.[61] What makes a lie odious to reason, then, Saadiah argues, is the clash between what one sees and what one says. God here is the guarantor of reality—not the arbiter but the Creator, proud proprietor, as it were, of reality and thus of the truth embedded in reality. Rejecting truth is an affront to God because it is an affront to reality. The heart of the problem is the logical disparity not *within* what is said but within the liar himself, between what he says and what he knows. God is the reality check, the hearer, as it were, of that dissonance. He is not the promulgator of arbitrary commands but the anchor of objectivity, the Truth itself, against which all claims to truth must be tested.

Our Gifford brief is not biblical, or dogmatic, or even civil but natural theology. That sets us squarely on the ground. Reason and experience, not scripture, must afford us our test of truth.[62] So the textual admonitions of the Bible or any scripture in behalf of love, justice, charity, truth, or compassion are not our authorities here. I cite them, nonetheless, as evidence of a historic investment in principles long canonized as worthy of ascription to God. But we do have knowledge of the good, not wholly independent, in its history, of what we've learned from sacred texts, although not radically, conceptually dependent, either. What revelation and the idea of God contribute to ethics is dialectical, not foundational. We bring our moral notions, suasions, customs, instincts, attitudes, and intuitions to the Law, and they enter into dialogue with what we read, informing our hermeneutic, as scripture itself and the conception of the God encountered in scripture, inform them in turn.[63]

Here's an example of that kind of hermeneutic. Tamar, we read (Genesis 38), played the prostitute. She disguised herself as a roadside whore, to trick Judah into giving her the heir his sons had failed in one case and refused in the other to give her.[64] Still unrecognized at the close of their encounter, she took Judah's staff, cord, and seal in earnest of payment. She then went home and resumed her normal role and clothing. So, when Judah sent to pay the prostitute he had visited, he could not locate her or recover his things. He did not press the search, *lest I be made a laughingstock*, he said (Genesis 38:23). But, months later, furious to learn that Tamar was pregnant—with twins, in the event—he ordered her burnt. Since she still had his sigla, the double standard stood to suffer a rare exposure. Hailed out for the barbaric punishment, she sent Judah word that the father in the case was the owner of these things.

The rabbis take a message from her obliquity: She allowed Judah to come forward, rather than simply name him. In effect, as the Midrash reads the case, she said: "If he won't freely own his act, let them burn me. I will not humiliate him." Rashi stands back to let the rabbis draw their moral: "It was on this basis that they said,'Better to be cast into a fiery furnace than to shame another publicly.' "[65]

Tamar's hope in sending Judah his things, the Talmud says, was that he would recognize God. How so? In Rashi's midrashic source (Genesis Rabbah 35.11), Tamar loses the identifying sigla, and God replaces them, in effect backing up her story. But Rashi, in retelling the story, retains the implicit appeal to God but suppresses the melodramatic and wholly fanciful loss of the seal, cord, and staff. As in his recounting of Joseph's vision of his father when the handsome youth repulsed temptation by Potiphar's wife, Rashi stresses the moral rather than the extraneous miraculous threads in the midrashic embroidery. Tamar, as Rashi reads the story, was calling on Judah's conscience.

Judah was not morally blind. It was he, after all, who had only recently urged his brothers to pull Joseph out of the pit and not leave him there to die.[66] Seeing things through God's eyes now meant that Judah must raise his gaze above the plane of his immediate ire and recognize that loss of face does not outweigh a human life. That larger perspective, as the Rabbis see it, made the truth luminous and cut away the ground from self-serving motives. The thought of God demanded and promoted a clear choice between the incommensurables, a human life or specious honor—a choice still troublesome today for many who commit or condone the ugly murders called honor killings. Tamar's dangerous ploy succeeded when Judah confessed that he had wrongly withheld a third son from her, after the deaths of Er and Onan. That matters genealogically.[67] But the rabbis glean from the tale not that God is the sole source of moral knowledge but that the thought of God's justice can realign our self-interested judgments and cut the ground out from under special pleading.[68]

Can we get the same clarity from other sources? Yes and no. Surely, social approval and disapproval are powerful motivators—fallible, of course, but so are human notions of God's will. Either source is subject to misprision; and misprision of God can be severe, since God's commands are deemed unexceptionable and often taken to be extreme. A crabbed, intolerant, fanatical, or dogmatic theism may need correction or modulation by the voice of conscience, personal or communal. But fads and enthusiasms, mob rule and hysteria, party spirit, libertinage, and secular fanaticism may also need to be curbed or gentled. Even noble quests may gain some guidance from a higher ideal than personal vision or cultural presumption. It's here that thoughts of God become most morally germane, enlarging our scope and expanding our horizon through the ongoing conversation between a religious tradition or ideal and the chambers of conscience, public or private.

Reflecting on the nexus between moral values and religion, A. C. Grayling quotes the Bloomsbury writer Leslie Stephen for the thought "that while religion flourishes, ethical inquiry is restricted to casuistry, that is, the science of interpreting divine commands." As Grayling himself glosses:

> The only justification for these is the *argumentum ad baculum* . . . The religious reply to the moral sceptic's question,'Why should I behave

> in such-and-such a way?' is simply, 'Because God requires it of you.' But this is merely a polite way of saying, 'Because you'll be punished if you don't.'[69]

But that account speaks more eloquently to the limitations in my fellow Gifford Lecturer's exposure to religion and religious ethics than it does to the actual dynamics (and diversity) of religious thought.

Epicurus treated any impulse not grounded in pleasure (or the avoidance of pain) as somehow unnatural. He judged appeals to the divine impious and immoral—impious, for assuming that the gods, who are blessed and immortal, would care at all about human doings or anything beyond their own perfect peace of mind; immoral, for tethering moral choices anywhere but to the natural promptings of pleasure and pain and the clear guidance of our own good sense of how best to maximize personal serenity. Nietzsche (having known little of serenity), took a different tack and strove to outdo Kant by making freedom not just a necessary but a sufficient condition of moral adequacy and authenticity. But the key notions here, whether Nietzschean or Epicurean, are variables, not fixed and opaque terms. Our ideas about the divine reflect our values, and our ideas of freedom echo our notions not only of human agency but also of moral responsibility and our attitudes about punishment and reward, praise and blame.

Just as people differ in their thinking about the divine, so do they differ as to the locus of the self. Epicurus finds our authentic identity in the hedonic and volitional. So it's no accident that Lucretius cherishes the assonance of *voluntas* with *voluptas*. Aristotle finds the authentic self in the mind, and Kant in the conscience. These philosophers agree in locating freedom in the congruence of choice with rationality. But they differ strikingly in what they understand by the dictates of reason.

Nietzsche, by contrast, locates the self that is worth realizing in the passions and freedom, in the will. Freedom, as he envisions it, is no longer the bright and plashing fountain of Epicurean spontaneity and creativity or the Aristotelian thoughtful rationality but a contrarian self-assertiveness that aims at self-invention. The Christian self, again by contrast, is often found in the human sense of creatureliness, acknowledging sin and accepting redemption. Nietzsche wants the moral actor to take God's place as moral arbiter. He is discontented with received values and still more with the very idea that values should be received. But that precisely is what many a scriptural theist embraces and celebrates, finding freedom in taking God's will and writ as one's own. Where Epicureans (if described in modern terms) saw alienation in conventional morality and heteronomy in theism, and where Nietzsche saw only oppressive conformity in religious tradition, scriptural theists often find joy, freedom, creativity, and liberation.[70]

So nontheists often feel uncomfortable on hearing scripture cited, especially in the public square.[71] All the same, what seems to irritate them most are moral suasions at odds with their own prescriptive bias. Value choices and value preferences, in such a case, seem to drive not just the choice of gods but even the choice of any god at all over none. Accordingly, religious appeals to charity, to fairness in the tax code, environmental stewardship, or racial equity may be welcomed in quarters where appeals against abortion or same-sex marriage are met with horror.

The natural history of such responses only confirms the linkage of values with ideas about God. From the defeat of the titans by the deities of Olympus down to today's struggles over Wicca and New Age spirituality, new gods are consistent harbingers of new (or newly confident) moral notions. In that sense, it seems, no-God is just another new god, and many an anguished appeal to ban prophecy from the public square, whether voiced as a Hobbesian fear of fanaticism or a Rawlsian banishment of all motives and motifs deemed "comprehensive," are heavily motivated by displeasure over what religions are seen or expected to teach or preach. They have little bearing on the practical relevance of a discourse, experience, or tradition that may work for good or ill in quite a variety of ways, depending on the integrity of the tradition, the moral openness of the discourse, the self-scrutiny of the experience. What I think we need to recognize about the nexus of morals to religion, even as we may continue to differ over both, is that our religion will be never be better than our values—or our values than our religion, by whatever name we may describe it.

3. *Stability*

Courage of a certain kind is part of what the thought of God contributes to morals. Again we recall Maimonides' instance: Moses boldly advancing to confront Pharaoh and demand release of his people from bondage, with nothing more than the staff in his hand, "because it was said to him, *I will be with thee*" (*Guide* II 38, quoting Exodus 3:12). The Israelite midwives, unprompted by any overt revelation, *feared God* and flouted Pharaoh's genocidal edict (Exodus 1:17). Their moral choice is constitutive: It arises not because God has ordered them to disobey Pharaoh's command lest they be punished. Rather, their stance contributes content and definition to the very idea of the fear of God—in much the way that Rosa Parks's refusal to give up her seat and move to the back of the bus contributes content and definition to the idea of human dignity. The thought of the Transcendent—not of power or punishment or protection but of transcendent right—led the midwives to risk their lives by sparing the infants. Esther, similarly, can say to Mordecai, *If I die, I die* (Esther 4:16). As Plato reasoned, it was because Socrates knew of things more precious than life and risks more dire than death that he could choose his own course as steadily as he did. That is piety; and Plato means us to see Socrates as a paragon of piety—not the impiety charged against him by enemies among his contemporaries, or credited to him by admirers among our own.

Do only theists show courage? Certainly not. But *anyone* who faces death unwavering on grounds of principle testifies to an awareness of higher values than are captured in the pragmatics of the day-to-day. Such actions point toward the Transcendent. They are paradigms of piety—whose Hebrew name, again, is *ḥesed*.[72] They demonstrate what piety is; we frame the concept around our understanding of such choices and the deliberations implicit in them.

Maimonides will argue that any Israelite who dies because of who he is or what he believes has perished in the sanctification of God's name. That is, such a person must be deemed a martyr. If we take seriously the idea that a martyr is a witness, we can generalize the Maimonidean claim in two ways. First, anyone who dies because of principle bears witness to the ultimacy of the principle for which his blood was shed. Second, lives, too, as the Jewish tradition has it, and not deaths alone bear witness. What this means is that we find testimony to God's truth not just in the beauty of the heavens or the bounty of the earth but also in every noble act, even when the actor does not clearly see the tenor of that testimony.

One sanctifies God's name, as the Torah calls on us to do (Leviticus 22:32),[73] the Rabbis explain, when one so lives and acts as to inspire others to recognize the blessedness of the Source of the values one lives by. And that recalls the traditional reading of God's promise to Abraham, that his people will be a blessing to the nations (Genesis 18:18, 22:18, 26:4, cf. Jacob's blessing at Genesis 27:29)—a promise itself bearing a blessing, along with an imperative: So act as to lead those who witness your actions to say, "Blessed is the person whose God is that person's God."

An important corollary, in these days of *jihād*, to the idea that noble and generous actions nourish a holiness that sanctifies God's name: A would-be *shāhid* who seeks to testify to God's transcendent mercy by acts of indiscriminate murder witnesses not the sanctity of the Ultimate but the perversion of his God-idea. Such martyrs desecrate the name they sought to glorify.

Halakha does not, of course, expect everyone to be bound by the commandment to die or live or risk his life for the sanctification of God's name. Still, every person's life bears witness to the values that he lived for. The world knows what the villagers of Chambon believed and how they lived by their beliefs. It also knows what the followers of bin Laden hold sacred and how they kill or die for their beliefs. The contrast is as stark as that between the ideas of piety and impiety.

A scholar of Torah, Maimonides writes, profanes God's name, desecrating the holy and violating the Law (of Leviticus 22:32), when his actions fall short of the exemplary. For the standard in which others' expectations of him are rightly fixed is the standard to which his learning points, if it is not mere empty rote. A Torah scholar's failure to live up to the standard to which the sacred books invite one to aspire, a standard that rises well above the bare minima of the Law, impugns not just his own character but the very principles he is thought to stand for. Among Maimonides' examples of such failings: purposeful delay in paying bills one could have paid promptly, addressing others harshly rather than gently, or confronting them quarrelsomely rather than cheerfully. One sanctifies God's name, Maimonides finds, through scrupulous dealings, affable manners, courtesy even to the scornful, and forbearance even in the face of an affront.[74]

Love thy neighbor as thyself is an open-ended command, an ideal, a target of aspiration. This results specifically from its conception as a moral demand of the Infinite. But the ideal is not, for this reason, to be treated as unattainable or meant only for the saintly and angelic. It is a target, not an unreachable goal—not in the heavens or across the sea, as the Torah puts it in its earthy way (Deuteronomy 30:12–13), a compass to steer by, but close at hand. God's nearness, God's intimacy, investing our words and thoughts with the pervasive moral presence of his command (Deuteronomy 30:14), make his core ethical imperative a source not of doubt but of stability.

4. *Universality*

Seeing *Love thy neighbor as thyself* as God's imperative gives the duties that enact the commandment a global reach not so readily won in contexts where the stark line between self and other may have hardened and deepened into a barrier between *us* and *them*. The stranger and even enemies are included in the God's-eye view adopted and commended by the Torah. Ben-Zoma articulates that outlook when he asks, "Who is worthy of honor?" and answers, "He who honors God's creatures, as it is written: *For those who honor Me, them will I honor*" (M. Avot 4.1, citing 1 Samuel 2:30).[75]

As Hertz explains, "The word *beriyyoth* [God's creatures] connotes the whole human family: there is one humanity on earth, even as there is but One God in heaven. The term *beriyyoth* often includes even the brute creation; and to spare animals unnecessary pain is deemed a duty of primary importance—*tzar ba'alei ḥayyim mi-d^{e}-'oraita,*"[76] that is, the prohibition against causing suffering to a living being is Biblical. But here, where honor is in question, the creatures singled out for special regard are our fellow human beings. Ben-Zoma's teachings of human fellowship rest on his recognition of our interdependence, as Hertz finds from Ben-Zoma's own reasoning:

> Not a mouthful did Adam taste before he ploughed and sowed, cut and bound the sheaves, threshed and winnowed the grain, ground and sifted the flour, kneaded the dough and baked it into bread; but I get up in the morning, and find all this ready for me.[77]

In the children's fable of the Little Red Hen, this sort of sequence illustrates the need for each of us to carry his own weight. But here the stress is on what Hertz calls "the web of social organism": Our interconnectedness was to Ben-Zoma "more than a mark of civilization; it was the basis of practical religion, of the ethical requirement to honour our fellow creatures."[78]

Glossing Ben-Zoma's equation of honor accorded with honor deserved, Isaac Abravanel remarks that a tree cannot bear luscious fruit if its roots are dry. His point: that the respect one shows others reflects one's self-respect, just as disrespect for others betrays insecurity. Honor sincerely given is a mark of confidence and self-esteem. Abravanel's psychology astutely recognizes how intertwined our identities are. A healthy ego, neither bloated with self-conceit nor quivering, like Uriah Heep's, between abjectness and resentment, has the strength to honor others without a sense of loss or diminution. It's that kind of self-respect that allows us to think constructively and work cooperatively, rather than enmesh ourselves in the self-defeating dialectics of emulous aggression.

But what can we say of Ben-Zoma's linking of the desert of honor with the honor accorded God's creatures? Clearly, the argument reflects the dignity of our fellow human beings as God's creatures. And respect breeds respect, as Jonah ben Avraham Gerondi argued. That imparts a prudential reading to Ben-Zoma's maxim: One is respected who shows respect.[79] But Ben-Zoma's prooftext refers to honor by God, not our human fellows. And the passive participle in Ben-Zoma's dictum (*Eizeh-hu m^{e}khubad?*—'What kind of person is honored') implies desert. The question was not just 'Who is respected?' but 'Who is worthy of honor?'

Ben-Zoma predicates honor fittingly given by God on our acts and attitudes toward one another. His prooftext proposes that we honor God by honoring his creatures—who are made in God's image. In other words, our human dignity calls on us to see in every human being sparks and marks of divinity. It is by recognizing that dignity that we attain the very dignity we impart. That is what we mean by global scope.

5. *The Reach of the Ethical*

The altitude that the divine perspective gives our moral obligations belongs to supererogation. There's an infinite variety of settings in which love might be shown and a loving character enhanced. That variety opens a field of infinite expanse for the exercise of imperfect obligations. Here the *mitzvot* are pedagogical, not coercive, the Torah working as a moral code, to open up our ethical sensibilities and humane talents.

What we need to recognize about imperfect obligations, however, is that they are real obligations. Standing at the edges of that field is not an option. Rather, the existence of an open ended field of self-development and service entails a *perfect* obligation to find and cultivate what is best in us and to grow and serve thoughtfully and creatively in the best ways that we are able.

The alternative is not merely satisfactory, as though all moral obligations formed a simple linear array, allowing us to quit, to retire from the field, once we have reached a certain mark on the scale. That kind of life or strategy is wholly unsatisfactory. For, as Naḥmanides observes, adhering strictly to the Law's behavioral demands, one might still live the life of a wretch. To rise above that level, we must live and act with grace and generosity, discovering or inventing the realm in which we can contribute most. Hence the commandment *Do what is right and good in the eyes of the Lord* (Deuteronomy 6:18). That open-ended imperative reflects God's infinite perfection, which we are called to emulate. It is for that reason that Naḥmanides can find it altogether proper that this commandment seeks to raise us above the plane of mere behavioral conformity to the statutory minima of the Law:

> The plain sense is "Keep God's commandments, ordinances, and statutes, doing strictly what is right and good in His sight. . . ." But our rabbis have a lovely, midrash on the verse in terms of supererogation:[80] 'First keep his statutes and ordinances, as God commanded you. But beyond that, even where He gave you no specific commandment, be sure to do what is good and right in His eyes, since He loves the good and right.' This is a major principle. For the Law cannot regulate every area of conduct—every interaction and transaction in every country and regime. It does spell out some things: *Do not go up and down as a talebearer* (Leviticus 19:14), *Do not take vengeance or bear a grudge* (Leviticus 19:18), *Do not stand idly by the blood*

> *of thy neighbor* (Leviticus 19:14), *Do not curse the deaf* (Leviticus 19:15), *Rise up before a hoary head* (Leviticus 19:32), etc. But in general, it says, in all things one must do what is right and good, and exceed the bare letter of the law—giving a neighbor first refusal (on a sale of property, B. Bava M^{e}tzia 108a), keeping the pristine reputation of your youth (cf. B. Ta'anit 16ab), being pleasant to people (M. Avot 1.16)—in short, deserving to be called good and just.[81]

Social usage is an index here but not the criterion. The true test is what is right and good in God's eyes, that is, objectively.

How can the Law, without paradox, ask more of us than it can command? The answer, clearly, is that the expectations are aspirational. As with any imperfect obligation, the modalities are neither minimal nor arbitrary. If one has a talent for music or painting, one does not answer its demands (moral demands in my view) by taking up ping pong or shuffleboard and proclaiming that one pastime is just as choiceworthy as another. Nor does one answer such demands by becoming a mediocre painter or musician. Thought and care, discipline and diligence, commitment and a pursuit of excellence set the standard. One who fails to study astronomy, if capable, Baḥya argues, is remiss.[82]

The same is true with service to our fellow human beings. Creativity is critical here, as David Novak urges. Introducing Naḥmanides' famous gloss on Deuteronomy 6:18, *do what is right and good in the eyes of God,* he writes, "*Imitatio Dei,* moreover requires imaginative application in concrete, specific circumstances, of the general principles of the Torah." Novak goes on to develop a Naḥmanidean conception of natural law, based on the idea that individual discretion in unique circumstances or moments of exigency is underwritten by God's acquiescence (or, indeed, approval), provided we actually *use* discretion in choosing and modulating our discretionary acts, framing and conceiving them as acts of *imitatio Dei.*

Novak's theme of divine acquiescence is especially germane when we think of supererogation in connection with the development and expression of our talents. But it applies, of course, to any human virtues.[83] That is why the Torah can fill out its positive, statutory code by projecting a virtue ethics. Concrete prescriptions illuminate a path toward better character. They guide us toward actions where there is merit in exceeding the letter of the law. Concrete as the steppingstones may be, the goal is to enhance our inner likeness to God. So it remains open-ended.

When Eliezer brings his camels to the well (Genesis 24:1–61), he is seeking not just a suitable but an ideal bride for Isaac.[84] Rebecca's cheerful offer, beyond slaking the traveler's thirst, to water his camels, reveals the kind of character that Abraham's faithful servant has traveled so far to find. As Samson Raphael Hirsch adds homiletically (at Genesis 24:19), Rebecca offered to water the beasts only when Eliezer had finished drinking. She had no wish to show off her kindness but was eager to act on it, in keeping with the maxim "Say little and do much."

Midrashic readings of the tale of Rebecca's wooing at the well make of that narrative a trope[85] that suggests how high and open the ethical sky may reach. Here's another: The Torah bans the use of iron tools in hewing stones for God's altar (Exodus 20:22). Iron is for swords. As Simon ben Eleazar explains: "The altar is made to enlarge man's days; iron, to cut short his years." Yoḥanan ben Zakkai[86] carries the symbolism a step further: "When it says *Of whole stones* [*sh^{e}lemot*] *shall it be built* (Deuteronomy 27:6) it means stones that establish peace [*shalom*, that is, wholeness, *sh^{e}lemut*] between man and God. The stones do not see, hear, or speak. Yet because they establish peace between Israel and their Father in heaven, the Holy One blessed be He said *Thou shalt raise no iron against them* (Deuteronomy 27:5). How much more so, then, should one be preserved from harm who makes peace between one person and another, between man and wife, or city and city, nation and nation, family and family, or state and state."[87]

Hillel captures the nexus between peace and love in his broad teaching: "Be disciples of Aaron, loving peace, pursuing peace, loving God's creatures and drawing them to the Torah" (M. Avot 1.12). Aaron's peacemaking was legendary, fulfilling God's charge to the Levites (Malachi 2:6) to judge in truth and justice and to keep the many from transgression. The Rabbis picture Aaron as shuttling between adversaries, telling each how sorry the other was to have given offense. Would-be wrongdoers stopped in their tracks, wondering how they would face Aaron if they did not overcome their enmity.

The Talmud tells that the rabbis Shemaya and Avtalyon, in taking leave of the High Priest in Jerusalem, possibly Aristobulus the Hasmonean, hailed him as a son of Aaron. Piqued at the love that the public lavished on them, he answered by calling them "descendants of the nations"—contemptuously alluding to their supposed non-Jewish origins. They retorted: Better than descent from Aaron is a life like his. Hillel, their disciple, took up their point when he urged his hearers to be disciples of Aaron.

Glossing the advice of the Men of the Great Assembly "raise up many disciples" (M. Avot 1.1), Hillel was stressing that scholars and sages need not be priests or prophets. He himself came from the humblest of origins. Those one should draw to the Torah need not be wise or keen, wealthy, well-born, or even righteous at the outset. As Hillel's followers taught: "One should teach everyone. For there were many transgressors in Israel who undertook to study Torah, and righteous, saintly, and worthy persons emerged from their midst."[88]

Thus, commenting on Hillel's "Be a disciple of Aaron, loving peace and pursuing peace, and loving your fellow creatures" (M. Avot 1.12), the Midrash remarks that many *mitzvot* become operative only under certain conditions, for example, the commandment to free the mother bird *If you come upon a bird's nest* (Deuteronomy 22:6). But one must pursue peace at all times. For the commandment *Seek peace and pursue it* (Psalms 34:15) carries no terms or conditions of application (Numbers Rabbah 19.16). The open-endedness of that task is indicative of the supererogatory reach that thoughts of God impart to ethical obligation.

6. *Inwardness*

Much of human ethics is social. Hence, the name of *ethics* in Greek and its Latin counterpart in the word for *morals* both refer to customs and to the intimate linkage of customs with character. But part of what is added by the thought of God as lawgiver and judge is an inward dimension, that is, conscience. Conscience does not mean mere remorse or regret but awareness and appropriation of values one can respect in oneself, even when no one is there to see.

In conscience God is thought by some to speak to us and by others to watch over us. But the nexus, I think, is closer than that imagery suggests—closer, as the vivid image of the Qur'ān (50:16) would have it, than our own jugular. That stands to reason, if I'm right in saying that the very idea of God is oriented by our idea of right (just as the idea of right is steadied by our idea of God). It's easy enough to drive a wedge between God's will and the dictates of conscience, but light shines between the two only when conscience falters or God's character is falsified. To the faithful monotheist, probity is as much an imperative of action as truth is of belief. The issue, then, lies not in spurious questions like 'Why should I be moral—Why should I do what is right?' but in the tougher question as to how to find or recognize or create right choices reliably.[89]

Some questions of conscience are readily answered. Leviticus (5:21) calls it *a trespass against God* to retain for oneself an object entrusted to one's care. Rabbi Akiva explains: God alone may know what actually transpired. Denial of a loan is tantamount to denying God. Can an atheist be conscientious? Of course. But the atheist who takes ownership of his own actions and guides them conscientiously is as much affirming God as the *soi-disant* theist is denying him by presuming that his defalcations are unseen. Not that the atheist imagines someone watching and holding him accountable. Rather, the atheist affirms implicitly what the false theist implicitly denies (even while paying lip service to the idea of a divine overseer): that the rightness of what is right is bone-deep in the fabric of being, without need of a watchman or scorekeeper. For the only proper reason that God is invoked in moral contexts is to underscore the objectivity of moral standards. As the Talmud insists, if you've wronged another, even God cannot forgive you until you've made amends.[90]

Thou shalt not covet (Exodus 20:14) is a subtler *mitzvah* than the prohibition against retaining an object entrusted to one's care, since it regards not just taking or keeping but speaking and thinking. Ibn Ezra (ad loc.) takes God's authorship of the command as the Torah's way of reminding us that God gave someone else, not us, this attractive object. The aim is not to squelch desire or stunt ambition but to curb greedy cravings and sidelong glances with a simple reminder of the facts and fate, property and propriety.

Ownership, of course, does not need God's endorsement—and does not always receive it. What's rightfully yours is not mine, and hankering after what another holds dear only breeds jealousy, rancor, possibly violence. One reason why adultery is wrong is that it can lead to murder—and does, far more often than would-be adulterers may contemplate. The Torah wants to nip that ugly blossom in the bud before it bears its deadly fruit. Hence the caution against coveting another's mate. But the commandment does more than caution, and the thoughts it seeks to stanch are destructive not just instrumentally and consequentially but intrinsically. They demean and degrade even those who fondle them quietly, quite apart from what they do to our relations with our friends and fellows: Covetous thoughts are rank and corrosive to the soul.

The commandment against bearing a grudge speaks to similar concerns. So does the duty the Rabbis draw from the *mitzvah* to judge each other favorably (Leviticus 19:15), that is, to give others the benefit of the doubt and not load oneself down with suspicions and negative presumptions. For a sour soul is just as nasty and unpleasant, just as precariously perched on the edge of illness, as a sour stomach.[91]

Still, the practical relevance of God in any of these cases lies in the need we may have for company when we start to plumb our thoughts and intentions. Since our attitudes are private, we might suppose, erroneously, that the rights and wrongs about them are wholly at our personal discretion (taking discretion now in a rather arbitrary sense that belies the underlying concept of sound judgment). Nothing could be further from the truth. Taking God's truth as the standard in the privy chamber of conscience is critical in theistic ethics—central to what the liturgy of the Day of Atonement intends when it calls God *boḥen k^{e}layot va-lev*—He whose scrutiny probes our hearts and kidneys.

Of course, the need for company, on this sounding, is no requirement of logic. There's no contradiction in the idea that one's personal judgment is quite adequate to one's moral needs, without benefit of counsel or clergy—let alone inner voices of obscure origin. Hypocrites and seers are equally attuned to thinking that they hear God's voice, and it's hard even for the best of us, since all of us are mortal, to distinguish God's actual commands from the rustling of our own passions and desires, hatreds, fears, or biases. Yet, that is the distinction that any of us must make if we are to seek divine guidance. Conscientious action calls for skill and insight, not just good intentions. And good advice is as relevant in that regard as good upbringing and self-demand. Conscience, it is true, *is* private and personal. But the pure conscience—the conscience that is not only clear but also sound—is not averse to company.

Discipline and tradition can help cleanse a human conscience of projective self-deceptions. That's one benefit of tradition, scripture, and faithful, uncorrupted counsel. What we're looking for when we seek to cleanse our conscience and turn to God for help is a way of overcoming the attachments that put ego on an animal plane (as Maimonides put it) and that twist our value judgments into self-serving rationalizations, robbing them of the detachment that might aid us toward a more universal, more objective, more Godlike vantage point.

One reason that we Jews fast on the Day of Atonement is to seek that kind of detachment. Perhaps it's no coincidence that, in Hebrew, the ideas of fasting, penitence, humility, self-affliction, answering, responding, giving testimony, even singing and focusing one's thoughts all meet and intertwine in the same tri-literal root (*ʿ-n-y/ʿ-n-h*).

Conscience is an inner dialogue. God does not interrupt with a thunder-and-light show—at least not usually. Unless one is a prophet, disembodied voices belong more to pathology than to virtue. Hearing voices without madness—that, I suspect, is the real miracle of prophecy. But sound character is more confident and better integrated than to take God's commands as anything utterly external. The *still, small voice* (1 Kings 19:12) pronounces God's commands, precisely through that integration. That's one reason why clarity of conscience and the absence of self-deception are so critical. We don't need to hear a sound to know what God is telling us. Objectivity does not demand objectification.

The Midrash takes up an image from the Song of Songs, calling God's Law *a hedge of lilies* (Song of Songs 7:3). The phrase is emblematic of the work of conscience. Reflecting on the doings of the conscientious person, who curbs the powerful demands of appetite or passion in deference to the Law, the Midrash asks: "Was there a wall of iron or a post to hold him back? Was he bitten by a snake? stung by a scorpion? . . . It was only the words of the Torah, soft as lilies!" (Song of Songs Rabbah, 7:3.2). The restraints here are border markers, mere reminders. The boundaries they set are neither arbitrary and coercive nor disruptive. To adherents of the Law, its ethical restraints and the ritual observances that are their filigree[92] are a hedge of flowers bordering a garden path, accepted and respected—cultivated for the beauty they impart to a way of life cherished for its lovely blossoms and its sweet and wholesome fruit.

7. *Imitatio Dei*

Thoughts of conscience and supererogation bring us back to *imitatio Dei*. Human subjecthood and self-awareness forge a moral link with God, conceived as the Source of all good. God becomes our model of beneficence; *ḥesed* becomes active and dynamic, rather than static and receptive. For Hebrew piety (as Spinoza well understood)[93] is generosity, the bestowal of grace and favor, not the mere acceptance and appreciation of God's bounties. The expectations are well framed in the Chinese call for rectification of names: If we are children of God, we should *be* children of God and live up to our calling as such.

Fashioned in God's image, the human person is holy, but not all-perfect. We are always *in statu nascendi*. We are, as the psalmist said, *but little less than divine* (Psalms 8:5). Yet, we are fashioned from the clay and infused with life. So we do not simply, statically exist as what we are. Indeed, what makes us holy is what makes inertness impossible for us, our dynamic, our conatus, our life and love—the love that is, as Plato would have it, the child of *poros* and *penia*, poverty and means (*Symposium* 203b). We need to act to realize our likeness to God. We can never just take shelter in it. Our creation in God's image is both more and less than a fact. It is, for each of us, a quest as well, something to be achieved and lived, lived by and lived up to. This is what is meant when we are charged to emulate God's holiness: *Ye shall be holy, for I the Lord thy God am holy* (Leviticus 19:2).

Holiness in the Hebrew Bible means transcendence, just as glory means immanence. We are called, by scripture and by our natures, to rise above our limitations and become more than we were when we began. That imperative, as biology reveals, is implicit in the life of every living being, manifest in the dynamic equilibria of homeostasis, in the dynamism with which living creatures cling to life, and in the higher-order dynamisms of procreation and evolution. It's what conatus means in living things. Every organism has a developmental history, and every species has its evolutionary struggle. But human striving, like the awareness of being created in God's image, is self-conscious and at many levels self-directed. We advance not just generationally, by evolution, or developmentally, in the pattern plotted in the DNA. Rather, we pursue goals of our own choosing and perfect ourselves (or fail to do so) along axes that our own creative choices help shape and define.

The moral onus, ultimately, is personal. But its theater is social, its foundations laid by parents and peers, its horizons undefined, but its upper, ethical stories reached not by what we take but by what we give. It's in the social realm that the commandment *Love thy neighbor as thyself* finds its theater of action. As Philo says, reflecting on the call to *imitatio Dei* that Plato and the Torah share,[94] a leader follows God by being creative and unstinting, bringing order out of disorder, and emulating God's generosity in giving being when there was none, harmony where there was discord, light where there was darkness.[95]

The Torah tells us to go where God manifests his Presence (Deuteronomy 12:5, 13:5).[96] Naturally, the Talmud asks: "How can flesh and blood follow the Shekhinah? One has to say, it means 'Follow the laws and the perfections of the Holy One, blessed be He: As He clothed the naked (when Adam and Eve were expelled from Eden, Genesis 3:21), so do thou clothe the naked; as He comforted mourners (blessing Isaac after Abraham's death, Genesis 25:11), so do thou comfort mourners; as He buried the dead (burying Moses, Deuteronomy 34:6), so do thou bury the dead" (B. Soṭah 14a). I cited these ethical instantiations of *imitatio Dei* in my first lecture. The Rabbis ceaselessly return to them. Midrashically, they say that the Pentateuch opens and closes with *ḥesed*, when God clothes the naked, by sewing garments for Adam and Eve, and models *ḥesed* in the burial of Moses. Generalizing on the same theme, Philo describes *imitatio Dei* as "following Him step by step in the highways cut by the virtues. For only those souls who make it their goal fully to follow in the ways of Him who brought them to birth can approach Him."[97] The *Ḥinnukh* adds a capstone to the rabbinic list: by tempering justice with mercy.[98]

The Ḥafetz Ḥayyim, with earthy starkness, silhouettes the alternative ethos against the backlighting of the virtues commended here: "One who thinks to himself,'Why should I help others?' estranges himself utterly from Godliness."[99] But, in a more positive vein, the commentators, noting that the commandment *Ye shall be holy* is addressed to the entire congregation (Leviticus 19:2), explain that this *mitzvah* sums up all the rest.[100] The Ḥatam Sofer explains: The *mitzvah* does not ask for an isolated quest of holiness but invites us all to pursue our likeness to God within our communities, sanctifying ourselves by the way we live and relate to our fellow human beings.[101]

Near the start of the Song at the Sea, Moses exclaims at God's epiphany in the moment of salvation: *Zeh 'Eli v^{e}-'anvei-Hu!* (Exodus 15:2). Often translated

"This is my God, and I will glorify Him," the ecstatic words challenge the interpreter in two ways. First, the sense of *anvei-Hu* is unclear: Does it mean glorify, enshrine, elevate, beautify? The rival etymologies and interpretative hypotheses are circumscribed by a context that clearly intends some form of exaltation. But that raises a deeper problem: How can mortals exalt God? Rabbi Ishmael in the M^{e}khilta,[102] taking beauty to be the core semantic referent of the unusual word, projects a ritual aesthetic: One's booth, citron, and palm fronds for Sukkot, the Feast of Tabernacles, one's scroll of the Book of Esther for Purim, one's *tallit* or prayer shawl and the *t^{e}fillin* or phylacteries bound upon the arm in weekday morning worship—all should be lovely, as befits the symbols that point to God's more than earthly beauty.

Rabbi José, choosing another etymology, specifies public and universal praise of God. Others propose other senses. But Abba Saul, playing on the Hebrew phrasing, groups the letters to read *v^e-ani v^e-Hu*,'and-I-and-He,' taking that odd coupling to mean "and I shall be (like) Him." That leads him back to our now familiar theme: "As He is gracious and compassionate, so must you be gracious and compassionate!"[103] God is adorned by emulation. Simon ben Eleazar caps the discussion, which has now moved far beyond the original occasion of Moses' song but not out of its range, still seeking concrete ways in which to express the awe and dedication that the experience of God's grace has evoked. He fuses public declaration with moral engagement, arguing that "When Israel do the will of the All-inclusive, His name *is* exalted."[104]

Allow me to sum up. As to the relations between God and morals, what I see in the Jewish sources is less an appeal to God's authority than a dialogue between our moral knowledge and the idea of God. The dynamic of that idea urges our moral thinking toward unwavering rather than compromised values—toward absolute rights most notably, but also toward unstinting generosity and unselfish love. Thoughts of God do evoke a sense of moral stability and courage. They do speak for universality and for positive, rather than merely formal, content in our ethical responses and undertakings. They call for supererogation, and they help define and enrich our sense of the directions in which the open invitation of the ethical can and should be pursued. They arouse and also answer to the sense of inwardness so critical in distinguishing the moral realm from mere etiquette or custom.

But in all these areas, divine imperatives do not fall on deaf ears or silent lips. No one capable of hearing what purports to be a divine command is without moral sense—a product, in part, of upbringing and experience, in part of our human endowment, as sensitive, reasoning beings. So we adjust the imperatives to fit our circumstances, ably or ineptly, honestly or invidiously, thoughtfully or mechanically. We scrutinize and criticize what we hear, adjusting our ideas about God as we learn, the better to express our moral, aesthetic, and other values—just as we refine those values in the light of what we learn about God from scripture, tradition, and history.

The dialogue between history and conscience sets up tensions and cross-currents between familiar and unfamiliar moral notions on the one hand and our dynamic sense of the divine on the other. But the moire patterns that arise as these currents intersect allow for mutual strengthening and not just undercutting. My focus has been on some of the ways in which our moral ideas are reinforced by our glimmerings about God and through the notions that we glean from scripture and tradition. For the hallmark of monotheism in ethics, and of ethics within monotheism, is the equation of being with value that is salient in our human affirmation of life and beauty, growth, thought, and creativity. What is right, as seen with the aid of this religious speculum, is not something arbitrary, changeable, or contingent but something bone-deep, as we have said—as deeply embedded in being as the fact of change and the reach of growth. For God, to the monotheist, is not some alien and arbitrary force or capricious personality but the Author of being, who created and affirms its goodness.

Do our moral obligations, then, derive from God's commands? I find that view simplistic. For not just any imperatives are worthy of ascription to God, and it is not by portents in the sky or rumblings in the earth but by their content that we recognize some imperatives as divine, others as human, and still others as impostures, desecrations of all that deserves to be held holy.[105] We test prophecy by its content, using our God-given reason, which is capable not just of noticing contradictions but also of recognizing truth and falsity, worth and beauty, striving and desert. Revelation, then, becomes an ongoing conversation; and our idea of God and of God's will grows pari passu with our recognition of value in all beings and of sacred worth and dignity in the human person.

We are not the authors of God's command *Love thy neighbor as thyself.* But we are its redactors, not scribally but in the practical sense that our lives write out what it will prove to mean to us in practice. When we take that commandment as our own, along with all that it entrains by way of love and care, universal scope, uncompromising principle and stability, the open sky of our emulation of divine perfection, and the silent counsels of a lively human conscience, the question 'Whose commandment is it?' gains a double answer: It's ours because we make it so. But it's God's because it points toward his perfection.

3

Q & A

Early on in your first lecture you say there's no such question as 'Why should I be moral?' You suggested that trying to tackle such questions only launches us into an infinite regress. You make an analogy of moral values with truth. If I understood you correctly, your argument is that we should accept what's true just because it's true and, in the same way, do what's right just because it's right. You seem to be saying that the question 'Why should I do what is right?' is a pseudo-question. But is it really? Does your warning of an infinite regress really cut much ice? A moral skeptic might see that outcome as confirmation that morals can't actually be justified. Shouldn't you accept the challenge of justifying moral claims? After all, many well-known philosophers have discussed the issue extensively—Christine Korsgaard, for one, not to mention present company.

I agree that it might seem imprudent to set aside a question that many moral theorists take seriously and that many who teach philosophy deem critical, at least to their students or their fellow theorists. Clearly, someone uncomfortable with a particular moral tradition, and especially with prescriptions that chafe, might ask, 'Why should I be good?' But *that* question relies on a particular moral backdrop. It assumes we already have a pretty good idea of what's supposed to be right. If taken generally as asking, 'Why should I do what is right?' the question does seem to me to lapse into triviality, as if it asked, 'Why should I do what I should do?'

There's plenty of contention about words like right and good—Where do they apply, how, and to whom? Are they uniform and universal in application, or do they vary in sense or force with time, place, and cultural context? What connection, if any, do they have to pleasure and pain, human suffering or fulfillment, money, energy, and other resources, animals and the environment, present, future, and even past generations? Faced with the dicta of a formal moral code, or with subtler, more pervasive pressures from an ethos or tradition, thoughtful people often ask, 'Why should I do what is good?' They mean 'Why should I do what is pressed or presented as good here, or assumed to be right by others in our community?' That kind of question gains currency, even urgency, in times of moral ferment. And what age in history was not a time of transition?

Questioning, challenging, seeking justification for the rules or for their use in a specific case can be exceedingly valuable. Asking 'How do I know what I know?,' not in a pyrrhonian spirit but to uncover the roots of knowledge, can motivate a critical distinction between knowledge and supposition. It can expose the pretensions of dogma and superstition. It can even keep journalism honest. Questioning moral norms and practices can lead to moral discovery—or at least help us frame good (or better) grounds for our commitments.

When we question ourselves in this way, rather than just turn the fire hose on others (whose fables and foibles are always plainer in our eyes than our own may be), the probing can provoke real changes—values clarification for those who do the questioning or encounter it and take it to heart. It can help us unsnarl confusions, reprioritize our goals, rethink nostrums or customs that have not firmly or steadily enough been held for questioning. It can expose tacit biases, calling on us to state the principles that would sustain our choices. That can be cleansing. Some norms won't stand up to the light of day. Explicitness is not always wholesome, of course. Social or societal pressures can make good norms sound bizarre if they're not widely shared. But the hope and trust of reason is that scrutiny of our norms is generally healthy. It's hard (to put it mildly) to find good reasons for racial discrimination in the distribution of goods or risks and often harder still to air such grounds publicly.

But normally, one who asks 'Why should I do what is right?' hopes to do what *is* right. The question is not whether any norms at all apply but about the pertinence of specific norms. When someone in all earnestness asks 'Why should I be moral?' the aim is not typically to question every ought but to hold certain norms at arm's length, for testing—usually against some other value—usefulness, perhaps, or consent, or sincerity, the moral counterpart of logical consistency.

College students sometimes probe familiar ethical dicta, perhaps encouraged by teachers who see in such questioning a gateway to maturity or critical thinking, or challenges to complacency, or entrée to theories about ethics that they fear may interest professionals more than their students. Pedagogy here may foment a kind of diglossia and confusion, if the teacher wants to know (or show?) what could ground (or revise?) ethical judgments and the students, perhaps, want to know whether or where specific norms about sex or alcohol apply to them, given their early tastes of moral freedom. But these last are questions about moral responsibility and human dignity in self and others, not the questions about meta-ethics or the metaphysic of morals that the instructors may have hoped to introduce.

The broad issue that philosophy instructors may have meant to raise is not typically about moral self-discovery, limits, and boundaries but about warrant. It's built on the assumption that morals at large need validation. But the question as put—'Why should I be moral?'—seems to lean on standards of just the sort that it professes to be looking for. The 'should' assumes that some sort of norms apply. Someone who thought that one's choices need not meet any standard would not ask such a question—unless, perhaps, to announce obliquely that he saw no reason to hew to what others regard as moral standards. In that case the question was rhetorical—the 'Why should I . . . ?' was a dismissal only slightly blunted by being phrased as a query. The real intent, perhaps, was to test, to challenge presumptive standards and to elevate personal preferences in their stead. But even that shift makes a moral claim, no less in need of warrant than any other. Moral skepticism, after all, can't privilege strong claims like those of egoism. And sheer amoralism is not self-justifying.

When philosophers seek validation for ethics, is the warrant they seek meant to come from inside the realm of values or elsewhere? If it's supposed to come from outside, it's hard to see how it would warrant ethical concerns. But if it comes from within, wouldn't it need the same sort of validation as it's called on to impart?[1] The ancient Skeptics posed just that problem about knowledge when they turned the search for a criterion of truth into an infinite regress, demanding a criterion for any proposed criterion. But the Skeptics were still invoking epistemic standards—high ones, in fact, meant to exclude any proposed solution to their problem, and moveable ones, typically filched from the armories of the adversaries they called dogmatists. They counted on their hearers' intuitions about what knowledge ought to be and do, even as they bored into all claims for a stable test of knowledge. The skeptical challenge to ethics is similarly parasitic. It presumes just the sort of standard that it challenges. So I do think it's misguided to ask how we can ground moral imperatives at large. It's asking for an answer that the question itself both precludes and presumes.

The epistemic parallel is instructive, I think. People may differ over what should count as truth or a standard of truth. But once we have the truth, *that* is what we should believe. In the same way, people may differ about what should count as right or wrong or about the best way of judging an action. But once we know what is right, it follows trivially, I think, that this is what we should do. People who say that expedience, pleasure, the law, the Party, history, evolution, destiny or convention, or any other power or principle should guide our choices are not denying that we should do what is right but proposing rival notions of right.

So what about Korsgaard?

Korsgaard sketches four main types of ethical warrant, under the rubrics voluntarist, realist, "reflective endorsement," and autonomy. As voluntarist, she classes all appeals to sovereignty, human or divine, deriving obligation "from the command of someone who has legislative authority."[2] She credits Hobbes and Puffendorf for moving (irresolutely in the end) from God's authority to that of an earthly sovereign. As moderns, they predicated morality on natural reason (albeit of a somewhat calculating stamp). But, in the end, they turned to God to project imperatives into a natural world that mechanism had stripped of intrinsic value. Korsgaard seems to admire these men for moving to secularize the source of command. But she does not lavish a lengthy discussion on command morality, taking it perhaps as a background theory looming up out of the mists of history.

So, did humans in olden times lack the moral or intellectual spunk or the military or political grit to question what was laid out as the will of God, or the ruler? I doubt there ever was such an age. Granted, laws and lawgivers have long been called divine, whether to enhance their authority or to affirm its objectivity. Were their edicts therefore accepted and obeyed without question? Disobedience is at least as old as laws. From the god kings of ancient Egypt or China to the crumbling of the divine right of kings, I suspect there were always questioners and yes-men, variously aware of serving or resisting a fiction that staked public or private peace on a willingness to presume or pronounce the Emperor fully clothed.

It's telling, I think, that papal infallibility was not proclaimed until 1870, when the Vatican was losing secular ground through the fall of the Papal States. Dogma is typically defensive, and dogmatism readily sees the best defense in a good offense. But I think theists are ill advised to peg moral standards to

God's will.[3] For, if we derive our values from God, we'll end up arguing in a circle when we turn to derive our knowledge of God from values. And I don't know any other way to reach toward God from where we stand. We need to start from the lives we live and the things we know in this intricate and subtle world if we hope to stretch our minds toward God's infinite perfection. We launch our quest from values we can recognize—beauty in the cosmos, a precious human face, the sanctity of love, the solidity of truth, the sheer exuberance of being.

I do see a vital link between God and morals—not quite the one-way ramp that Korsgaard sketches but a dynamic, dialectical relation, as my image of chimneying suggests. Every moral revolution, after all, is heralded by new thoughts about the divine—be it the Titans' expulsion by the Olympian gods,[4] the rise of monotheism in the Torah, the birth of Christianity, or Buddhism, or Islam, the Reformation, the philosophies of Locke, Spinoza, or Leibniz, the deism of the philosophes and their counterparts in the fractious American colonies, down to the birth of pragmatism, Marxism, existentialism, postmodernism, the mantras of today's "Brights" and fideists, and the neopagan followers of wiccan.[5] The marks of a tandem revolution show up vividly when the Decalogue sets parental honor on the same tablet as God's mandate of exclusivity, conjoining two kinds of reverence. Filial deference is not cut off from the fealty that belongs to God. But parents, alive or dead, are not divinized. Linked and not competing, the two kinds of piety gain color and body as each helps limit and shape the other.

Of course religions quake when moral ideas are in flux. Value notions are constitutive in our thoughts about the divine.[6] Traditionalists hold tight to the old gods for stability. But moral challengers contest received religious ideas and play on their complexities and perplexities, seeking warrant for their own commitments in new gods—or the downfall of the old. So there's no clean inference from 'So saith the god' to 'So shall it be done.' Human practices and values invariably intervene.

Likewise with secular sovereignty. Piety, reverence, patriotism, loyalism—all invoke allegiance. But allegiance is fluid and flexible, even at its most stolid. Traditions are never static. Indeed, images of stability are among their most powerful motors. Traditionalism, for its part, is typically reactive, often revolutionary, as today's Islamic Salafiyya movement clearly shows. The quest to recapture painted glories from the past makes traditionalism both a symptom and a cause of social, moral, and religious change, at times stunningly swift or violent.

Appeals to the authority of God, or the king, the ruling class, scripture, or tradition are effective only where that authority is recognized and in tune with what is asked of it. So telling people to do *x* because *A* wills it or commands it differs little over time and across a population from telling them to do it because it's right. That's the wisdom in Max Weber's idea of the legitimation of authority. But legitimation, as Alexander Bickel stressed, is a process, dynamic, never static.[7] Politics works the chinks between enthusiasm and resentment, embrace and disappointment, sometimes with a breeze or a wind, sometimes with a pickax. To ignore the draft or the tools poking in from all directions—moral, social, religious, baldly aggressive—is to miss history's most constant lesson. It's also to lose the ability (so keenly honed in the biblical prophets) of sensing, in the failure of legitimation, the critical moment in any revolution—as our modern vatic class so egregiously failed to do in Iran in the 1970s or the Soviet Union in the 1980s.

Sheer power—the use or threat of force, sometimes imputed to God or the state—promising rewards for compliance or punishment of disobedience, is of limited pragmatic impact if isolated from legitimacy, and of little moral relevance. God does not rule that way, as the story of Noah eloquently proclaims.[8] State coercion will sway some of the people some of the time—but more the venal than the virtuous. A professional criminal learns to cope with the threats of force he faces, the occupational hazards of his line of work But even a nonprofessional can be pretty unimpressed with such threats when he or the society he lives in is demoralized. And the oppressed in a tyrannical regime can grow desperate enough to ignore sanctions and stop caring about the ears and tongues of the secret police, even as the decay of legitimacy saps the will of the enforcers. Hence the vivid images of 1989: the youth who placed his body in the path of a tank in Tiananmen Square or the pregnant woman who braved Ceauşescu's troops and shouted, pointing at her belly: "Here, shoot here!" Robbed of dignity, she and the many who stood with her in the square and in many another place and time no longer heeded the fear of death.

Sanctions do yield prudential imperatives. But these sunder obligation from the sovereign's will and paste it to a bundle of promises and threats. Conformance becomes contingent on externals, alien to the ideals of those called to embrace it, and even to those who do the calling. Fear and greed stay on the job, but love, loyalty, and piety erode. So even the faithful may fall away. Even in the Tsar's palace, trinkets disappear. The notion of a command morality, then, is inherently unsound: viciously suppositious if it pins legitimacy to a sovereign's orders, leaky and incoherent if it looks elsewhere, say, to sanctions.

Moral realism, as Korsgaard describes it, rests on the claim that there are moral facts. She classes Samuel Clarke and Richard Price as moral realists of the eighteenth century; H. A. Pritchard, G. E. Moore, W. D. Ross, and Thomas Nagel, of the twentieth. The weakness of the approach, as its critics tend to agree, lies in its troubles about what makes for the truth of moral facts. Are there natural properties or states of affairs whose very occurrence makes the world a better place? If so, the realism becomes a kind of naturalism, subject to the critique leveled by Hume and, later, Moore against all attempts to reduce the good to natural terms. But if 'good' is meant to name a nonnatural property, as some moral realists have urged, it falls into a mare's nest of issues about how any property of natural beings could be nonnatural and how nonnatural properties are to be identified, compared, appraised. Do we need a nonnatural faculty—intuition, inspiration?—even to spot them, let alone distinguish or describe them, or gauge their relative worth?[9]

I think there are moral facts—that the world is a better place for the existence, say, of human virtues. But I don't think the good reduces to the sort of mere facticity that Hume's and Moore's arguments targeted. Clearly, not all that happens is good just because it happens. But I do think it's better that something exists rather than nothing. I can believe that because experience gives me a pretty concrete idea of what sort of somethings there actually are: It's good that life exists, and better for there to be sensation and awareness than just, say, vegetation.

Part of what I see in the world is that natural beings, by nature, tend to reach beyond themselves. The conatus that is the essence of each being makes claims that deserve consideration, even respect. If so, the *is/ought* contrast projects a false dichotomy, and so does the natural/nonnatural distinction. Philosophers who treat reality at large as value neutral neglect the dynamism of nature. They fail to see the inherent value of beings. In effect, they strip the claims that beings make of their prescriptive force—partly by ignoring the transcendent dimension that makes all things in nature more than merely natural.

Value, as I see it, is not a property supervenient on the being of things. It *is* their being and the project of their being. I see value in the very existence of things, because that existence is dynamic and conative. Beings make claims, and those claims establish prima facie deserts. The equilibration of such claims in relation to each other lays out the basis of actual deserts. In the resultant hierarchy, persons, by dint of their subjecthood, reach a moral plateau that grounds human worth and dignity, existential rights and equality.[10]

The search for value as a nonnatural property was an artifact, a hangover, I suspect, of the logicism of an era when the work of philosophy was widely supposed to be linguistic analysis and values were sought by parsing value judgments—as if the good were to be found (or found missing) in a term.

That, I think, was a category error, perhaps connected to another: trying to derive value judgments deductively, from a propositional or linguistic source—as if justification meant implication. But, just as causal laws will never be discovered by deductive reasoning, so will prescriptive principles never be unearthed as mere properties of a predicate. If value is real, it must reside in the only things that are real, not in sentences or terms but in beings.

The approach I'm taking is as old as the verse in Genesis that tells of God beholding the light and seeing that it is good—not just calling it good and imposing that description, and not making its goodness dependent on anyone's opinion, or use, or appreciation. God (in the poetry of Genesis) sees that the light itself is good, as a work of art might be judged good, not for its uses but for what it is. The worth of beings, I think, is what validates their claims; their worth advances in the measure of those claims—their projects, purposes, creative activities. It's the merit of those projects and the promise of their potential that warrants ethical response.

But no response follows analytically from the sheer making of a claim. Ethics arises not by implication but out of invocation, invitation, receptivity and response. Claims ask for a response, nuanced, attuned, sensitive, and itself creative. But such responses are not a given, and the fact that what is right is what we ought to do does not necessitate ethical action. It's still up to us to act and choose. Even *modus ponens* does not *determine* a response. It just specifies what an appropriate response *should* be.

Beings are not norms any more than they are propositions. Most of the claims beings make are unspoken. Recognizing those claims, insofar as they are not overridden, is like acknowledging a truth. It, too, is a response to what is there. But it is we, the conscious subjects, moral agents, persons in short, who make the response. We do not find it ready-made for us.

The realism I propose, in short, is not a realism of predicates, properties, and propositions but an ontic realism that can lead on to varieties of virtue ethics and perfectionism. It finds value locally, in the strivings of all beings, not just in their utility. This kind of realism is too readily overlooked by inquirers who imagine that physics somehow dissolved the values resident in beings or who presume that Darwin killed off teleology. The entities that physics studies are all, in fact, dynamic. And adaptation, the linchpin of evolutionary biology, is as teleological a concept as any advanced by Plato or Aristotle or the Stoics. For we cannot describe, let alone treat medically or explain in evolutionary terms, any organ or physiological process without reference to its function—the benefit afforded to the organism or the type, now or in the past. Biology, inevitably, points to the good of organisms. Even the most primitive have a "sake"—an interest, not just to us or for us but for the organism or the population it belongs to. All things have and, indeed, affirm some value. It is that very general fact, the worth of beings, that I think should ground our norms.

When I point to the worth of all things and to the precious worth of the human person, who is, with all our human failings, the best of the beings we find in nature and the most worthy of our regard, not for our mere kinship but for what a human subject really is, am I, too, trying to give warrant to ethics? On the contrary. I'm only pointing to loci of value, not trying to say why we should do what is right but endorsing a specific ethical approach that I find to evoke a catena of familiar norms: respect for the works of nature and of human hands, love of life, and reverence for the sanctity of persons. The obverse of the honor that is the due of being is the aversion for destructiveness presaged in the Torah,[11] which rises to a high pitch of horror at acts of wanton destruction and sounds a shrill tocsin when the victims are human. The norms expand naturally, organically we might say, into new situations. Even if we find new life forms as we explore the cosmos, what we know already of the deserts of persons and of beings susceptible to pain or disruption tells us much of what we would need to know morally.

My brief is not to try to warrant 'should' statements, as if saying, 'One really should take "should" more seriously.' I simply fear that many a moral realist is barking up the wrong tree by looking for value in predicates or properties when it should be seen and sought in beings, whose projects call for a response by anyone who can recognize effort and achievement.

Under "reflective endorsement" Korsgaard groups Hutcheson, Hume, Mill, and Bernard Williams, since they all seek warrant for morality in the idea that morality "is good for us."[12] Eighteenth-century sentimentalists, she notes, reversed the polarities set out by the realists: It is not because an act is vicious that we disapprove it, Hume holds; we call it vicious because we disapprove. That sounds a rather subjectivist story, and that is how it's often understood.[13] But Korsgaard finds an objectivist kernel in the suggestion that we "have reason to be glad that we have such sentiments and to allow ourselves to be governed by them." It suggests that morality might be "a good thing for us."[14] That links Hume's celebration of benevolence with Fielding's praise of prudence. Mill, too, "turns to the method of reflective endorsement," having found nothing in his naturalism that "settles the question of the normativity of obligation."[15] Bernard Williams becomes the poster child of the approach for his efforts to build "an absolute conception of the world," a vision of life and value that rises above personal or parochial assumptions. His model is the relative objectivity of science. He finds the roots of ethical objectivity not in "thin" notions like 'right' and 'good' but in 'thick' ones like 'cowardly' or 'brutal.'

What makes terms thick, of course, is their cultural embeddedness, a marked feature of all terms that name human virtues and vices. Different contexts and cultures set varied valences on thick notions like pride or pity. So it's hard to see how thick notions escape the fate of the commonplaces that used to pass for intuitions and that so readily roll and twist themselves into varied shapes to accommodate casual or casuistic demands. Intuitionism came to grief when the seeming truisms that cushioned it began to split along the bias, exposing bigotry, triumphalism, sexism, and other prejudices that helped fill out and puff up familiar moral notions. To qualify as Korsgaard's jockey, flying fast and free over the exclusionary slough, Williams jettisons such stuffing, the prejudices born of gender or background, and holds fast to a *human* viewpoint, *universal enough* for ethical use but never knackered by unseen biases about what 'human' means.

That's a tall order, fraught with risks of slipping into relativism, or chauvinism, when familiar values are celebrated as human and their alternatives caricatured or ignored. Many aspire to universality, and many may claim it. But one thinker's catholicity is another's parochialism.[16] Rawls is one casualty. His reach for the universal does not quite satisfy the universe. It's too thick for some, too thin for others, and altogether the wrong flavor and ingredients for many more.

The paragons of thick virtue are the heroes of songs and stories. But the strop that gives thick values their sharp edge is often hanging from the belt of some alien oaf or ogre, or lying near the hearth of some witch or hag, the bestialized or demonized other evoked as a foil to the idealized or romanticized values of ego or ego's group. Reflective endorsement, in a word, is only as open as the sensibilities of its users. Sterne's Uncle Toby in *Tristram Shandy* is the soul of gentle tolerance. But Dr. Slop receives as ungenerous a portrait as any in Dickens. Melville is at pains to humanize Queeqeg and then paints Ahab's Malay boat crew in lurid tones of racial loathing. Hawthorne cannot find it in himself to show kindness to a Puritan.

Reflection, we read, is supposed to involve conversation, eased by the tact that certain conventions of certain polite societies expect of conversation partners when they're face to face. Such dialogue can be fruitful if those who engage are broad minded—more open and less prone to polarization and digging in their feet when challenged than most real people are. But even on the best assumptions, conversation adds no warrant to the quality of the judgments brought to it. Open-mindedness is no remedy for ignorance or confusion, and the authority of expertise can often breed tunnel vision. Even the finest whetstone can't make an earthworm into an épée.

'Reflection,' clearly, is not a success term, and the universal sensibility Williams pursues is a virtue to be won, not the sure output of clapping on one's thinking cap and chatting with friends or colleagues, or enemies and rivals. But beyond that, there's a structural problem: Catholicity, insofar as it's attainable, is most often won at the price of vagueness, compromise, etiolation of just the sort that Williams resists in thin moral notions. There seems to be a tradeoff here: Specify what you're after well enough to make it thick, and you're in the cultural soup—perhaps not yet a prisoner of its particularities but well dredged in its flavors and scents. Extricate yourself, and you're wielding abstractions, or even rules of thumb, laws, proverbs, now shorn of the contextual cues that made them usable in practice. Aristotle knows the problem well. It's not a strict dilemma but a practical issue that everyone must face who wants to live thoughtfully and think critically in a community. Thinking, we can say, is always preferable to thoughtlessness, and talk is better than many an alternative. But neither is a panacea.

But Korsgaard raises another problem: The method Williams preached or practiced (assuming it is a method and not just a new call upon shared sensibilities), his appeal to our shared humanity, collapses in the end into teleology, a refuge Korsgaard stoutly rejects.[17] Teleology, regularly linked with essentialism, may look procrustean to her or to her imagined audience. But, beyond that, as she sees it, teleology (as typified in Plato and Aristotle) finds the world we live in wanting vis-à-vis its ideal. Only modernity, she says, faces the world forthrightly, as it is.

That's a strange criticism, since morals would seem remiss merely to settle for what it sees and not hold out for better. A hurdle too high, of course, will not be tried for, and some hurdles are too high in absolute terms. No one should be pressed to leap tall moral buildings in a single bound. Ethics, it seems, should seek a middle path, not asking the impossible or even the highly unlikely but not just settling for the status quo—or there'd be no point in any prescription. Humanism, in that case, does not seem unfair or unrealistic at all: It asks us only to be what we can be. If that's the human goal, teleology seems far from overly idealistic.

Korsgaard's preferred mooring for morals, Kantian in inspiration, is the view that "autonomy is the source of obligation."[18] Our capacity for reflection allows us to think critically about our actions, indeed, demands it: "The reflective mind cannot settle for perception and desire, not just as such. It needs a *reason*." And then, mysteriously: "If the problem springs from reflection then the solution must do so as well."[19] More simply stated: If our problem is want of reasons, it's solved by having them.

Terms like 'good' and 'right,' Korsgaard argues, *are* success terms, signaling the happy resolution of a quest for reasons:[20] "'Reason' means reflective success."[21] That leaves behind the problem of the complacent cad. But "Reflective distance from our impulses makes it both possible and necessary to decide which ones we will act on: it forces us to act for reasons . . . it forces us to have a conception of our own identity, a conception which identifies us with the source of those reasons. In this way it makes us laws to ourselves."[22] Reasons have "an intrinsically normative structure."[23]

That sounds like pulling a prescriptive rabbit out of a syntactical hat—until Korsgaard confesses: "But there is still a deep element of relativism in the system. For whether a maxim can serve as a law still depends upon the way that we think of our identities. And . . . different laws hold for wantons, egoists, lovers, and Citizens of the Kingdom of Ends."[24] Evidently, Korsgaard does not mean quite the same thing by a law as Kant does. For him, a law, unlike a maxim, can never be bad or neutral. Kant's high silk hat, perhaps, was more semantical than syntactic: reliant on the richness (thickness?) of the German *Recht*—for right cannot be wrong. Onora O'Neill replicates Kant's reasoning when she speaks of "acting on principle." For a principled person, in modern English, is one whose principles are good and who acts on them.

Korsgaard knows that there are bad rules, but she thinks (or hopes) that something in human psychology demands that reasons be inherently good, not just speciously appealing. Granted, reasons have an inherently normative *syntax*; they do, in intent, prescribe. But whether they do so legitimately is quite another question. There's no more necessity in a rule's being right or a prescription's being prescriptive or a norm's being normative, just because it's a rule or norm or prescription, than there is in a king's command being just or an officer's order being sound simply because he's a king or an officer in charge. Newly unearthed photographs show the SS personnel of Auschwitz having a fine time. They knew the rules and clearly thought they had excellent reasons for doing what they were doing.

Struggling to advance from relativism to anything properly normative, Korsgaard proposes: "We could, with the resources of a knowledge of human nature, rank different sets of values according to their tendency to promote human flourishing."[25] There's the teleology again that Korsgaard has forsworn—not, of course, Aristotle's culture-bound and gender-marked ideals but still the structure he anatomized—now trimmed selectively:

> It is because we are human that we must act in the light of practical conceptions of our identity. . . . so long as you remain committed to a role, and yet fail to meet the obligations it generates, you fail

> yourself as a human being, as well as failing in that role. And if you fail in all your roles—if you live at random, without integrity or principle, then you will lose your grip on yourself as one who has any reason to live and act at all.[26]

The homiletical tone grows more strident and more insistently secular as Korsgaard sums up:[27]

> I have argued that human consciousness has a reflective structure that sets us normative problems. It is because of this that we require reasons for action, a conception of the right and the good. To act from such a conception is in turn to have a practical conception of your identity, a conception under which you value yourself and find your life to be worth living and your actions worth undertaking. That conception is normative for you and in certain cases it can obligate you.... you are a human being and so if you believe my argument you can now see that that is *your* identity.... And that is not merely a contingent conception of your identity, which you have constructed or chosen for yourself or could conceivably reject. It is simply the truth.[28]

How does this differ from saying "Just let your conscience be your guide"?[29] Does saying that "in certain cases" the truth of one's humanity confers obligations help one find, for self or others, the cases where bad conscience or bad faith has waylaid or misled one's reflective identity?

Our varied identities and roles, Korsgaard argues, are contingent—and therefore readily (or not so readily) shed (or re-ordered): "Being human, we may at any point come to question the normativity of one or another of our practical identities... citizenship, or motherhood, or my profession." We cannot "be bound" ultimately "by conceptions of our identity which are not in themselves necessary."[30] But our common humanity is another matter. Here we encounter (or fail to encounter?) our reflective nature, the source of our *moral* identity, "which stands behind the others" and "in a special relationship" to them. For it governs them "in a way," gives them their importance and "part of their normativity." The claims are halting but backed by a stronger claim: that without moral identity, without reflective awareness of our membership in the Kingdom of Ends, none of the rest of our roles would be normative.

That brings us full circle. We're admonished to live as human beings and live up to the roles implicit in that identity—some of them self-chosen, others thrust upon us socially, or exigently, economically or existentially, or (dare we say it?) by our essential nature. "Thrownness" may sound better to postmoderns, but 'givenness' is a more neutral term and closer to the truth. Our humanness dominates our other roles, apparently because this one, being more general, is unescapable. Would that every person committing suicide or suicide by degrees through drug use and other forms of self abuse—including those millions who still use tobacco—were as aware of that as Korsgaard seems to assume we must be. Would that every economic man and woman knew that their humanity comes first and calls on them to reflect and not let their more contingent roles as milkman or mother or politician or entrepreneur commandeer their personhood. Somehow, between the empiric and the normative, Korsgaard has projected her wishes onto the human condition, as if our sheer humanity (shorn of thick normative content?) gave each of us clear guidance about which roles come first, or later, or last, or not at all.

Still, the human given includes our embodiment (and so not just our species membership but our sex and sexuality, and, yes, our gender and even our parental drives and roles, at the interface of identity and embodiment, and reaching beyond the fringed boundaries of individuality). Our awareness includes but is not confined to reason. It does contain the roots of creativity, as well as sensibility, spirituality, and, yes, susceptibility to moral claims—which is, I believe, a part of reason. Our experience and our repertoire of roles and motivations do include some actions that are self-serving in the narrowest of senses, along with an ability to learn and grow, relate and connect, that enriches and enhances the idea of human flourishing and lifts it above the soil in which the flags are planted and the flowers take root, the soil from which the imagery of human flourishing was plucked.

Korsgaard's analysis returns us to the Socratic idea that the unexamined life is not worth living and to the Socratic hope that self-knowledge can be redemptive. It even chimes with the Gospel thought that the truth can set us free. But Korsgaard forswears any overt reliance on scripture or salvation or on what Plato discovered at the heart of the Socratic hopes for self-knowledge, the expectation that what one finds once one knows oneself is no poor, bare, forked animal, no mere creature of conditioning, but something, someone divine.

Thinking about reason in substantive, rather than merely formal, terms, not as mere reflection on our own thoughts and those of others but as a capacity for knowing value when we see it, brings us back to Plato's finding about the practical role of reason in the internal politics of the soul and his recognition that there is strength in the integration of our values and weakness in the contention of desires. But there's not much use in recognizing reason's capabilities for recognizing and integrating values if we're barred from seeing the worth of psychic coherence and integration. Shouldn't something be said (if the quest is for a warrant of moral values) about why we should prize health over illness, or sanity over madness, or flourishing over dissolution? That, it seems to me, would call for some claims to be made in behalf of beings, and in particular for the special worth of living, conscious beings as compared with any others. But such claims can't warrant morals. They only point it toward its proper objects.

Like the Chinese mandate for a rectification of names, Korsgaard's argument, in effect, says, If you're a man, *be* a man! She even echoes the Stoic counsel to embrace our roles. But she lacks the Confucian reverence for roles (with its attendant rigorist downside), and she has not paid the price (in terms of resignation) for the Stoic harnessing of dignity to our situation. For both nature and culture can set trammels on our free expression and even on our moral obligations, if virtues like diligence and discipline, loyalty and follow-through prove insufficient to define the path of duty. Korsgaard's recipe for virtue is to urge us to embrace our roles, but 'Not too narrowly!'—as if the rightful boundaries were somehow resident in a shared ideal of humanity somehow capable of fine-tuning and applying itself, even when stripped bare of cultural elaboration—stripped even of gender roles and the filial or parental norms that vary so widely and yet span so wide an arc in the identity of most of us human beings.

But assuming our access to so fittingly substantive (but not overparticularized!) a vision of our humanity, what have values like these concretely to do with autonomy? Of course our human strengths and capabilities (virtues, in short) strengthen us in the exercise of autonomy and lend worth and weight to the acts and choices we call our own. But how does autonomy, per se give birth to substantive moral dicta, as Korsgaard seems to expect? That hope seems to split the notion into equivocal moieties, suggesting at least on one side of the idea that our faculties of choice and action somehow guarantee their rightful use.

If autonomy means mere willful self-rule, it lacks the moral power Korsgaard wants to give it. But if it stands for something richer, for moral adequacy or integrity, or the kind of mature and situated judgment that Aristotle called *phronesis* and that Maimonides called *kamāl*, maturity, gravitas, insight—or that the Chinese, Greek and Islamic philosophers called refinement of character or greatness of soul—then what have we gained from all the paeans to autonomy? Has Korsgaard added anything to what traditional ethicists have said all along—beyond the pretense that sound moral thinking is somehow resident in the fact that we ourselves are the ones who make the choices?

Reflection and reflectiveness do indeed depend on the reflexivity of our thought; and they are necessary (but hardly sufficient!) for moral seriousness.

Critical reflection is especially needful when it comes to our human penchant for rationalization. But the advice 'Be human' adds little to what a morally grounded person already knows; such counsels gain little purchase in the thinking of the facile, self-indulgent, self-deceiving hypocrite. For such a person, humanity is more often an excuse than a shining ideal; and even as an ideal, its light is more readily adjusted to flatter than to probe. The extreme generality of maxims uttered in the name of humanity alone readily dilutes the specificity that practical counsels most need. Thick gets watered down to thin.

Efforts to warrant moral claims face deeper problems than superficiality, however. There's also the risk of arguing *pro obscurum per obscuriora.*[31] It's long been known that someone who shrugs off all moral prescriptions (or selectively rejects the ones that chafe) will hardly be awed by appeals to God. As the psalmist says, the wretch (*naval,* whom the Psalm goes on to describe as one who commits all sorts of heinous acts) *saith in his heart "There is no God!"* (Psalms 14:1; cf. 53:1). But the same is true of roles, large or small, including our common human identity.

Even if a would-be wrongdoer were to hesitate long enough to weigh a qualm, he could still readily revise his notions of his role and set aside the broad and abstract, putatively overarching mandate of humanity, in favor of the greater immediacy of some competing role, or guise, or mask. A speculative sort might (like Nietzsche) urge that even the idea of humanity is too much with us and needs to be outgrown. The freedom that the youthful Augustine was seeking by vandalism in a neighbor's pear orchard is as readily made a paramount value as is the deeper felicity that the older Augustine found in Christ. The license that masquerades as liberty can also adopt the name of autonomy. Many a would-be follower of Nietzsche will label it as such.

Consciousness, *pace* Korsgaard, is not conscience, and plenty of people (with or without the help of moral critics, sophists, or philosophers) find warrant enough for their choices in the fact that they are choices. Many confine the warrant of a choice to the case in which it's made. Some look to custom or convention, morals by agreement. But others simply laugh at such earnestness. Our talent for setting the base of thought or action now here and now elsewhere but, often, where we want it is as much a part of human reason and autonomy as is reflection.

Korsgaard finds merit in all four of the accounts she tables as to the groundings of normativity. Indeed, she judges all of them as true—if only partly so. Puffendorf and Hobbes were right to see that "normativity must spring from the demands of a legislator" with powers to punish and reward. What they did not see, or did not see clearly, as Kant did, she writes, was that, in morals, the legislator is the self: "The fact that we must act in the light of reflection gives us a double nature. The thinking self has the power to command the acting self."

Nagel was right in holding reasons to be "intrinsically normative entities." For "Reflection has the power to compel obedience, and to punish us for disobedience."[32] So reflective endorsement is also true: "In the end, nothing can be normative unless we endorse our own nature, unless we place a value upon ourselves," as "animals of a certain kind," self-legislating, reflective, autonomous agents: "That is, in the Aristotelian sense, our human form."[33]

All three alternatives, then, reduce to Korsgaard's version of autonomy. My problem with *that* view, to give you the executive summary, is that it tries to spin the gold thread of caring, the love mandated in Leviticus, out of the sheer logic and structure of the thought process.

So is there no way of justifying ethics? Did Kant and all other ethicists fail?

Well, what I've been arguing, of course, is that ethics doesn't need to be justified. Only values could justify it, and to see worth in any value is already to commit to some sort of ethical standard. The question, then—the proper question, as I see it—is what sort of values should we commit to, what sort should guide our choices and our lives?

Kant's argument, I think, like that of Socrates, was ultimately dialectical. It works well over the critical but limited terrain of moral rules, when addressed to someone who is already well disposed to doing the right thing. Fortunately, that description applies to many people much of the time—but not to everyone all the time. It's prone to wobble, regrettably, just where and when we need it most. And it seems least effectual in cases of the gravest evil, with those who have convinced themselves that what others may take to be wrong is right in fact or so overwhelmingly attractive, resplendent, or expedient as to be worthy of their preference.

Say a little more about that. Doesn't Kant free ethics from the arbitrary control of God or his self-appointed and pretentious, all too revered spokespersons?

Well, let me say first what I *don't* think Kant achieved in ethics. His hope, as he describes it in *The Groundwork of the Metaphysic of Morals,* was to be the first to discover what he called "the principle of morality," the moral basis of obligation, which he believed had lain long hidden in our capacity to self-legislate. That kind of discovery, evidently, was not possible until the Enlightenment had cleared the ground of all appeals to mere authority,[34] and Kant's own Stoic-inspired deontology had set aside, as irrelevant at best, all appeals to interest, be it one's own or that of another.[35]

The moral law, as Kant saw it, was a priori and universal, so it could not be arbitrary. Its rationality and objectivity, its very transcendence of all appeals to interest, made it intrinsically binding and gave it sufficiency as a motive of action. As I argued long ago, Kant's purism, so strongly reacting against the consequentialism of his contemporaries, isolates the moral realm from the general sphere of choice and action. Beyond that, his strictures against eudaimonism lean too heavily (albeit understandably) on well-founded fears that the notion of enlightened self-interest might slide into self-serving and self-deceiving rationalizations. Kant's one-sided deontology was, in my view, goaded by his overreaction to that possibility. My slogan, paraphrasing a famous remark of Kant's and echoing the intent of his first Critique, to integrate formal with material concerns, was this: "Morality without interests is empty; pragmatism without principles is blind."[36]

Kant's great achievement in ethics, as I see it, was in undermining the claim that all ethical imperatives are subjective or conventional, the notion of many an apologist of human willfulness, that no authority can be objective. Just as Kant sought to vindicate our scientific and our everyday understanding by showing that the categories of causality and substantiality and the related ideas of possibility, necessity, continuity, and interaction are not products but preconditions of experience, presupposed in the formal structure of our explanations and judgments of fact, so he championed the logic of ethical discourse, by showing that some imperatives do not boil down to mere counsels of prudence but apply unconditionally. That is what makes them matters of principle.

Kant's claims for the categorical imperative rest on the Socratic discovery of an internal contradiction in wrongful choices, between the good one seeks or presumes and the ill one devises. That discovery affords the iron bracing of Plato's Socratic dialogues: When a speaker misconstrues a virtue, the error is laid bare by a dialectic that cuts to the good which that virtue, as a virtue, is expected to pursue and reveals its inconsistency with anything unworthy of the name of virtue: Courage cannot be harebrained, or piety thoughtless.

Thrasymachus will try to define justice as the interest of the stronger, a more formidable challenge than other, more casual or inadvertent confusions. His carefully plotted equivocal notion of justice serves both rebels and defenders of the status quo: Justice is as the powerful would have it. Their dictate is an imposition reveled in by those who profit from it but a sucker bet cravenly accepted by the weak. Thrasymachus struggles to avoid admitting that justice is a strength. Giving the word a stable, objective meaning would rob it of the iridescence that Thrasymachus uses to dazzle his hearers.

But Socrates turns the tables and uses the sophist's weight against him: When Thrasymachus admits that the stronger is stronger only insofar as he judges well of his interests, he has acknowledged corrigibility as to this value. So justice is a strength after all, an objective matter subject to good or bad judgment, and not a mere preference of the chooser. Even in a band of thieves, effectiveness depends on mores that would look a lot like virtues if applied more broadly—loyalty, discipline, tact, trust, even selflessness. If virtues are strengths and people can discriminate traits conducive to the well-being we seek, virtue is not a sucker bet or a mere matter of opinion, convention, acquiescence. So it is not just an imposition.

The Socratic dialogues always probe for an inner contradiction in the false conceit of wisdom. They find it, typically, as I've indicated, in the cross-pressures between the putative goods that motivate a choice and the real outcomes of that choice. There's a nice analogy between the Socratic probing question and what I've called prophetic irony, the device by which the prophets of ancient Israel expose the latent tensions and overt contradictions between goods sought with base or vile motives and the ultimate yield or outcome of those motives.[37]

Kant's ethical achievement, as I see it, was to lay bare and vindicate and put to use the core assumption underlying Socrates' probing questions, showing how pursuit of some good, real or perceived, contradicts any ill or unworthy intent in the means or motive of its pursuit, making the maxim of a wrongful act implicitly incoherent. If ends are to justify their means, the means themselves must be worthy, and worthy of their ends. Kant's insight into that moral truth led him to two main ways of formulating the moral law. One was formal, based on exposing the logic of that contradiction and pursuing its mirror image in the holy grail of all rationalism, the inner coherence of the truth. The other sort of formulation was material, based on the tacit assumption Socrates probed for, the assumption that all actions pursue some presumptive good. The material statements of the categorical imperative rest on the interests imputed to subjects; the formal statements, on the idea of moral consistency and the logical solidity expected of a moral rule.

Kant brilliantly outflanks the relativists who suppose that 'good' and 'right' are mere terms of praise, assigned to what is socially or privately approved. By articulating the formal structure and material terms of choices that pretend to moral standing, he spells out the logic of the Socratic elenchus. Universalizability is his lens, magnifying maxims to display their inner coherence or incoherence. But, beyond that, he seeks to derive the biblical law of love from the logic of universality. That is, he essays to ground his own rephrasing of the biblical *Love thy neighbor as thyself* on the formal structure of the very idea of law.

Retracing Kant's steps here has not proved easy. Korsgaard tries, by seeking to derive a general and genial humanism from the fact that we are human. She takes the given of our autonomy to demand respect for autonomy in others. Following in Kant's footsteps by seeking the roots of altruism in the very formalism of the moral law, John Hare focuses on the "exclusion of self-reference." That, he argues, forces on us a kind of generality, "in which the roles of the parties" self and other "are exactly reversed.[38] John Rawls claims a Kantian mantle for his notion (again Socratic in origin)[39] that the veil of ignorance, by obscuring the strengths and interests of the rational subjects in his contractual thought experiment, forces even the most grasping of choosers to put themselves in one another's place.

I confess, these attempts do not look cogent to me. The law of love, I think, adds something to the sheer rigor of the demand for consistency. Besides, not every maxim is meant as a rule. Kant makes his own case easier by assuming that the choosers in *his* thought experiments at least pretend to propriety: They would like their maxims to be recognized as rules; they admit, far more freely than Thrasymachus, that what they seek is some kind of good. They *hope* (as Kant spells out their motives for them) to *justify*, say, theft or suicide, neglect of one's talents, or refusals of charity. Kant can show how their rationales trip themselves up. But by allowing vice or moral weakness to pay tribute to virtue in this way, he posits far too generous a set of premises if the aim is to give a warrant to morals for someone who does not already see it.

Kant's thought experiments assumed no mean measure of moral earnestness and intellectual honesty on the part of those who bring a maxim for testing. Their admission that some good is sought was critical to the argument, as was their moral seriousness. Without those stipulations, Kant could simply dismiss the petitioner as a louse and the nominated maxim as a counterfeit, of course. But an avowed immoralist would not make the concessions Kant requires and indeed might feel no need for self-justification—or might, if explanations were demanded, simply appeal to his role or station, background or circumstances. Self-deceivers and moral philistines, the wretch of the psalm and the sociopath whose mind is made up or whose appetites are unbudging, would not—do not—successfully plumb and probe their own motives in the way that Kantian dialectic calls for. A situation ethicist might not acknowledge the worth of moral consistency—might vigorously deny it. But consistency is clearly not quite enough for morals. It is not the same as love, or even the bare civility that can serve as an outward acknowledgment of dignity. Henry Higgins treats a duchess the same as flower girl. Colonel Pickering treats a flower girl the same as a duchess. That's not the same.

The Torah's moral law embodies both the material and the formal side of the categorical imperative: *As thyself* speaks to formal equity, but the demand for love honors the material side. I have not yet succeeded in understanding how Kant was able to extract material interests from the formal versions of the categorical imperative. He brilliantly formulates the moral demand that we treat others as ends and not mere means. And upon this rock he rests the sacred mandate of humanity at large to work toward building a kingdom of ends. But I have as yet to see how he derives this mandate from the sheer logic of universality. I suspect that efforts to derive the love of persons from the logic of choice are just another phase of the Enlightenment drive to secularity, paralleling the consequentialism that Kant abhorred and echoing in logicist terms the psychologism of the sentimentalists, which Kant outgrew when he saw that resting ethics on a theory of sentiments would make moral imperatives contingent.

Kant did not wholly secularize his ethics. His ideas of duty are redolent of Christian appeals to conscience; the primacy he gave to truth telling, promise keeping, and self-scrutiny bears the impress of the values he held fast from his Pietist upbringing. But Kant subtly transformed the Protestant idea that conscience is the voice of God, recasting it in his own more inboard terms by saying that the pure will of the genuinely pious takes moral imperatives as divine commands. Still, conscience, and even conscientiousness, is not infallible. Evil, too, can be conscientious, as it was in the dutiful discipline of Adolph Eichmann, the Latin American death squads, the Red Guards in China, the Revolutionary Guards in Iran, Pol Pot's Khmer Rouge, the Serbian snipers, Tutsi machete-men, and the mounted janjaweed in Darfur.

I don't think Kant turned ethics into logic, and I don't think it's a terrible thing that he did not. The scrupulous inquirer posited in Kant's thought experiments does seek the guidance of a rule and does at least profess a desire to act on principle. He's also penetrating enough to know his own motives, articulate enough to state them, and well-intentioned enough to find them at least tacitly aligned in pursuit of some real or apparent good. Tragically, those parameters aren't enough to rule against an Eichmann. And among the many who actively reject them are all those who in effect have said, like Milton's Satan, "Evil be thou my good."

Fortunately, that last is a maxim rarely uttered, unless by those arch-romantics who find a perverse charm or wild freedom in flouting what others take to be the good. But if an actor cares not at all for moral coherence, or doesn't see incoherence in his own, say, selfish motives, Kant's powerful arguments will not move him. Kant has no answer to him, and neither have we. We can urge that every breath one takes reaffirms how precious life is. As the Hebrew liturgy puts it, *The soul of all that lives blesses Thy name, Lord our God*. But the psalms in our breathing are silent psalms, like the message the psalmist gleans from the sun in its course. To translate such silent voices into words of praise and acts of reverence is the task not of morals but of religion.

That's where I have a problem with what you're saying. In making a metaphysical appeal to the deserts of beings, aren't you still suspending human values from God? Isn't Nietzsche right in calling all supposedly objective moral standards ghosts of God, and aren't the postmoderns on sound ground when they generalize the point to include values like the claim to objective truth, or political or aesthetic standards?

I'd say lights and shadows, not ghosts. I don't believe in ghosts, but I do believe that light of various kinds comes from God. I think it's interesting that one would speak about finding solid ground for postmoderns. Solid foundations would seem to be the last thing they'd want to claim. I do think that moral standards, and all values, as you suggest, spring from God. But I don't think we should simply peg or pin our valuations on our idea of God. That's why I'm proposing the dialectic I've described, allowing the values we encounter *here*—truth or striving, beauty, creativity, unity, or love—to lead us to God, and then allow our idea of God, as it grows within us, to lead us back to our world, enriching the values we live by here, with one another. I think we find God by discovering value in beings. But religious ethics reflects the value found in God back onto those beings, viewing them as his children, servants, works—creatures and creations.[40]

So, if all values stem from God, by your account, shouldn't we just follow God's lead and take our values at his direction? Isn't it the height of hubris to make ourselves the arbiters?

I see several reasons for avoiding that approach. Prominent among them, as I've stressed, is the way it leads to circularity. But, beyond that, no matter how strenuously we turn to God with creaturely acceptance, we can't escape our own responsibility as arbiters. After all, there's more than one tradition that professes to articulate what it is that God asks of us, and no tradition is self-authenticating. When we choose a tradition or pursue a familiar or exotic articulation of what we take to be God's mandate, we're still, inevitably, following human thoughts. The norms we accept and the practices we pursue are still filtered through human texts and customs, and human minds and mores, including our own. Even if we take as God's *ipsissima verba* the dicta of a particular scripture that we call our own, we still choose and commit to that canon and the reading we give it. Morally, I would argue, as earnest of our intellectual honesty, we still need to test any such norms and notions to see if they're worthy of attribution to a being that merits being called divine.[41]

But isn't it the Jewish view that our obligations come to us as God's commandments?

Certainly it is. That's the language of the Torah, and the Rabbis follow it. The *mitzvot* are God's imperatives, and also his blessings, meant to sanctify our lives. We acknowledge that each time we voice our gratitude for the *mitzvot* in the benedictions of God that accompany their performance. But let's consider what the idea of a *mitzvah* means to us. Does it mean that God counts on his power or his ownership of the world to impose duties on us? If God did that, there'd be little reason to think of the resulting commands as *moral* obligations. And we'd still have to judge, as best we can, whether the *mitzvot* we've got really are commands of the All-perfect and not some illusion or imposture.

The Torah prefaces its laws by telling of God's creation of heaven and earth. I think that means to show us that God embedded his laws in the very nature of things. God blesses and in the same act commands all living creatures to be fruitful and multiply. God sees that it is not good for a human being to live alone and gives Adam a counterpart and ally, a *helpmeet, ezer k^{e}-negdo,* as the Hebrew puts it. The text graphically proclaims that men and women are not of alien kinds, not from Mars and Venus, but of the same flesh and blood and bone. So we are capable of aiding and understanding one another, living together, forming families.

When positive laws are built on foundations of this sort—based ultimately on the love of life and human dignity, the beauty and bounty of nature, and the inner drive of all things to persist and seek perfection—we can see the themes of justice and mercy spelled out in God's laws. We can recognize the authority of those laws on that basis, because (and insofar as) they worthily express God's love and can be applied and interpreted in that spirit.

So when the psalmist hails God as King, he says: *Right and justice anchor Thy throne; love and truth go before Thee* (Psalms 89:15). God rules not because He is almighty but because He is all-perfect. His throne is braced not by lions and leopards (cf. Song of Songs 4:8), but by love and truth. Truth here means justice. Love (*ḥesed*) is its consummate expression.[42] If worshipers harbor a mental picture of God's splendor, the psalmist resolves the imagery of such visions, treating power and glory as mere expressions of the justice and truth that make God's rule eternal:

> The Lord reigns, robed in glory,
> Girt with power,
> So the earth stands firm, unyielding,
> Thy throne, assured, of old,
> Thyself, eternal.
> Rivers may rage, O Lord,
> Rivers may lift their voices
> And raise their pounding waves.
> But above the sound of thronging waters,
> Mighty breakers of the sea,
> The Lord on high, in solemn grandeur:
> Thy testimonies, most faithful,
> Thy rule, rightly sacred,
> O Lord, forever! (Psalm 93)

The testimonies here are God's commandments.[43] The stability of God's rule is the counterpart of his justice, expressed in his governance of the world, whose emblem, poetically, is the limit He sets to the unruly might of the flood (cf. Jeremiah 5:22). Saadiah Gaon stands on biblical ground, then, when he reverses the familiar order, grounding God's sovereignty in his justice: "the King deserves to rule only for his justice. So it is absurd that He be a rightful king and yet be vicious. Such a thing could only occur among humans, through a struggle for power."[44] And, on the same page: "the doings of the Creator cannot be impugned," for "it is absurd to impugn the Truth itself."

God's goodness, Saadiah argues, is known through his acts, most tellingly, from the creation and sustenance of the world. For the generosity of creation answers to no prior desert.[45] The Psalms (19:10) confirm Saadiah's approach when they call God's laws *truth* and balance the line by saying: *tzadku yaḥdav*, "they are just in their entirety." That hemistich complements and amplifies the psalmist's acknowledgment of the justice of God's laws with the further thought that, in the Torah (as in nature), the stability of God's laws springs from their integration as a sound and coherent system.

Clearly, the biblical tradition is not at ease with the ancient notion of arbitrary monarchs. Moses saw more than enough of god-kings, and Samuel resists the petitions of his people for a king (1 Samuel 8), although what they ask for is protection and not for the flamboyant self-aggrandizement of a pharaoh. The Torah gives little comfort to the more modern fiction of the divine right of kings that Christian monarchs once called on to prop up their fortunes. David and Solomon are, of course, anointed, but their weaknesses are no less visible in scripture than their strengths, and the prophets will confront them and their far less glorious successors with stern reproofs or condemnations in the measure of those weaknesses. Kingship, biblically, is a concession.[46] So it is not surprising that even God's rule must be justified to his stiff-necked people by the justice that gives it legitimacy along with strength.

Theocrats may swoon at thoughts of surrender to God. But even they make choices; and what they choose, inevitably, is a human institution. Pietists may pursue devotion to God's will. But they, too, must put into practice what they think God asks of them. Is it fasting, penances, hairshirts? Is it God in fact who speaks in such mortifications? Or is it self-loathing, or a certain image and appropriation of tradition? Is it machismo, or a perverse triumphalism, when Shīʿites crowd the streets of Najaf or Karbalah to score their flesh with barbed wire and showy knives? Is it God again, or ancient custom with long-forgotten pagan roots and still flaming emulous impulses, when Spanish youths run with the bulls?

Moral skeptics sharpen their critical poniards to puncture the precepts others hope to live by. But, if they hold true to their doctrine, they leave themselves without a standard by which to judge the choices that all of us must make each day. Habit and custom move in and take over by default. Yet, much the same is true of theocrats and pietists: They follow a tradition or a lifestyle, a text and its interpreters, a practice and its avatars. And any of these may lead in sound or senseless, loving or insular directions. A word from God is not amiss in charting our course. But God's word, as Elijah found (1 Kings 19:11–21), is clearest not in the thunder, the storm wind, or the earthquake, not even in the fire that might herald it, but in the still, small voice whose moral message is readily acknowledged even by those who were not the first to hear it.

It's in that vein that Isaiah, in God's name, can challenge vulgar confusions of piety with idle fasts and vain petitions: *Is such the fast I favor, a day of self-affliction, head bent like a bulrush, spreading sackcloth and ashes? Is that what you call a fast, a day pleasing to God?* (Isaiah 58:5). Only on the Day of Atonement is fasting biblically ordained (Leviticus 16:29–31, 23:27–32; Numbers 29:7). But if fasting means contrition (Judges 20:26; 1 Samuel 7:6; 2 Samuel 12:16), God Himself will critique the gesture when its backdrop is complacency:

> *Daily do they seek Me, eager to know my ways—as if they were a nation that did justice and had not forsaken their God's law. They seek just treatment, eager for God to be nigh: "Why did we fast if Thou seest not? Why afflict ourselves, if Thou takest no notice?" Look, on your fast day, you do just as you please and drive all your workers hard. You're*

> *fasting for strife and contention and to smite with a wicked fist—a fine day for your voice to be heard on high!* (Isaiah 58:2–4)

God calls on Isaiah to redirect a misplaced piety: *Cry thy throat out! Don't hold back. Raise thy voice like a trumpet, and tell my people where they overstepped and the house of Jacob where they erred* (Isaiah 58:1). To the prophet, God's voice resounds in the moral commands we spoke of in our first lecture:

> *Isn't this the fast that I prefer: to strike the wicked fetters, loose the yoke's cords, free the oppressed, and snap every yoke! Isn't it sharing thy bread with the hungry, taking the homeless poor into thy home, clothing the naked when thou seest him, and not making thyself invisible to thine own flesh!* (Isaiah 58:6–7)

God's command, ringing in Isaiah's ears, is the voice of justice, generosity, and care. It's in that vein that Micah issues his stirring indictment and exhortation:

> *What shall I bring to the Lord and present to God on high? Shall I come before Him with burnt offerings, yearling calves? Will the Lord take satisfaction in thousands of rams and myriad rivers of oil? Should I give my first-born for my transgression? The fruit of my womb for the sins of my soul? He hath told thee, O man, what is good and what the Lord requireth of thee—Just this: to do justice, to love kindness* (ḥesed), *and humbly to walk with thy God.* (Micah 6:6–8)

There is no mystery here about God's desires, and no division between his will and what is right.

Given your openness to religious texts, I wonder what you think about your fellow Gifford Lecturer, John Hare's alternative to Korsgaard's way of giving warrant to our ethical obligations?

Well, Hare, like Korsgaard, has reviewed quite a range of efforts to find an anchor for morals. His decision, as your question suggests, is to appeal to God and thoughts of God's command—God's call, as he puts it.[47] Only this, he argues, gives authority to moral obligations. He starts with a critique of intuitionism, which was once quite the fashion in philosophical circles and still appeals to many, through the idea of conscience. Hare raises the concern that intuitionism seems to press an analogy of moral knowledge with sense perception, as if some counterpart of Plato's Forms presented us with unwavering objects of moral knowledge. Beyond that, Hare argues, intuitionism seems to imply that moral doubt and controversy, and even cultural differences in moral norms, cannot exist.[48]

That last argument, I think, doesn't allow for the social and psychic fitting and filtering that may affect our moral judgments. In other words, I think there could be moral unity at a rather deep level, even where there is diversity of implementation: I think most people (and most peoples) value kindness and consideration more highly than cruelty and rudeness, even though cultures and personal styles may differ in their ways of showing kindness and avoiding rudeness.

As for moral knowledge, I'm not quite as leery of rational intuitions as Hare may be. I don't think Kant ever quite dissolved them when he showed that all human consciousness must be temporal. Clearly a time-bound consciousness can intend nontemporal things. That's presumably what we do when we think of God. But even in mathematics, I don't think we have to *hypostatize* things like numbers and ratios to be able to claim that mathematical knowledge is objective. So I don't think we need Platonic ideals if moral knowledge is to reach (or grasp for) objective truth.

I know that Hitler and Saddam Hussein and Idi Amin were evil and that Gandhi and Schweitzer and Mother Theresa were good, without turning to some archetypal class of goods or evils as objects of that knowledge. On my own scheme, of course, the truth-makers for moral judgments are the beings in which value resides and *for* which supportive actions are undertaken—not Platonic Forms. Forms make no claims in the way that, say, living beings do. They have no needs that my efforts might serve.

Seeking further, Hare, like Korsgaard, turns to the appeals to human nature typified in Aristotelian ethics. These he finds wanting not on her grounds but because they seem to say no more than 'Be what you are.' I don't find that advice quite as vacuous as it may sound. It's not always easy even to find out who we are, let alone to become that person and live that life. I can't help thinking of the Hasidic story of Zusya, who wept as he pondered his final accounting: "I'm not weeping," he said, "because I'm afraid to be asked why I was not Moses. But what if I am asked, 'Were you Zusya?'"

Taking his own tack, Hare argues (against the naturalism he finds in Aristotle) that nature is deficient: It does not always tell us to do what is morally right. Often, it seems to press us to give preference to happiness over duty. That may be true, of course, depending on how we understand nature, happiness, and duty. But I'd be chary of equating human nature with sheer self-assertion. That's certainly a facet of our nature, what the Rabbis call *yetzer ha-ra*^{c}, our bad bent. But there's more to human nature than that. We also have a penchant for love and generosity, a desire to share. We're drawn toward transcendent values, including ideals of duty that might be wholesome or vicious. It's our penchant for the transcendent that Plato describes poetically in the *Symposium* as a ladder of love. I don't think Plato is wrong to find the base of that ladder here on earth, in our drive not just to survive but to procreate—and teach. Nor do I think Maimonides is wrong to find in Jacob's ladder a biblical counterpart to Plato's—a ladder mounting to the heavens, with God at its summit. Looking at human nature in this way, I don't find it wrong to link morals to what we are—given our projects and potentials and the emergent capabilities of a larger and more giving self.

Hare does see the better side to our humanity, of course. But he balks at ascribing its potentials to our nature while we remain unredeemed. That looks sectarian to me, a product of taking too literally Christian readings of the idea that Adam and Eve fell from grace and dragged down with them all the rest of humankind. I don't think natural theology can do much with the idea that all of humanity is damned for a sin we did not commit and saved through a sacrifice we did not make. I'm troubled by the metaphysics and the morals of that model. But if Hare follows Kant's (Pietist/Enlightenment) reading the story of the Fall as emblematic of our penchant for giving precedence to happiness over duty, we still need to credit human strengths as well as debit the weaknesses and not package only weaknesses in our idea of human nature, reserving all the strengths to the work of grace—as if nature too were not an act of grace. Any ethics of human nature, of course, will only be as adequate as the idea of humanity it deploys. But the same is true of an ethics built on ideas of God. Bad theologies yield bad ethics—and vice versa.

I share Hare's concern that appeals to human nature slide too readily into reductive visions. The cynical exposés projected in the name of what is called naturalism (at least in fiction) often oscillate between shock value and permission giving. I'm reminded of Spinoza's charge about those who would rather ridicule or decry our nature than faithfully describe it.[49] But such appraisals, as Spinoza cautions, arise in the assumption that mankind disturbs the natural order rather than belonging to it. It's easy to ascribe all that one loathes in oneself or others to some inborn flaw in nature and not to simple moral frailty. But the outcome is a skewed vision and a homiletical ear that (as Spinoza puts it) hears shrill condemnations as if they were divine inspirations. The vice of writers, as Plato warns (*Republic* X 599–602), is to pursue impact at the expense of balance. So it's easy to overlook the conative reach of nature and assign the name of nature to just one view of the human face. That kind of writing may win credence from the alienated or draw pleas for help from the disheartened, but it lacks the broad but never uncritical sympathy for human nature that great writers and great humanitarians find in their love of the human animal

Hare lends bite to his dismissal of naturalism by singling out Larry Arnhart's menu of natural desires—a list of drives for status, rule, war, and wealth. That bill of fare affords a striking example of what Hare finds troubling in efforts to build ethics on an account of human nature. The chauvinism and machismo he uncovers in that model do little to lend it credit as a beau ideal. If we build our morals along these lines, Hare writes, "We will not need, for example, to love our enemies or to feed the hungry in the rest of the world."[50] But I'd be wary of making an extreme and self-consciously cynical case the paradigm of the idea that human nature tells us something of moral relevance.

Clearly, we won't agree with everything that Aristotle has to say about what human nature reveals of human ends. But there are two or three points that we can learn from Aristotle about human nature. One is that we humans are social by nature. For human life is not actually possible—let alone fulfilled—without some form of society. Second, what a nonreductive naturalism commends is not the mere pursuit of unexamined ends but the development of human potentials, including our potentials for nobility and generosity. Third, human nature is not a finished product. Its strengths are not a settled check list, as if all we had to do were touch the bases or collect the tokens in some peculiar game or scavenger hunt. Our properly human aims form an open-ended set, pointing toward transcendence in ways that rise beyond the narrow interests of the atomic individual and that often open up to intellectual, aesthetic, and spiritual as well as social goals. Such aims are not base. But they are as much a part of human nature as the many weaknesses to which we, as humans, are vulnerable. It's toward these better aims, the potentialities of our higher nature, that the Torah points when it teaches that *a man does not live by bread alone, but by all that issues from the mouth of the Lord does a man live* (Deuteronomy 8:3).

Still, in Hare's critique of Arnhart, I wonder about the order of the argument: If we don't yet know the sources of moral obligation, can we appeal to dicta like "Love your enemies" or "Feed the hungry and clothe the naked," to expose the weakness of some rival claim? That sounds like question begging. If we need to know and do not yet know the basis of moral obligations, how can we deplore the modest proposals of, say, social Darwinism in its new or classic forms, or the evolutionary ethics of sociobiology, or eugenics, or lifeboat-earth ecology, or other programs that we may find repugnant? To be in a position to denounce such ethical impostors, we must already know a good deal about our moral obligations. Hare presumes on that sort of knowledge even as he challenges us to find it unwarranted without the underpinnings he expects to find for it in the religious tradition he has chosen.

Turning to efforts to ground moral concerns in reason, Hare, like Korsgaard, typifies these by the Kantian claim that the categorical imperative is a command that reason addresses to itself—that is, to all beings who are finite, rational, and therefore free and subject to a moral law. Noting that Kant finds the rationality of the moral law in its universality, Hare derives reciprocity from that formal character, specifically, as we've noted, from the demand that I abstract from the particularities of my situation or, more pointedly, from the narrow perspective that makes my own interests paramount. Abstracting in this way, Hare reasons, should put me in the situation of the others whom my choices might affect.

But not all moral obligations, he observes, fit the model of a universal law. Calling Duns Scotus to witness, he affirms that we have individual essences and argues that "what distinguishes humans from each other is more valuable than what we have in common."[51] I think that's sound and part of what the Rabbis were urging in the Mishnah when they anchored human dignity in human uniqueness. But, as I argued in the lectures, the imperative to cherish one another's uniqueness belongs properly to what a universal moral law commands. It was in this sense, supported by the Jewish texts, that I read the obligation to love our neighbors as we love ourselves.

Some universal rules, Hare argues, can be odious, even if we accept their application to ourselves. Again I agree. Sade's willingness to suffer the abuses he deals out, as I argued years ago, does not make him a paragon of virtue.[52] He apes and mocks the formal principle but neglects the material content of the moral law. What that shows, as the difference between Professor Higgins and Colonel Pickering underscores, is that formalism is not enough in ethics. Kantians are tempted by that idea—and even by the proceduralist notion that the very structure of the law as law is somehow a sufficient warrant of its justice. But Kant himself saw that the categorical imperative needs material as well as formal formulations. If he erred in thinking that the former are implicit in the latter, the mistake is venial, since he did not omit either kind from his account.

Kant did make a powerful case for the idea of a moral law. If his thoughts about universality do not exhaust the scope of morals or the mandate of reason, even so, testing for the lacunae in Kant does not confound or demolish reason as a source of moral knowledge, especially if reason is not artificially debarred from the recognition of values—be it the normative force of facts (in the demand that we accept them)[53] or in the claims of beings (in the demand that we pick up the baby in the basket and not leave it on the doorstep in the snow).

I don't think a caricature does sound service as a *reductio ad absurdum*. So funhouse mirrors like Arnhart's model of human nature, or haunted house projections like Sade's parody of the Golden Rule reveal only the limitations of some especially crabbed or perverse constructions of the idea of reason or the ideal of humanity. Clearly, it is not reasonable in the morally relevant sense to derive odious notions from a rule on the sheer grounds that one is (devilishly) consistent. And what calls itself reason does not look very reasonable if it demands, say, that we ignore our loved ones or steamroller our commitments or slight any of the things that are both precious and unique about ourselves or others. Reason, like piety or courage, should not be harebrained. Calculative reason like that of terrorists, tyrants, and torturers is not what morals needs and not at all what moral rationalists like Plato, Aristotle, or Spinoza had in mind when they assigned reason a crucial and critical role in human ethics.

Hare's fourth instance of efforts to find a warrant for morality is the appeal to community. He cites Hegel here, and the organic idea of the state. That leads him to recall the prescriptive and invidious use of class terms like 'gentleman' in his childhood. He presses the distinction between authority and power to drive home the sound point that what's *expected* of us need not be what we should do. Fortunately, however, the communities we live in are not static or monolithic but labile. And most of us, as Hare notes, belong to more than one: So "when I consider the various communities I belong to, I am faced with a battery of competing norms and values."[54]

What Hare draws from that welter of claims is support for the idea that "mere membership" in a group does not impart legitimacy to its dicta.[55] But that's a foregone conclusion. The inference I would draw pushes a little further. I see competition among values as one vital way in which critical thinking is awakened. In that sense, our engagement in multiple, overlapping communities and the corresponding tendency to disengage are not just sources of noise but, for those who are sensitized by cognitive dissonance, wakeup calls to judgment and the need for trustworthy sources of moral counsel. Perhaps that's why cross-cultural experience can stimulate moral growth and not just stir up moral confusion.

Hare does not follow Hegel's path to reason as the dialectical resultant of the babble of history. He finds reason, at least as Hegel construes it, unreliable for the task of sorting and sifting the claims we face. In its place he puts God's call, "a source of attraction and repulsion outside us . . . the quasi-magnetic center" that draws us to value some things as good and reject others as bad.[56] Does this mean that reason and God's word are rivals?

Hare sees three components in a moral judgment: an objective reality, an internal response, and a decisive endorsement of that response. By finding an objective counterpart to our valuing, he means to ally himself with moral realists of varied stripes. By speaking of the quasi-magnetic attraction of a good action "like the firefighters' going up into the flaming skyscraper," he finds common ground with intuitionists. By speaking of endorsement, he leaves room for critical reflection on our immediate responses. But he fights shy of an intellectual account of that reflection. Like Plato in the *Ion*, he sees God as the ultimate source of attraction in what we value—and of the other two components, as well: "all these things hold together in a coherent whole, because they are signals from a single source."[57] Is reason, then, lost sight of? Endorsement, he writes, at least for a Christian, "is an attempt to discern whether a particular attraction that she feels toward something is consistent with God's will."[58]

I too believe, with Plato, that all sound values stem from God. But I also think, as Aristotle (and Spinoza) did, that it's a mistake to rush to ultimate causes at the expense of proximate ones. The mistake is all the more telling when the ultimate cause is always the same and the proximate causes differ strikingly. Clearly, one needn't be a Christian to affirm the objectivity of moral values and our own key role in endorsing or critiquing our immediate responses. But, philosophically, I don't find it very helpful to set our God-given reason at odds with God's internal call.

The language of call chimes with my own take on the *mitzvot* not as blunt imperatives (although they are, of course, commands) and not as implications but as invitations, specifically, to pursue perfection.[59] That language evokes the open-endedness of the imperative of Leviticus to emulate God's holiness—which means the pursuit of our perfection as human beings and, indeed, as the unique human individuals that we are. *Love thy neighbor as thyself* is an application of that obligation, a very special special case, based on a rather broad generalization of the underlying principle of self-love, that is, the recognition of inestimable worth in *every* human being. All the ethical obligations that flow from this command to love one's neighbor, the obligations sketched out in our first lecture, are concrete imperatives that body forth that principle, not letting it float off into the empyrean of abstraction but cementing our connection to God and to each other in the here and now.

Hare's pursuit of moral warrant gets a distinctively Protestant flavor from its focus on individual acts and choices, rather than the general tenor of our actions and the life that gives them context. So does his centering of God's call within the human heart—as he puts it, echoing the Sermon on the Mount: "Where your treasure is, there your heart will be also" (Matthew 6:21).[60]

Clearly, it is in the heart that our shared tradition expects God's call to be heard. But, for a Jew, that call is addressed not to individuals alone but to a people. And it will not be sought in the example of a single idealized figure but is laid out in the fabric of the *mitzvot* and the life they open up for the individual and the community.

But can the mitzvot really free us?

I think it's fascinating how the images tangle one another's cords. Just a moment ago we were speaking of hearts that could *hear*. But it's only the *ictus* of God's word that strikes the heart. It takes a human messenger to set that beat to music and to give it words that we can ponder—and even choose to live by. But your question isn't asking about obligation and what can bind us to obey. You've shifted to a language of liberation, and intimations of salvation. Still, we have to remember that when Jesus said he was the way, he didn't mean it in a Taoist sense. His hearers, often, were looking for a way *out*. The world, as many of them saw it, was an airless crypt, a trap one needed to be saved from. Life *here* meant being buried alive, and salvation meant escape. In Judaism those ideas do not take hold. We celebrate life and hold it precious. Our striving is to sanctify it.

Leaning on Paul's effort to disengage Christian faith from Jewish practice, Hare at one point speaks of the slavery of the Law.[61] I don't think we can begin to reach for real dialogue among religious traditions until we find a way to drop that sort of talk. Judaism is not a fossil. We Jews are here, part of the conversation, living bearers of a living tradition. Committed Jews do not see the *mitzvot* as a bondage or a burden but as a privilege, a blessing, an opportunity to serve God and do the good that is his will. That's what is meant normatively, as we've noted, by the idea of Israel's chosenness. Life in or even close to God's commandments is a relation of intimacy and trust, as Halevi describes it.[62] The biblical poets, in bolder imagery, speak of Israel's relations with God as a love affair and marriage.

There's an ethos in that relationship and no mere set of guilty choices. God's partner is the whole people of Israel. Our mission (should we choose to accept it!) is to build that ethos for ourselves—and, by example, for other nations, whom we never expect to dominate but do expect to influence, as we have historically, in profound ways.[63]

A life (as Aristotle teaches) is a mosaic of actions. But the actions that make up a life interpret and sustain each other—as Hare agrees: "The various parts of the moral law belong together in a single integrated whole." That idea is a vital thread connecting the monotheist traditions. And it connects those traditions not only with one another but also with the great tradition of philosophy that was founded by Plato and Aristotle. That's one reason why the philosophers of that tradition found a home in monotheist thinking. The humane ideals of Western civilization were forged in part by the welding together of Greek philosophical and monotheistic ideas: We do not accept the tragic view that diverse goods can never be integrated in a coherent way of life for individuals and the community.

But the doctrine of original sin, which Hare, like Kant, reads in terms of the human penchant for choosing happiness over duty, reinjects into this more integrated vision elements of the tragic view that had so powerful an impact in the *odea* of ancient Greece and in the teachings of the ancient sophists. Hegel preserves that vision of conflict in his notion that the affirmation of identity in each being contains the dynamic of its own destruction. Isaiah Berlin revives the tragic idea in his claim that every exercise of liberty is pregnant with some corresponding moral loss. Martha Nussbaum puffs her own breath into the same thought when she suggests that nothing excellent is won without the loss of something precious.

Hare paints the tragic idea in Christian colors: The failure of integration among values is an inevitable outcome of our unredeemed nature. The vanity of human wishes here, like the memento mori of a Christian ascetic, serves not as some merely macabre emblem of pessimism but as an entry gate to salvation, since it shows us, Hare argues, that "We need something other than the human nature we are born with to tell us what fulfillment to seek and what not to seek. We need something that transcends our nature to play this role, and in the Christian tradition this is God's selection of the route toward our final end and God's revealing this in the life of Christ."[64]

Let's lay our cards on the table. I don't think, and the Jewish tradition does not think, that God left nature so radically deficient that only magically or mythically can its wounds be stanched and healed. Our trust in God's unity, creation, rule, and justice reflects and reinforces our shared confidence that tragedy is not inevitable, that one good need not undermine another, that the good life is possible.

But how can life be perfect if human beings are not perfect?

I'm not saying that the lives we live will ever be perfect. Even in the messianic age, it's the changing of human hearts, the reform of character, that will yield peace and justice.[65] Life itself is constant interchange. It does not become static. There's always give and take. Close that down and you get not Elysium but death.

What I'm arguing is that tragedy is not inevitable. Choosing one good may foreclose another, but the choice itself is not inevitably destructive or self-undermining. Nature itself is good. It is not the absolute, not a god but a good, bounteous and commodious, opening possibilities of learning and growth that make life itself worthwhile, choice possible, and wise choices fruitful.

The Jewish sources are keenly aware that human finitude does not measure up to God's perfect goodness. They do not ignore human frailty and fallibility. But neither do they overlook the mercy and grace by which God scales his demands to the order of magnitude of our moral capabilities—just as He scales his theophany to our intellectual powers. So when the Rabbis read that God instructed Moses: *They shall make an ark of acacia wood, two and a half cubits long and a cubit and a half high* (Exodus 25:10), they marvel that God's Law could fit in so small a space[66]—or any finite space—let alone reduce to words! They address the seeming paradox by quoting from Judah the Prince, appropriately enough, since it was he who compiled the Mishnah. His mind turned here to Job's recasting of the God-stricken ejaculations of Elihu, his youthful interlocutor: Elihu had called God unapproachable and unfathomable (Job 37:22–23). But Job saw his companions' praises of God not as errors but as mere outcroppings of God's acts (Job 26:14). Elihu was not speaking as an agnostic. What he meant, as Job more judiciously and more charitably understood him, according to the gloss of Judah the Prince, was simply this:

> We will never find God's power fully unfurled upon his creatures. For He does not overtax them with his laws but visits each according to his strength. As you know, had God come upon Israel with the full dint of his power when He gave us the Torah, we would not have been able to withstand it, as it says: *If we hear the voice of the Lord our God any further, we shall die* (Deuteronomy 5:22). So God came to them according to the strength of each of them, as it says: kol ha-Shem ba-ko'aḥ, *the voice of the Lord in power* (Psalm 29:4). It does not say "in his power" but just *in power*, that is, in keeping with the strength of each one! (Exodus Rabbah 34.1)[67]

What would be the point in God's burying his creatures beneath an infinite burden—or with any charge that they were not, in principle, equipped to bear?

But when you speak about pursuing holiness and even emulating God, isn't that really an unattainable goal? If the Torah makes that kind of demand of us, isn't it in fact asking the impossible—casting us, inevitably, in the role of sinners?

Well, the Torah does charge us to pursue an open-ended aim, to emulate God's holiness. In biblical language, God's holiness, as we've noted, is God's transcendence. And we do pursue transcendence in many ways—in each breath we take, in our endeavor to stay alive, to raise and teach our children, to grow intellectually and cultivate our talents, but, morally, most tellingly, in reaching out to one another, to seek one another's good, not out of any desire for profit but for the others' sake. We do emulate God in this, and yes the aim is infinitely high. But I don't agree that this makes it futile, that we are somehow, ultimately, inadequate, born unto sin and incapable of generosity, nobility, and growth, both morally and intellectually. Levinas, a great champion of the moral outlook in the past century, often spoke of the infinite demand upon each of us that is made by the other. But I think we best understand just what it was that Levinas intended if we read his text alongside the Mishnaic texts that he knew and loved so well: Infinite here does not entail moral paralysis, crushing our powers under an unbearable burden. Rather, I think, it should be taken as the opening lines of Mishnah Pe'ah would suggest, to imply that there is no clear upper limit to the charge that *ḥesed* gives us. And, beyond that, we should be heartened by our capacity share and collaborate with others in shouldering the responsibilities that our subjecthood sets before us.

Once again I think we need to listen to the good moral advice of Rabbi Tarfon, who saw the immensity of the human moral and spiritual task but counseled not that we give it up in frustration or confess our inadequacy and turn to a surrogate to bear our guilt. For that would risk moral abdication and could yield an outcome little different from complacency. His words: "The day is short, the task huge, the workers slack, the pay steep, and the master pressing." Still, he would say: "It's not your charge to complete the task, but you are not free to give it up!" (M. Avot 2.21–22).

We need to remember that the Torah sees itself not as an onerous charge but as a law of life. Its aim *is* human flourishing. So, of course, its project is open-ended, but its means are near to hand. If we know what is worthy of being taken as God's law, it's not by knowing what obligations would be hardest or most tedious but by reflecting on the norms that best aid us—all of us together—in realizing our humanity. We build on what we have, on the institutions we know and on our grasp of human nature—not on our penchant for atrocities or banalities or fads but on what reason, experience, and an open mind teach us will aid us in our growth and in our task.

I'm still troubled by the idea that God is somehow bound to do (or to command) what we human beings think is right.

Again, I think "bound" is the wrong image here. It's the same sort of slip that people make when they suppose that civil society impinges on our freedom—failing to see that civil society is the major guarantor of our freedom and of the power to exercise it—or when they imagine that the tyrannical man is free and that power is seen only in violence and perversity—forgetting that these are symptoms of weakness, not sources of strength.

There are plenty of thinkers who worry that if ethics is objective it does not need God and that if it needs God it's not objective. But I think that worry is specious, largely the product of polemics and apologetics by those who profess to have cornered the market on values for their own sectarian or secular outlook. The dogmatic, authoritarian, or rigorist tendencies that often attach themselves to theism and the relativism, libertinism, or excess that theists find alarming among professing humanists polarize this division of the house. Hypocrisy, false consciousness, complacency, and self-righteousness on both sides deepen the divide. Such faults are often plainer to outsiders than to those who bear them and less tolerable and more scandalous in adversaries than in allies.

Still the choice demanded is a false one: God is inseparable from the good, and our concepts of divinity reflect the adequacy of our values. Hence the prominence of self-portraiture in all theologies, noted at the very dawn of philosophy, when Xenophanes observed that the Scythians and Ethiopians depicted the gods in their own image, arguing that if cattle and horses or lions could draw, they, too, would paint the gods in their own likeness.[68] He might have said, the likeness of their ideal. But perhaps ideals vary too much for alien ideals to be readily seen as such.

The God of Aristotle is, of course, a mind, supremely active and fully actual, drawing all beings to emulation and admiration. The Epicurean gods enjoy perfect *ataraxia*, untroubled among themselves and untroubling to others. The Stoic gods are models of good governance and concern, seeing to the needs of their wards, designing all in benevolence, and facing us all with trials that test our mettle, blessed opportunities for the growth and exercise of virtue. Ideas of God shift as our values grow and change. Values, in turn, ethical or intellectual, political or aesthetic, are honed and chastened by the concepts of divinity we encounter or embrace.

So, far from giving us a stark choice between defining the good (or any value) in isolation from our idea of God or submitting that idea to some external, putatively divine determination, critical reflection points to an active (and inveterate) dialectic in which our values are informed by our idea of the divine and enrich it in turn. This dialectic is what I have called chimneying.

You seem awfully chary of theistic subjectivism? Why is that?

Well, this concern of mine is nothing new in Judaism. Perhaps that's part of what sets apart our tradition from many Christian and Muslim approaches. Avi Sagi and Daniel Statman have searched the texts of Jewish ethicists and decisors and found little support among them for treating moral standards as the sheer reflex of God's command.[69] Isadore Twersky and Marvin Fox,[70] they note, do voice a discomfort with moral autonomy and even speak up for heteronomy, which Twersky fuses with theonomy in what he calls the traditional Jewish view.[71] In the same spirit, they might have added Immanuel Jakobovits, who wrote that Judaism "emphatically insists that the norms of moral conduct can be governed neither by the accepted notions of public opinion nor by the individual conscience" but only from Sinaitic revelation.[72]

That last, however, was written in a bioethical context, where, as Chief Rabbi of Britain, Jakobovits was setting himself at odds with widespread moral fashions. He pictures public opinion as swaying in the breeze, which it does, and calls personal conscience frail and fallible, which it is. But his appeal assumes that morals ought to be clear and objective, qualities that he expects loyal Jews to find in revelation and its authoritative interpretation from Sinai down to the present day. He appeals, then, not to authority but to loyalty and a sense of duty, backed up by steady moral principles that are hardly halakhic alone.[73]

If the notion derived from such thoughts of God-given moral standards is that God might capriciously ask us to do just anything, that inference would undercut the call to clarity and stability and moral objectivity that underlies Jakobovits's case. The fact is that most Jewish writers are pretty firmly committed to the objectivity of ethics. Even when they speak of God as the ultimate moral authority, it's ethical objectivity that they're seeking to underwrite. Thus, Marvin Fox writes: "without the divine moral standard, there is no standard at all"—but then adds, tellingly: "What God commands must be good; otherwise the commander is not God."[74]

Heteronomy was Kant's name for an improper reliance on external sources of moral authority, sources other than one's own freely appropriated, rational will. Self-enslavement to one's appetites or passions was Kant's paradigm case. But fears of moralistic buck passing led him to treat slavish deference to divine commands as another type of heteronomy.[75] G. E. Moore and many a subsequent twentieth-century philosopher followed up on this idea, treating divine commands as just another grotesque in the rogue's gallery, just another way of reducing moral judgments to facts—now, facts about God's commands.

It was Hume, of course, who sniffed a problem in the attempt to jack up factual claims into moral prescriptions, to derive an *ought* from an *is*. What Moore argued was that all attempts at naturalistic definitions of 'good' must fail, since one can still intelligibly ask—when 'good' is defined—'But is it really good?' Paradigmatically, it makes sense to ask, when a Utilitarian defines as 'good' whatever is productive of the greatest pleasure for the greatest number, 'But is *that* really good?' A successful definition would be an analytic truth, and questioning it would make no sense. For to question a claim is to entertain its denial, and it makes no sense to deny an analytic truth.

But does Moore's open-question method scuttle God's commands? That depends, I think, on how we understand the relation of those commands to the ideas of right and good. Some critics of theistic ethics—and some theists, too—like to speak of God in ways that problematize God's goodness or its nexus to the human, moral good. But that preempts the familiar and well-entrenched equations of God with love and truth and goodness itself.[76] What's the Jewish view here?

Observant Jews introduce the twice-daily proclamation of God's unity and uniqueness in the *Sh^ema*ʿ (Deuteronomy 6:4–9, 11:13–47; Numbers 15:37–41) with the exclamation *The Lord God is Truth!* Truth here, once again, entails justice. And prefaced to the *Sh^ema*ʿ in the morning liturgy is the acknowledgment of God's great love in teaching the Patriarchs his "laws of life" (*ḥukkei ḥayyim*), the norms crystallized as rules in the *mitzvot*. In the evening, the *Sh^ema*ʿ is preceded by a parallel acknowledgment of God's "infinite love," again manifested in his teaching us his "Law and commandments, statutes and ordinances." Thrice daily, near the end of the silent devotion called the ʿ*Amida*, comes the benediction *Blessed art Thou, O Lord, whose name is Good and whom it is seemly to praise.*

If God is understood in such terms, the notion that any equation of the good with God's will is somehow reductive falls to the ground. The question 'But is God really good?' does not stay open. It's more like asking 'Do four quarters really make a dollar?' We can force sense into the question about God and good, but only by bracketing the monotheist's idea of God, the idea that Genesis relates was revealed to Abraham and, through him, to the nations of the world, when God rejected pagan notions of divinity and revealed Himself to Abraham and all his heirs and successors, by making clear that holiness is not won through violence and does not demand the immolation of all that a human being rightly loves and cherishes. It was at the binding of Isaac, when the angel stayed Abraham's hand, that the God of monotheism revealed Himself (Genesis 22:14) as the God of love and justice, charity and kindness—*ḥesed*, in a word.[77]

Any notion of divine arbitrariness or "teleological suspension of the ethical" distorts and displaces the monotheist's reasoning, the same reasoning that traces all bounties, blessings, and beauties in the world to God's infinite goodness. When Moore's question has meaning in the case of a deity, it's a clear sign that Abraham's God has been quietly replaced with a fickle power, known only through dogma—as if sheer authority could somehow command sincere belief and as if a capricious power were worthy of worship and celebration as the source of divine grace. Such notions are alien to the spirit of monotheism and sharply at odds with Jewish tradition. As Abraham Joshua Heschel put it years ago:

> To inquire: is a particular act holy (commanded by, or dear to God) because it is good or is it good because it is holy (commanded by or dear to God)? would be just as meaningless as to inquire: is a particular point within the circle called the center due to its equidistance from the periphery or is its equidistance from the periphery due to its being the center? The dichotomy of the holy and the good is alien to the spirit of the great prophets. To their thinking, the righteousness of God is inseparable from His being.[78]

So you're saying that the God of Abraham has nothing to do with the sacrifice of Isaac?

Isaac wasn't sacrificed. Abraham's trial, as Maimonides teaches, took him to the limits of loyalty and showed the world where those limits lie (*Guide* III 24). It's in that sense that Genesis can say that the Lord revealed himself on that mountain—and still does (Genesis 22:14). But we need to take to heart the discovery Abraham made there: that holiness is not to be bundled up with violence but finds its authentic expression in justice and love. It's through that discovery, which becomes the message of Abraham's successors and heirs, that they—that *we*—become the conduit through whom all the nations of the world of the world are blessed.

But what about the implacable violence of the Old Testament God—the genocidal warfare, the command to destroy Amalek?

The commandments to destroy Amalek root and branch (Deuteronomy 25:17–19) and to blot out the memory of the Amalekites, as enemies of God, from one generation to the next (Exodus 17:14) remain troublesome. But they make a far better test case for those who look for moral conflicts with divine commands than do the familiar, often tendentious, readings of the binding of Isaac. For the treatment of this episode as the tradition unfolds reveals just how seriously halakhic authors struggle with imperatives that they find morally problematic.

As Amy-Jill Levine writes:

> no tradition is pristine. As a Jew I am appalled by the sanctioned genocide suggested by passages in Deuteronomy and Joshua. I take no comfort in such passages as Deuteronomy 20:16–18: "But as for the towns of these peoples that the Lord your God is giving you as an inheritance, you must not let anything that breathes remain alive. You shall annihilate them—the Hittites and the Amorites, the Canaanites and the Perizzites, the Hivites and the Jebusites—just as the Lord your God has commanded, so that they may not teach you to do all the abhorrent things that they do for their gods."[79]

Levine is horrified by the order to devote Jericho to utter destruction (Joshua 6:21). She acknowledges the rabbinic readings that "denounce the violence" and that reinterpret passages that later generations found repugnant. "But the texts are still there," she adds. And she takes neither pride nor comfort in that fact. Hers is one type of response to what we might call moral dissonance. That of the Rabbis is another, like hers moral in motivation. The halakhic authorities do not simply say: If this is what God wanted, this was what must be done. They are at pains to bracket and contain a mandate that seems so violently to conflict with the Torah's larger moral vision.

Polemics will naturally focus on hard cases. Enlightenment thinkers like Tom Paine reveled in passages like this one, and Christian polemicists have done the same before and since his time. But it's important when we consider biblical texts like these to remember the good counsel of Salo Baron about any comparative work and to resist the temptation to run (invidious) comparisons of "our" ideals against "your" history (or "theirs"). We also need to recognize just how little we know historically about the episodes these passages address. The same critics who doubt even the existence of many a scriptural figure and event—including the Exodus itself—are much less skeptical about the destructive mandates ascribed to figures whose standing as moral paragons they hope (for reasons of their own) to discredit, even if they doubt their existence.[80]

Taking a historic view of scripture, it's not difficult to consign to the past the horrifying commands about Amalek—in causes of war and ways of warfare that we can fondly hope are long forgotten, or will be, perhaps, in an age when nuclear war, carpet bombing, and terrorism have also become foreign to our consciousness. Some may balk at ideas of ongoing revelation, perhaps fearing that such thoughts subject halakhic norms to moral fashions quite alien to the Torah's outlook. Still, the ways of war, like those of peace, do change, and we can't help but hope that they—and the norms about them—will one day make our familiar moral standards seem as savage as the military practices and war rhetoric of our ancestors may seem to us.

Viewed historically, the unfulfilled order to King Saul to blot out Amalek might well be a back projection, meant to legitimate David's and Solomon's succession and to explain Saul's loss of God's mandate. That's the meaning Samuel gives the episode, guided by God's word in a sleepless night and the portentous tearing of the Samuel's garment when the king snatches at it: *the Lord hath ripped the rule of Israel from thee this day and given it to a better man* (1 Samuel 15:28). Even so, one ancient rabbi, Samuel bar Avdimi, noted somberly that Samuel's hewing down the miscreant king was not in keeping with halakhic standards. For it was done without witnesses or warning, and the mode of execution was not among those sanctioned in the Law.[81] The exigencies of a war long past in Rabbi Samuel's time may have helped him to explain his namesake's severity and the condign punishment that the prophet/judge meted out. But Rabbi Samuel's subtext is also clear: There is no normative force or precedent to be drawn from Samuel's example here.[82]

Where prescriptive lessons are drawn in rabbinic readings of the story, they are often even handed, even in their severity. The *M^e^khilta*, commenting on Amalek's ambush of the Israelites in the desert, reasons that Israel must have deserved the attack: The Israelites were ungrateful and had fallen away from God's commandments.[83] Even so, in keeping with the rabbinic rule of measure for measure (M. Soṭah, 1.7), the same source adds: "The early sages [*ri'shonim*] say: 'The principle applies in every generation that Israel's scourge will in the end itself be smitten. Every man can learn ethically from Amalek, who came to harry Israel but was destroyed by God, in this life and the next.' "[84]

The economy of retributions here is moralistic, if not moral. It is certainly not final. Later writers continue to struggle with the mandate to destroy Amalek. They do not simply prostrate their moral sense before God's command and say: 'God said blot out Amalek, so it must be right.' Michael Harris writes that he hears a deafening silence about Amalek from many later exegetes.[85] But the comment rings strangely, given the prominence of the episode among the exegetes troubled by the dire command or seeking its warrant. They do not simply say that because the order came from God, it was therefore right.

Sticking close to his text, Naḥmanides (at Exodus 17:16) stresses that Amalek's attack on Israel was unprovoked—and exacerbated by the assailants' descent from Esau, which made the aggressors Israel's cousins.[86] Rashi tells of Amalek's sexual laxity and blasphemy and stresses that nation's failure to fear God,[87] as the Torah itself records: *Remember what Amalek did to thee on the march when you were leaving Egypt, how he waylaid thee on the road and massacred all thy stragglers when thou wast faint and weary—not fearing God* (Deuteronomy 25:18). The Torah itself here seeks to justify its sentence: *So, when God giveth thee respite from all thine enemies about the land that the Lord thy God giveth thee as thine own estate, thou shalt blot out the memory of Amalek from under the sky. Do not forget* (25:19). Yet the warrants Rashi and Naḥmanides offer hardly suffice in our eyes to justify the desolation that Rashi believes God ordered: "*Man and woman, infant and suckling, ox and lamb*" (1 Samuel 15:3)—so that the name of Amalek is not remembered even through an animal, of which it might be said: 'This animal belonged to the Amalekites.'"[88]

The Midrash characteristically embroiders: The Amalekites mutilated corpses on the battlefield and mocked the covenant of Abraham.[89] The sense of outrage voiced in such claims is intended, once again, to make the biblical severity morally understandable. But the effort to bring the ancient texts under moral control does not stop here. One line of approach trades on God's omniscience. Locating the respite anticipated in Deuteronomy in the reign of King Saul and his Amalekite campaigns, the Midrash identifies Agag, the Amalekite king that Saul spared, as the ancestor of Haman—who is, after all, called "the Agagite" (Esther 3:1). Haman's forefather, we are told, was conceived the very night that Saul spared Agag, who died the next day at Samuel's hand in requital of his crimes (1 Samuel 15:33). The pedigree is fanciful. But the crimes Samuel cites to justify the execution are real enough. The Midrash means to suggest that Haman's genocidal plot might have been forestalled had Saul faithfully obeyed God's order and not tried to substitute his own ill-informed sense of sympathy for a fellow monarch.[90]

One way of locking enmity with Amalek in the past was to invoke a kind of rabbinic statute of limitations. Rabbi Joshua in the Mishnah (Yadaim 4.4, citing Isaiah 10:13) voids the Torah's ban on marriage with Moabites and Ammonites (Deuteronomy 23:4), arguing that the depredations of Sennacherib so confounded the genealogies that the remnants of these peoples are no longer identifiable. Joseph Badad, a nineteenth-century halakhist, rules similarly as to enmity with Amalek.[91] But Joseph Soloveitchik takes a different tack. Maimonides, after all, calls the seven nations Israel was mandated to displace in Canaan "by now gone and forgotten." But he does not say the same of Amalek, implying, Soloveitchik reasons, that they must have survived. Hence the Torah's declaration that God is at war with Amalek *in every generation* (Exodus 17:16).[92] But that pushes enmity with Amalek into the realm of allegory.

Rabbi Joshua in the Midrash finds messianic portents in Exodus 17:16, and Rabbi Eleazar reasons that Amalek will never be destroyed until God's eternal kingdom is established.[93] So Meir ha-Kohen, in thirteenth-century Germany, locates the respite promised in Deuteronomy not in Saul's days but in the Messianic era.[94] David ben Zimra (called Radvaz) disputes his gloss. But Maimonides, for his part, holds that Amalek remains a threat until the coming of the Messiah. That does not, however, place the Amalekites beyond the moral pale. For, by the laws of war, even these inveterate enemies must be spared if they accept terms of peace.[95]

Soloveitchik, in tune with the rabbinic allegorizations, reasons that if Amalek endures throughout history, *any* nation that seeks to destroy Israel must be the halakhic Amalek. Citing his father, Moses Soloveitchik, he names the Nazis as the Amalek of our day—not by genealogy but for their role in history. Amalek, after all, never emerges as a clear ethnicity in the historic or archeological record. The Torah itself is vague about the land from which the Amalekites came to attack the Israelites, a fact not lost on the ancient rabbinic exegetes. So Amalek readily becomes an archetype. That may be what it was from the start. Sublimating the biblical account into symbolism allows Soloveitchik, as a halakhist, in a way to fulfill the paradoxically paired imperatives to blot out the name of Amalek forever yet never forget what the Amalekites did.

The semiotic response to the moral challenge posed by the biblical text may seem strikingly modern. But it is well represented in the Midrash and clearly announced in Haman's fanciful pedigree and in midrashic images of Amalekite mockery of Abraham's covenant. As Louis Ginzberg notes, "Even the early Tannaitic sources use Amalek as a designation for Rome, and in the legend Amalek's sneering at the Abrahamic covenant characterizes the attitude of the Romans (especially during the Hadrian persecutions)."[96] Amalek readily becomes imperial Rome, since Rome, rabbinically, is Esau, the Red, eponymous ancestor of Edom. And the name of Amalek is assigned on the same pattern to other enemies, as well—much as any avatar of evil might be called a Hitler and as Islamic usage calls oppressors pharaohs, generically. Indeed, the commentators on the Qur'ān say that 'pharaoh' was a hereditary title of the kings of Amalek![97] Israel's enemies, historically, were real enough, of course. But genealogy was hardly to the point, and the Torah's verses were often read for their promise of respite rather than as a focus of anger.

Carrying sublimation a step further, the Kabbalah makes Amalek not a nation at all but Sammael, evil personified, or rather, demonized.[98] Samson Raphael Hirsch, the founder of German neo-orthodoxy, shifts that thesis into a higher register: "It is not Amalek who is so pernicious for the moral future of mankind but *zekher Amalek*, the glorifying of the memory of Amalek which is the danger."[99] As Harris sums up the view:

> The crux of Hirsch's position lies in the radical idea that the Amalek commandment is not to be interpreted as mandating the physical annihilation of the Amalekites.... the struggle of Israel against Amalek is not a physical confrontation but rather an uncompromising contest between two conflicting sets of values: between peace and militarism (the sword), between spiritual-moral values and brute force, and between "building" and destruction.[100]

Clearly, the focus of the halakhic authorities is on the norms of the Torah. They moralize the account of Amalek and neutralize the ancient norms of battle that it may preserve. Their interest is not in history but in the ongoing project of building a way of life on the Torah's constitutional trellis. Whatever the ancient laws of war and customs of proscription or devotion, these have no more relevance in practice than the fractional census of slaves announced in the American Constitution.

We see a similar rabbinic bracketing of the law of *soṭah*, the suspected adulteress;[101] another, in the revision already underway in biblical times, of the ancient norms of *ḥalitza*, making ritual release from levirate marriage more an expectation than an exception;[102] again, in Hillel's introduction of the *prosbul*, to ease the shift from a subsistence to a cash economy; and in Rabbi Gershom's rejection of polygamy. All these are instances of the general practice in halakhic exegesis, of bringing to bear the full weight of biblical and extra-biblical moral themes in shaping the Law, smoothing its asperities and contouring to its larger principles any rules that seem to jut out and jar against its broader humane thrust. Similar dynamics continue today in efforts combat a man's willful refusal to give his ex-wife a *get* or certificate of divorce and in efforts to address the problem of the *agunah*, or straw widow.[103]

A striking instance of the force of moral reasoning in the framing of Halakha is the rabbinic response to the Torah's sentence of stoning for the recalcitrant rebellious son (Deuteronomy 21:18–20). Rabbi Shimon asks, pointedly, is one to be stoned for mere refractory behavior? We can only infer, he insists, that no son ever has existed or ever will who falls under the biblical sentence. Such laws, he rules, were placed in the Torah only for study (B. Sanhedrin 71a). They are regulative ideas, as Kantians might say. Similar mitigations are underway within the Torah itself, in the establishment of Cities of Refuge (Numbers 35:6–32),[104] in the Law of the Fair Captive (Deuteronomy 21:10–14), in the provisions for military deferment (Deuteronomy 24:5), in the qualification to the institution of slavery (Exodus 21:1–13), in the laws of debt and land tenure (Leviticus 25),[105] and even in the regulations that demand an acknowledgment of communal responsibility for bloodshed outside a town (Deuteronomy 21:1–9).

The canon, in short, has never excluded moral considerations from the weighty task of interpreting Halakha. On the contrary, those who interpret and apply that law as the articulation of God's will pretty consistently use any moral insight they can bring to bear, and they have done that throughout the history of that Law's elaboration. Whatever moral knowledge they feel they have has proved critical and constitutive in their elaboration of the law. This moral thread—along with the commitment to continuity itself, which is characteristic of any juridical tradition—gives a sense of unity and organic development to Halakha and allows the free and playful use of prooftexts as pretexts—since the moral thematics are the real rabbinic guidelines. The words of the founding texts, of course, are sacred, portentous, even oracular in the eyes of these exegetes. But the most basic themes that shape their halakhic interpretations are the core values of the Mosaic ethos. That is why Maimonides can confidently say of the "Men of the Great Assembly" that their authority is tantamount to that of the prophets, whose poesy they unfold and whose mandates they give concrete, practical application (*Guide* I 59).

Aren't you just saying that morality is autonomous, that we have moral knowledge independent of God or revelation, and that the Torah is otiose at best and often in need of correction from our superior, human standpoint? But isn't autonomy sheer willfulness? Doesn't piety demand surrender? Isn't that what theonomy means?

On the contrary, I think human moral thinking needs all the help it can get, from scripture and tradition, society and revelation, whatever form it comes in. Hubris can take a variety of forms, and one of them is that of thinking that one's preferred tradition alone is self-sufficient. That was not the view of Moses. He was in intimate communion with God but did not refuse advice from Jethro, his Midianite father-in-law. Jethro, for his part, while remaining very much a Midianite (Numbers 10:29–30; cf. 1 Samuel 15:6), did not arrogantly assume that his insights would inevitably be at odds with what Moses had by way of inspiration. He predicates his advice on the concurrence of God's command (Exodus 18:23).[106]

In the biblical sources, human moral autonomy is presumed—axiomatically, as Maimonides puts it, in the very issuance of a command—for commands make sense only when issued to someone who is capable of choosing whether or not to heed one's words. We see the presumption of autonomy also in the Torah's appeals for the acceptance of its laws. It's true that no less a scholar than Ephraim Urbach scores Moritz Lazarus's efforts to read Kantian standards of autonomy into biblical law.[107] But Urbach was relying on Hermann Cohen's definition, "that an autonomous ethic means one that emanates from man and from him alone."[108] That's too lopsided an account to apply to acts of piety, since the religious spirit, as Kant says, takes the moral law as God's command. The spiritually minded, we must add, finding God's commands precious and uplifting, take them to heart and make them their own. Rabban Gamaliel III, the son of Judah the Prince, saw appropriation of that kind as the heart of piety. He hints at this kind of harmony and not just at some external reward when he says, "Make His will your own, that He may make your will His" (M. Avot 2.4).

Hermann Cohen addresses the complementarity we need in ethics between reason and revelation by citing the concurring appraisals of Saadiah Gaon, the first systematic Jewish philosopher, and Baḥya ibn Paqudah, the great exponent of Jewish philosophical pietism:

> Saadyah significantly states that no real discussion is possible with anyone who asserts that only the Torah, and not also reason, is a source of ethics. This shows how unreservedly reason is upheld as a controlling principle of the Torah. Similarly, there is a statement in Baḥya ibn Paqudah's *Duties of the Heart* to the effect that man's blind acceptance of revelation as the sole source of knowledge, to the exclusion of his own reasoning power, might well be the work of his evil inclination. Thus reason, that inexhaustible and indispensable source of all morality, is acknowledged as the inviolable basis of religion.[109]

For it is reason, after all, that adopts moral principles as its own, uniting God's will and moral truth with one's own intent, as piety demands.

As for theonomy, I think there's been a fair amount of confusion about that word. Let me try to untangle that a bit. Paul Tillich coined the term in his very first public presentation. His aim was to preempt Kantian worries about heteronomy as a source of inauthenticity in inspired ethics. Ethics, like science, Tillich agreed with Kant, must be "purely autonomous, entirely free of all religious heteronomy." That means that ethical obligations, to be properly ethical, need to be our own, not sheer impositions.

Still, in the mind and heart of the monotheist, moral obligations are divine commands—as Kant urged. Theists do make God's commands their own. So autonomy merges with theonomy: "The possibilities of conflict are radically eliminated."[110] Autonomy now does not mean willfulness, and theonomy does not mean moral abdication. Self-legislation is not moral subjectivism, and harkening to God's commands does not mean separating God from his own goodness.

Often, it is true, religious people don't freely and joyously make their own what they see as God's commands. Sometimes they do intend surrender—as the word *islām* implies. That kind of yielding of will or willfulness is a natural outcome of the vigor and rigor, the enthusiasm and momentum of a conscientious commitment, an intent to be not just devoted but devout. Many a pious seeker, as Joseph Soloveitchik wrote, finds his very identity and life's project in God's imperatives. Soloveitchik is not alone in applauding such choices.[111] But in any merger there's a risk of domination by one side or the other: Morals can be swamped by piety or its markers; devotion can collapse into ethics or its polite or politically correct surrogates.[112]

The genuinely devout are rightly alarmed in that latter case, and righteous secularists are properly outraged by substitutions of the other sort. They think that piety professed but not practiced is all too typical—since they find faith itself unwarranted, its objects not credible. They suspect all professions of faith of pretense or naïveté. When outward piety betrays itself in acts of dishonesty, even acts sincerely intended as witness to God's holiness become, as the tradition puts it, a desecration of God's name. Still, when authentic piety grafts itself to the God of goodness, truth, and justice and when moral and social choices are in dialogue with critically refined values worthily traced to God's word, moral inauthenticity vanishes. And so does the imagined conflict between God's command and what is right.

Theonomy means not the loss of moral freedom but only the surrender of willfulness and the illusion that choices are right just because they are ego's own. Nor does theonomy entail a loss of creatureliness but only the recognition that God's commands are not capricious fiats but articulate expressions of what is right and holy—holy because it is right, and chosen by God because it is holy. The God who loves love and chooses holiness is the God worthy of worship. And the affirmation that this God is good or loves justice and *ḥesed*, beauty, mercy, and generosity is not a tautology. For part of what it means is a denial of gods that might have demanded that we do just anything, or anything bizarre or cruel, in sheer assertion of their power and human subservience.[113] But, biblically, as Saadiah rightly argues, we distinguish a true prophet from a false one by the moral tenor of his precepts. A god that asks for cruelty is not a real or a worthy god.

Theonomy, as Tillich sets out the concept, is "what happens to culture as a whole under the impact of the Spiritual Presence." Not "that culture is dissolved into religion"—as in a would-be theocracy. Rather, the outcome is "the self-transcendence of culture"; the moral law becomes a force for creativity, allowing the culture it leavens to strive toward ethical and spiritual perfection.[114] People may differ as to just what shape such a life should take and debate the means by which it might be sought. But, if internalizing God's commands does foster thoughtfulness and openness, such virtues should be a bulwark against the loss of conscientious and creative moral energy that is the great threat of heteronomy.

Fox and Twersky seem to have little more in mind when they seek to rescue and privilege 'heteronomy' than a powerful sense of commitment to God and his commandments. They see the issue in terms of personal, rather than societal, commitment. For American political oratory does not echo tunefully to the Christian socialist overtones of Tillich's prewar rhetoric; American Jews are chary of any Christian triumphalism that might cling to Tillich's early formulations. But what Fox and Twersky are after boils down to a traditional attachment to the abiding authority of the *mitzvot*. That's not the same as saying that God's commands have nothing to do with what we human beings, at our best, understand by right and wrong.

I still want to press you on this. Is it your position that divine commands are otiose, since we have within us sufficient moral knowledge to confront the choices we must make?

Not at all. It's pretty clear from the course of human history that neither internal nor external admonitions (or constraints!) suffice to meet our human moral needs. That's why I hope for a complementarity and dialogue, for chimneying between reason and tradition, and for triangulation among traditions, as means of enhancing our ethical objectivity. I don't think it follows from the recognition that one source is not sufficient in itself that therefore another must be. I think we learn a lot from the biblical idea of a covenant. Start with what Kenneth Seeskin says:

> the normal metaphor for the relation between God and humans is not the making of an edict but the joining together of two people in matrimony. I submit that what philosophers typically call "revelation" is more complicated than a list of imperatives saying "Do this" and "Don't do that." At the very least, it is an agreement that takes into account the dignity of both parties. Without this agreement, we may have lightning, thunder, and a booming voice from the top of a mountain, but we would not have action worthy of a divine being.[115]

The biblical covenant idea grows out of ancient norms about pacts and treaties. But notice the difference, say, from modern legal contracts: Israel's covenant with God is in part a gift. But also, like a marriage, it needs consent—intelligent, informed consent, as David Hartman argues:

> I allow that the Torah may challenge some accepted current patterns of behavior, but I cannot imagine that it requires us to sacrifice our ability to judge what is just and fair. The covenant invites a community to act and to become responsible for the condition of its human world. This invitation to full responsibility would be ludicrous if the community's rational or moral powers were relegated in the very act of covenantal commitment.[116]

What's most distinctive in the covenant idea is that our relations with our fellow human beings are not simply the object of a bargain that we strike with them. The primary relationship is with God, and the obligations we owe each other are grounded in the recognition of the preciousness of all of us in God's eyes. That is, they're grounded in the real worth of real beings and the dignity of persons—not their social standing or market value or negotiating posture. So it's not the case that whatever one agrees to is acceptable just because it is accepted. And the interests that need to be regarded ethically in all our undertakings are not confined to those of the contracting parties or proportioned to their bargaining power or status. The helpless are included. So are past and future generations, other peoples, living beings, the creatures of God, and the works of human hands. All wasteful and destructive acts are rejected, and love is to be extended to our fellow human beings, not in proportion to their influence but in the measure of our own self-love.

That does sound like a version of natural law thinking. But isn't it the Jewish view that we are all supposed to accept the mitzvot *simply because they are God's commands?*

Well, let's look at the Jewish texts and see if they find the only real reason for keeping the *mitzvot* in the fact that God ordained them. Sometimes that sounds a little like the Karl Barth's idea, so skillfully addressed in James Barr's Gifford Lectures. Barth didn't think much of natural theology. He liked what he thought of as the plain sense of the Bible. But Christians who want to eschew natural theology in favor of an opposing biblicism have their work cut out for them, Barr showed, since the Bible itself is filled with natural theology.[117] Natural law is equally anchored in the canon. And Jewish philosophers from Saadiah and Maimonides to David Novak and beyond have not had to invent it or read it into our texts.

The Torah repeatedly argues for the merits of the Law and the blessedness of the life it ordains. God warns Israelites not to *go awhoring* after whatever draws their hearts and eyes. Fringed garments are instituted as a reminder—as if all Israel were to tie a string around their fingers—*to remember to perform all My commandments.* In the same breath the Law continues—*and be holy to your God* (Numbers 15:39–40). Holiness is the freely stated aim of the *mitzvot.* Those who hear God's commandments are to try to become godlike (Leviticus 19:2), *a kingdom of priests, a holy nation* (Exodus 19:6). That might include Kant's idea of a kingdom of ends. But it seems to ask and also to offer a great deal more.

The life the Law lays out for all those who receive it is the means God affords for that open-ended pursuit: Ethical *mitzvot* are the broad avenue toward its ideal. The ritual commandments are the flowering borders along that highway, its hedge of lilies, in the midrashic image, as we've seen. So nothing in the Torah is a sheer test of blind faith. That, it seems to me, would be the real display of human willfulness. All of the commandments are laid down to serve a purpose, and the moral commandments in particular form a fabric designed to foster a good and holy life within this world for the individual and the community.

The aim of the Torah, far from being sheer imposition of an arbitrary will, is clearly stated to be enhancement of our lives. Human righteousness and wrongdoing, after all, as Elihu argues in the Book of Job (35:6–7), don't touch God.[118] Rather, as the Torah insists (Deuteronomy 6:24), the commandments are given for our own good. It is in this vein that Moses exhorts his people:

> *And now, Israel, what doth the Lord thy God ask of thee? Just this: to revere the Lord thy God, walk wholly in his ways, love Him, and serve the Lord thy God with all thy heart and all thy soul—keeping the commandments and statutes of the Lord that I command thee this day for thine own good.* (Deuteronomy 10:12–13)[119]

God *asks* and Moses persuades, speaking in God's behalf. He urges his people to accept a way of life that will benefit them.[120] The system includes the statutes, God's *ḥuqqim,* a favorite sticking point of Jewish legal positivists—just as (and just because) they are a favorite sticking point of those who carp at the particularities of the Law. When even these are said, biblically, to be for our own good, we can see how slight the hold of legal positivism is on Jewish norms.

The Rabbis distinguish *ḥuqqim,* statutes, from *mishpatim,* ordinances, saying of the latter that we humans would have found ourselves obliged to institute such rules had they not been revealed (B. Yoma 67b). Of the statutes they say that these are the butt of criticism, but still authoritative.[121] Here is Maimonides on the topic:

> Religious thinkers differ as to whether God's acts arise in his Wisdom or his sheer Will and serve no purpose at all. They differ accordingly as to the laws He laid down for us. Some seek no grounds for these whatever, holding them all to stem from his sheer Will. And some say that every one of these commands and prohibitions springs from his Wisdom and is meant to serve a purpose—that all of them can be explained and were instituted for the sake of some good. But all of us, lay and learned alike, agree on the view that all of the laws *have* grounds, some of which we do not know, since we cannot make out just how wisdom is expressed in them. The biblical texts are clear on this: *Just statutes and ordinances* (Deuteronomy 4:8); *The ordinances of the Lord are truth; they are just in their entirety* (Psalms 19:10).[122]
>
> With those called statutes (*ḥuqqim*)—like *sha'atnez* [the ban on wearing garments of wool interwoven with linen] (Deuteronomy 22:11), milk and meat [their dietary separation] (from Exodus 23:19), and the scapegoat (Leviticus 16:10, 16:21), of which the text of our blessed Sages states clearly: "One may not disparage[123] them, though Satan denounce them and the nations of the world reject them" (B. Yoma 67b)—most of the Sages do not see them as sheer groundless commands for which no purpose is to be sought. For that would imply pointless actions on God's part, as I've explained. Rather, the bulk of the Sages believed that these commandments definitely do have grounds, some beneficial purpose, albeit hidden from us, by our own intellectual limitations or lack of knowledge.
>
> They deemed all of the *mitzvot* rational, then, in that a given command or prohibition serves a useful purpose.[124] With some, the benefit is clear to us, as in the prohibitions of homicide and theft; in other cases, not—as in the ban on first fruits (Leviticus 19:23) and planting seeds of mixed type (Deuteronomy 22:9). Those with benefits clear to the commonfolk are called ordinances [*mishpatim*]; those whose benefits are unclear to the commonfolk are called statutes [*ḥuqqim*]. Still the Sages say "*It is no idle thing*[125] (Deuteronomy 32:47)—and if it is idle, that's your fault!" (J. Pe'ah 1, J. Ketubot 8). That is, this body of laws is not pointless or purposeless, and if any of the *mitzvot* seems so to you, the failing lies in your own apprehension.

> You have studied their well-known tradition (Ecclesiastes Rabbah 7.23) to the effect that Solomon knew the reasons for all the commandments except the red heifer (Numbers 19:1–10), and you know their dictum (B. Sanhedrin 21b) that God concealed the grounds for the *mitzvot*, lest they be taken lightly—as did occur in Solomon's case with the three commandments [among those affecting kings] whose grounds *are* spelled out. (*Guide* III 26; cf. 28, 31)

Kings are forbidden (Deuteronomy 17:16–17) to assemble a large harem, collect a big string of horses, or hoard silver and gold—lest their hearts be diverted from their charge. Solomon, notoriously, did all three. Knowing the reason for these commandments, the Rabbis infer, led him to think he could maintain his obligations without restraining his appetites—a complacency that resulted in his lapse: *And it came to pass that in old age Solomon's wives did turn his heart* (1 Kings 11:4). Hence, as the Rabbis reason (B. Sanhedrin 21b), the biblical reticence as to the grounds for the *mitzvot*: If the wisest of men could lose focus, must we not all be on guard? Yet, biblical restraint as to the grounds for a prescription does not make the *mitzvot* arbitrary or unmotivated.

Confirming Maimonides' thesis that all God's laws are meant to confer benefits on those who live by them is the exhortation of Moses that we cited more briefly in our second lecture:

> *Ye who cleaved to the Lord your God are all alive today. You see that I have taught you laws and rules* [ḥuqqim], *as the Lord my God charged me, for you to follow in the land you have come to inherit. Keep them and practice them. For that will be recognized as wisdom and insight on your part by other peoples, who will hear of all these laws and say: "What a wise and discerning people is this great nation!" For what nation is so great as to have the Divine as close to them as the Lord our God is to us whenever we call upon Him? What nation is so great as to have laws and rules as just as this entire Torah, which I set before you today.* (Deuteronomy 4:4–8)

The lawgiver appeals not to an arbitrary authority but to the wisdom and justice of God's laws, the enduring mark of God's accessibility: God did not just save Israel from Egypt or protect us in the desert. He remains actively, intimately at work among us, through the wisdom of his laws.

The canon is crystal clear on this: *The Lord was pleased, for his justice's sake, to make the Torah great and splendid* (Isaiah 42:21)—not just complex and copious but splendid, honorable, a vehicle of justice. Such reasoning grounds Rabbi Ḥananiah ben Akashya's inference that keeping the *mitzvot* imparts merit:[126] The laws make us worthy by making us better persons. Hence Isaiah's dismay at his people's falling short of their obligation (42:22–25): These laws *are* laws of life; they lay out a course of virtue that strengthens our character, enhances our lives, buttresses our communities, and guides us to our destiny as individuals and as a community.

Not only do all God's laws serve beneficial purposes, Maimonides insists, but the Torah's prescriptions are ideally balanced to promote and preserve the health of the soul. It is in this vein that he reads the reference in Psalm 19 to the perfection of God's Law: Its wholesome aims are not advanced by tinkering. Those who hope to improve on it by pushing its restraints to ascetic extremes are like naive valetudinarians who dose themselves with medicines while in good health, foolishly presuming that if a little helps the ill, heavy doses must be all the better, even for the well.[127] But if the Law is a system, adding or diminishing, turning left or right, only subverts its life-giving intent (Deuteronomy 4:2, 5:29–30, 13:1).

The Torah, of course, is not the only law or way of life that inspires and informs an ethos, and when Maimonides reads the psalmist as calling it perfect, he does not infer that no other system pursues such goals. His claim is simply that the Torah's norms, working as a system, reach an optimum. Historical and anthropological study might reveal whether other cultural modes define goals as worthy of choice and as fitting means of seeking them. But, as we have noted, anyone who denies that biblical laws have purposes is implying, in Maimonides' view, that revelation is vain, frivolous, or futile (*Guide* III 25, 31). Still, as the Rabbis say, seeing the purpose of a law no more cancels its authority than does failure to grasp that purpose. Thus, Maimonides concludes his discussion of objects consecrated in the ancient Temple service:

> If sticks and stones and earth and ashes can become holy by words alone, sheerly because the name of the Lord of the Universe was pronounced over them, and anyone who treated them as a profane thing, even unwittingly, committed a trespass demanding atonement, how much more must we guard against any disobedience of a *mitzvah* ordained for us by the Holy One blessed be He, just because one fails to grasp its reason, or to cavil against the Lord, or regard the commandments as one might treat secular matters.[128]

Prescriptivity and reason do not conflict. One should contemplate God's laws, seeking, to the fullest of one's capacity, to grasp the meanings they embody:

> All the statutes [*ḥuqqim*] in the Law are divine edicts, as we explained at the close of the Laws of Sacred Trespass. But one should study

> them and give reasons for them, as well as one can.... For the Law has plumbed the depths of man's mind and the furthest reach of human inclination.... [Even in the minutiae of Temple practice] these laws aim to control that inclination and improve our character. Most of the Torah's rules are *counsels of old [faithful and true]* (Isaiah 25:1), from One who is *great in counsel* (Jeremiah 32:19). They make us better human beings and keep us honest in all our doings, as He says: *Have I not written sound counsel for you, and knowledge, to make known to you how to answer with truth those who send unto you?* (Proverbs 22:20–21)[129]

The specific circumstances underlying the institution of a given biblical ritual, Maimonides explains—why a lamb or a ram is sacrificed, say—might well be long forgotten. But the broad purposes of the *mitzvot* are not mysterious or obscure: They all aim to enhance our civil security and welfare, improve our character, or aid us in realizing our inner affinity with God by perfecting our spiritual and intellectual natures.[130]

So is it true that normative Judaism holds that all mitzvot have reasons?

I think it is. But Maimonides is a far better authority on Halakha than I. He clearly thinks that the majority of the rabbinic Sages confirms his view. He cites a striking test case, where the Midrash asks: "What difference does it make to the Holy One, blessed be He, whether one slaughters a beast by cutting its throat or chopping off its head? One must say the *mitzvot* were given solely to refine [*l^e-tzaref*] mankind" (Genesis Rabbah 44.1). *L^e-tzaref* here is sometimes mistranslated or misunderstood as "to discipline." But the image, drawn from the silversmith's craft, is one of assaying and refining.[131] The concern is with the refinement of character: Even in their seeming minutiae, the *mitzvot* are vehicles for the improvement of character, not for God, of course, but for those who receive the Law.

Naḥmanides, who is commonly contrasted with Maimonides, sometimes too sharply, strongly agrees with him in holding that all God's laws have purposes.[132] He cites Proverbs (30:5) in support: *Every word of God is proofed* [*tz^{e}rufah*]. The verse continues: *He is a shield to those who trust in Him.* And that leads to the caution: *Do not add to his words, lest He try thee and thou be found wanting* [*pen yokhiaḥ l^e-kha v^e-nikhzavta*].[133] Echoing Maimonides, Naḥmanides assigns the general purposes of every *mitzvah* to God's wisdom and lays to God's will the concrete modalities that launch an obligation into the realm of practice.[134] True we do not know the purpose of every law. The

Midrash rightly allows that some of the Torah's ritual symbolisms are obscure even to the wisest of men, as the story about Solomon suggests.[135] But the Rabbis call God's *ḥuqqim* royal edicts, Naḥmanides argues, not to paint them as purposeless but to compare them to the commands a king promulgates for his subjects' good, even when they do not know the benefits of each ruling.

But aren't many of the mitzvot *plainly pretty arbitrary on the face of it?*

What we learn from Maimonides' analysis and its warm second by Naḥmanides is helpful to us here: All the *mitzvot* of the Torah, indeed, all laws, are underdetermined by their broad purposes. The modalities filled in to flesh out norms and create an operative system thus become a richly primed canvas for the symbolic gestures that are the subtext of a legislative canon. That gives all laws a ritual dimension.[136] The ban on murder voiced in the Decalogue sets human life on a high plateau, as human deserts would lead us to expect. The biblical specifications as to intent and as to penalty gauge that elevation. For the Torah introduces empiric tests and presumptive boundaries to isolate murder from manslaughter. It also sharply distinguishes crimes against persons from property crimes.[137] The differences in legal response set up a hierarchy of values and speak to the ordering and magnitude of the values in that hierarchy, even as they keep the core concerns in all these cases strictly in the moral realm, aiming to deter bloodshed and preserve the peace.

In *ḥuqqim,* however, the subtext regularly becomes the message, and the ritual, expressive dimension of a practice may carry its chief intent. Christians familiarly dismiss such laws as mere ceremonial. Certainly the negative valence Paul gave to that idea as he sought to roll out the ethos of monotheism among nations not attuned to the ritual practices of the Torah[138] was intensified by the Reformation, with its distaste for the baroque and its abhorrence of the presumption of a merely behavioral gateway to grace. That negativity was heightened by the Enlightenment revulsion against religious warfare that seemed only to be goaded on by the ritual markers of confessional allegiance.

But, if we dredge through the layers of history that may may silt over and obscure our view of a living and dynamic ethos, the biblical intent emerges clearly: Worship, as Saadiah argues, is a fitting response to God's generosity and grace.[139] The modalities of worship, however, are underdetermined by that general principle.[140] Indeed, Maimonides argues that the entire elaborate cult of sacrifice laid out in the Torah was regulative and concessive. That is, its aim was to confine and control the modalities of sacrificial worship, setting spatial and temporal boundaries to the practice and clearly proscribing all that was morally repugnant or symbolically reminiscent of pagan piety—even as it sought to accommodate the spiritual infancy of the early Israelites. For they were, as Maimonides put it, in need of breast milk and not yet ready for solid food. One could hardly expect newly freed slaves radically to alter their ideas of worship even as they adjusted to new ideas of God and to the new laws that would govern their lives as free men in a new land (*Guide* III 32).

All the same—all the more so—the modalities of worship in such a circumstance were hardly arbitrary. The Torah chooses clean and pacific beasts for sacrifice, to be offered by a body of priests whose garments and implements are as pure and chaste as their practices and thoughts. Later, prayer and meditation may displace animal sacrifices. But the symbolism remains powerfully evocative. The sacrificial cult eschews the violence and license of its pagan counterpart, even at the cost of allowing its contrast with pagan rituals to leave their imprint, in reverse, upon its own modalities.[141] So the ancient symbols of the Temple cult gesture toward the Transcendent just as plainly as prayer does, albeit not through words. For their purity and chastity point toward God in the language of linen, gold, and honey, grain, and, yes, sheep, goats, and bullocks, even as they leave the door ajar to prayers like the outpouring of the heart that Hannah offers in the Temple, in the face of an uncomprehending High Priest (1 Samuel 1:12–16)—and just ajar as well to the meditative silence that Maimonides, taking up a hint from the psalmist (Psalms 4:5), pictures as a still higher mode of worship (*Guide* I 51, 59, II 5).

Ritual conditions belief at least as powerfully as belief conditions ritual. It's that fact that shows us the real function of the Torah's ritual laws: There are laws that regulate our social interactions, a damper on force and fraud and a stimulus to material well-being. Biblical laws go further when they command actions designed to improve our moral character. But even character, on Maimonides' account, is not the ultimate goal. Good character does better our lives with one another. But it is also the substrate of our spiritual and intellectual perfectibility. The Torah's ritual laws lay out a structure of symbolisms that can guide us toward the idea of divine perfection. Their function, then, is pedagogical. They teach without direct recourse to words, inculcating not mere piety (as though undirected piety had any better claim on the name of virtue than unfocused discipline, or blind faith). Their cynosure, itself beyond the familiar reach of language, is God's transcendence.[142] They allow Israel, as a people—rich and poor, wise and simple—to share in an apprehension of God, to know God, as Maimonides puts it, and that without heavy reliance on the abstract language and logical apparatus of professional philosophy.

The paradigm case of a ritual commandment, then, is not *sha*ᶜ*atnez* or even *sh*ᵉ*ḥiṭah*, although these do contribute to the ethos, but *Shabbat*, the Sabbath, since it takes the simple if revolutionary and transformative idea of a day of rest and imbues it with spiritual and intellectual meanings. Shabbat becomes a vehicle through which human consciousness can be elevated and brought closer to God. For, as the Torah teaches, the Sabbath day is a symbolic reminder of God's transcendent grace in the act of creation (Exodus 31:17); as the Sabbath *Kiddush* attests through its reference to the observances that commemorate the Exodus (cf. Deuteronomy 5:15), it is a sign, as well, of mankind's transcendence of any merely menial or pragmatic role. By fusing those two meanings and reading the content of each into the significance of the other, the Sabbath becomes, in the rabbinic phrase, *me'eyn 'olam ha-ba*, an emblem of eternity.[143]

Blind faith, faith without a content specified, is not a virtue in the rabbinic canon.[144] Nor does the Torah ask for simple or simpleminded obedience. Hence the stringent tests for probity and veracity in any self-declared prophet (Deuteronomy 13, 18:22).[145] Obedience without understanding too readily sours into a vice. Indeed, as we have seen, Baḥya ibn Paquda and other classic Jewish thinkers stress that many *mitzvot* require diligent and penetrating exercise of understanding for their adequate performance.[146] All of the ethical and spiritual commandments do. Naḥmanides goes so far as to say that "one who performs a commandment without understanding it has not fulfilled it completely."[147]

It's easy to see how that's true in many cases, since the heart, in the Torah's idiom, is the seat of understanding, commitment, and conviction. So how, without intellectual engagement, can one fulfill the commandment to love God with all one's heart and soul (Deuteronomy 10:12, 13:4)?[148] In the moral sphere, where the commandment *Love thy neighbor as thyself* is at work, we have seen how widely the Law prescribes supererogatory obligations. Clearly, these will not be undertaken without the right understanding and intent. Indeed, without such mindfulness and zeal, even the direction in which enlargement is to be pursued will not be found.[149]

I think the distinction between mechanical and mindful observance closely tracks your question of arbitrariness. Doing something because one has been told to do it *does* show obedience. But, as I indicated in the lectures, I think that some acts or tasks need to be done thoughtfully or with spirit or brio—or kindness. There are biblical commandments about rejoicing, some about delighting others—one's bride, in particular. Others still admonish us to afflict (and interrogate) our souls. Acts like these can't be done mechanically, as Isaiah's cautions make very clear. The obligation to love our neighbors as ourselves, with all its ramified applications, looms significantly among the *mitzvot* that demand penetrating thought. Here, mere mechanical obedience cannot fulfill the *letter* of the law. And obedience out of a sheer sense of duty, without commitment or intelligence or joy in the doing, will not only fail to answer the spirit of the law. It can be flat or empty—or even deadly.

Virtues, as Aristotle taught, are won through habituation.[150] But they are not therefore the mechanical sort of habits like thoughtlessly flicking on a light when we enter a room or flicking it off when we leave. They cannot be. For the middle ground to be sought in virtuous actions and made habitual in virtuous dispositions is not the sort of mean that might be picked out by some mindless algorithm. It's a disposition to choose appropriate responses to the situations in which we find ourselves, to respond with sensitivity to numerous (often incommensurate) concerns as to the outcome and intent, manner and implication of our actions. These are the concerns that make an act fair or foul, noble or ignoble—concerns about our circumstances and those of the others who are affected by our choices. Human virtues, in short, are habits of acting thoughtfully, as a wise and considerate person would act in the varied situations we confront.

In understanding the Torah's precepts as a school of virtue, Maimonides is not reading into scripture some alien concern but spelling out authentic biblical themes in the language of Aristotelian ethics: The Torah prescribes behaviors meant to foster a character that reliably yields actions together constituting a life worthy of being called just and true, generous, loving, fulfilled, and holy. Admirable actions of this kind are naturally emulated by those they touch and inspiring to those who witness them. That is how they fulfill God's promise to Abraham, that through his seed shall all the nations of the earth be blessed (Genesis 22:18). The blessing flows through the pattern of justice and fairness that the patriarch sets for his progeny (Genesis 18:18). In Maimonides' view, much of that promise had already been fulfilled by his own time. The scriptural paradigm had led most of the civilized nations of the familiar world to their own encounter with the God of Abraham, regardless of their diverse laws, theologies, and modes of worship.[151]

Convinced that virtues are acquired through action, the Rabbis encourage following the dictates of the laws even for external motives. Like Aristotle, they believe that what is done at first for extrinsic reasons will in time be done for its intrinsic worth, valued and enjoyed for its own sake (B. Pesaḥim 50b and B. Soṭah 22b). Correspondingly, they say that once a person has repeated a sin, it becomes licit for him—not that habit makes a wrong right, but rather that usage inures us to a pattern and makes the forbidden familiar and seemingly permissible (B. Yoma 86b)—as if one had broken down the Law's delicate fence and trampled its hedge of lilies. But the object of the Law, as we've seen, extends far beyond the behaviors it prescribes: Far from seeking mere obedience, the Torah aims to foster human and humane sensibilities and to open up to us the prospect, ethically and intellectually, of realizing our inner affinity with God. That goal, the Torah pleads, is not beyond our reach—not in heaven or beyond the sea but near at hand, in our own mouths and hearts, ready to be grasped and lived by (Deuteronomy 30:11–14).

That's all very well, but it seems to be only part of the story. In the Talmud, the Rabbis say that a person should be hushed if he invokes God's mercy by citing his compassion for the mother bird or the calf and its dam (B. Berakhot 33b). *As you know, Maimonides offers two conflicting explanations of that ruling. What he says in the* Guide (III 48) *seems to support your approach and reject what you call a positivistic reading of the Torah, because he does specify mercy as the reason for these* mitzvot. *But in the* Yad *he leans on the sheer imperatives and denies that mercy explains them* (MT II 11, Laws of Prayer, 9.7)—*since, if mercy were the issue, the Torah would forbid animal slaughter altogether. But, as we all know, the Torah allows meat eating and actually commands the sacrifice of animals.*

I'm glad you asked about that, since I think it's easy to miss the difference between those two passages. It's true that the Rabbis hush a person who appeals to God's mercy by citing those two *mitzvot*, the prohibitions against taking a mother bird with her eggs or young (Deuteronomy 22:6–7) and against slaughtering a calf and its dam on the same day (Leviticus 22:28). Maimonides, of course, includes these rules when he codifies Halakha. But the issue in the Code, as I see it, is the need to avoid essentializing emotive portrayals of God. That's why Maimonides, in the passage that you mention there, goes on to cite Rabbi Ḥaninah's famous reproof of a student who had tried in his prayers to expatiate on God's greatness, "since human powers cannot exhaust the praises God is due."[152]

Rashi's sensitivity to nuance helps us here.[153] He explains that prayerful appeals to God's care for the mother bird wrongly treat the attributes revealed to Moses, with mercy paramount among them (Exodus 20:6, 34:7), as though they were properties, when in fact they're norms![154] Context supports Rashi's reading. For God's "attributes" (*middot*) were revealed when Moses sought to learn how he should govern (Exodus 33:12–14). He was seeking norms, and the *middot* revealed to him, couched in human language, were ideals to emulate, not exposures of God's "face" or essence.

So Maimonides can agree with Saadiah that laws like that of the mother bird seek to foster a humane ethos.[155] But the fact remains that the Torah does not endorse vegetarianism. Its concerns with a humane ethos are balanced, Maimonides argues, against a recognition of the human demand for meat and against the claims of economy and convenience (*Guide* III 17, 26, 48). That delicate balance, on Maimonides' account, is itself an expression of God's grace. And, of course, it is by drawing fine lines of this sort that the Law's principles become statutes, which are never merely deducible from broad themes like kindness.[156] For, as we've noted, the specific modalities that make a law an institution rather than an abstract ideal are always underdetermined by the general principles that give the law its general warrant.

In the Code, then, Maimonides focused on anthropomorphism and the illusion that human thoughts can somehow capture and contain God's essence—or even command his act. But the theme of mercy robustly survives that concern—especially, as the Code itself makes clear, if we do not expect to move deductively from the broad theme of mercy to our own inferences, say, about vegetarianism. There are other needs and values for the Law to address. But slaying the young in the presence of their dam, Maimonides reasons, is unfeeling enough to be singled out as barbarous. Mercy *is* the issue. And it's not inconsistent for Maimonides to reject the sheer positivism that denies its relevance or to argue, as he does (*Guide* III 48), that if mercy is due even to animals, all the more is it the due of our fellow human beings—toward whom an ethos of compassion is expected to spill over. The Torah's aim, as Maimonides consistently argues, is to modulate Israel's ethos, not to push it to extremes[157]—still less to mark an essential property of God that one might draw upon as if on a bank account.[158]

So is legal positivism a nonstarter? Is it inauthentic in the Jewish tradtion?

Clearly there are texts that stress the positivity of the *mitzvot*—especially of the ritual laws.[159] Each Passover, Jews read in their Hagaddahs how Rabban Gamaliel explained the symbols on the Seder plate, *matzoh*, bitter herbs, and the emblematic reminder of the Paschal lamb. Maimonides speaks of the awe inspired by the sound of the ram's horn, and allegorists find in its quavering tones an echoing allusion to the ram sacrificed in Isaac's stead. But others will say: "Why do we blow the shofar on Rosh ha-Shanah? Because God commanded, *Blow the shofar*!" (B. Rosh ha-Shanah 16a). Ben Ḥai-Ḥai says: "According to the trouble is the wage" (M. Avot 5.26), as if to imply that merit is proportioned to the burden of an obligation, drawing a sharp, Kantian sort of line between obligation and inclination and suggesting that there is merit in following orders one fails to understand.

The Rabbis do find merit in keeping God's commandments just because they are God's.[160] Such devotion is a natural expression of piety, as Saadiah argued. That helps to explain many a ritual—as does Maimonides' thesis about the ethical and spiritual pedagogy of ritual practices. To this Naḥmanides adds a commemorative motive.[161] But when the Rabbis say that performance of a *mitzvah* because it is a *mitzvah* is worthier than performance of the same act for some other reason (B. Kiddushin 31a),[162] Maimonides explains that such estimates apply only to the ritual obligations, where the *mitzvot* are *radically* underdetermined by an adequate conception of the human condition. The *virtuous* accept and observe the moral and intellectual imperatives of the Law with delight[163]—as well they might. For they see how their observance of the laws of righteousness and truth enriches their lives and those of the community. Even observance of ritual laws, as Saadiah stressed, can be both a duty and a delight, insofar as their performance is a mode of worship—and, ideally, a joyous celebration of the Divine.[164]

Such laws, then, are not demands for sheer displays of discipline. The notion that no reason should be sought for them beyond the fact that they are given is purely apologetic, an effort by the self-nominated defenders of tradition to bolster their authority. It is thus external to the laws it seeks to guard.[165] All the caveats and cautions that might be cited in support of legal positivism about the *mitzvot,* from the Deuteronomic admonitions against adding or removing laws or turning to the left or the right down to Fox and Twersky's rhetoric, seem clearly to spring from the same motive: the worry made explicit in the Midrash about Solomon's wives, wealth, and horses, that those who know the reasons for a commandment might be tempted to think of it as a norm of merely human manufacture readily set aside by anyone who sees another pathway to the same presumptive ends—or, for that matter, by anyone who chooses some rival goal.[166]

The protective concerns that stress the givenness of the Law are understandable, of course. But halakhically they add little; and tactically the effort to sustain commitment by banning inquiry affords a feeble defense at best to tradition for tradition's sake: The apologetics reach only the committed, strengthening their resolve, perhaps, or quieting their doubts. But they prove unhelpful to anyone who wonders why in the world a certain ritual should be practiced or preserved. And that includes many who are deeply committed but in search of spiritual depth and intellectual understanding of the practices they pursue.

Rationalism about the commandments can be apologetic too, of course, since it tries to make sense of the norms presented as laws revealed by God to Israel. Traditionalists often find the rationales offered for the *mitzvot* hokey, especially when the explanations seem ad hoc or forced or when they try too hard to sound trendy. But the quest for *ta^camei ha-mitzvot,* the good sense of the commandments,[167] has two advantages over legal positivism: Dialectically, it addresses the committed and the uncommitted alike, and, perhaps more pertinent, it respects the Torah's own praises of its laws and the continuous efforts within the tradition to seek the wisdom inherent in its precepts and the goods inherent in their practice, whether in an effort to optimize one's own adherence to the Law or in the efforts needed to interpret and apply its norms.

Well, aren't there many voices in the Jewish tradition? Isn't the multiplicity of voices the essence of our tradition—the constant dialogue and conversation? Doesn't it suck all the life out of the tradition to say that there's just one right way to read the texts, one final answer? Surely there's a place for positivism, as you call it, alongside the rationalism that you seem to favor so warmly.

You're making an important point, and I agree with much of it. Dialogue is vital in Judaism, and the conversation goes on not just at a given moment but across the centuries. Old ideas are constantly taken up, revised, reinterpreted, translated into a new idiom, tested against alternatives, home grown and exotic. But I think it's going a bit overboard to *equate* Judaism, as some do, with mere discussion and debate or, for that matter, to assume that a mere survey of disparate opinions must be the fairest way of discovering what you call the essence of Judaism. There is a coherence in the ongoing dialectic, not just an unresolved cacophony.

If we think of the Talmud, where the core of Jewish tradition finds its forum, we can see both the process and the products of that dialectic, as Louis Jacobs describes them:

> The Talmud consists almost entirely of arguments having as their aim the elucidation of the law, ruling, religious teaching or ethical idea. Theories are advanced and then contradicted. They are examined from many points of view and qualified where necessary. One argument leads to another when logic demands it. The claims of existing theories are investigated with great thoroughness and much subtlety. Fine distinctions abound between apparently similar concepts. The whole constitutes reasoning processes which have received the most careful study on the part of generations of Jewish scholars and have contributed more to the shaping of the Jewish mind than any other factor.[168]

I'd say 'Jewish thinking' here, rather than "the Jewish mind," as if there were a single univocal and uniformly molded Jewish intellect. What Louis Jacobs teaches, drawing on his lifelong study of the rabbinic literature, is not the welter of voices that a casual passerby might overhear but a conversation carried on across the centuries and one that shapes a definite body of practice and a coherent body of thought. Just as Aristotle teaches that philosophy begins in wonder but does not expect it to end there, so the Talmud, as its adepts know well, begins with its own distinctive problematics but does not end there. Its living conversation aims to answer the questions it raises—and often succeeds. The same is true, although the idioms vary widely, if we extend the point to include the biblical literature and the post-Talmudic literature of commentaries, poetry, responsa, liturgy, and other genres.

Every religion takes on a variety of forms—sometimes, it seems, as many as the adherents it attracts and holds, sometimes as diverse as the moments of their experience. Judaism is no exception. But Jewish tradition has not split as sharply as Christianity did, and its varied strains have not diverged in the kind of polymorphism that we can see in, say, the many forms of Buddhism. I think the effort to take seriously what we receive from the past is one reason for this relative coherence.

The conversations of the Rabbis, which are sometimes cited as if their whole message were diversity, do reach pretty firm conclusions on normative matters. Even in theology, where there's a lot more latitude than a strictly doctrinal creed with normatively enforced dogmas would allow, there's a rather high degree of consensus. Rabbinic liberalism as to human thinking has proved fruitful, not just in fostering creativity but in promoting intellectual harmony. One reason is the rule of charity, the degree of respect that Jewishly committed thinkers have shown for one another's efforts. Like Aristotle, they strive to save the opinions of their predecessors. Exegesis works hard to motivate and situate a revered antecedent's views. So the thinking is synthetic rather than exclusionary; change has been organic and the tradition's evolution, relatively continuous rather than abrupt.

What do the Jewish texts have to say about the nexus of our obligations to divine commands? Sagi and Statman make a persuasive case for the congruence of the Jewish canon with ethically responsible and indeed generous moral norms. They are not, of course, alone in this. Summing up the normative tradition, Leon Roth writes: "The Torah is a law of life and kindness and love and decency and pity. This being the guiding principle, whatever appears contrary to it must be explained away. And it *was* explained away."[169] Roth's language echoes that of the Talmud (B. Gittin 59b), which rests in turn on a biblical text: The entire Torah, Abaye says, "is for the purpose of promoting peace, as it is written, *Its ways are ways of pleasantness, and all its paths are peace* (Proverbs 3:17)." The passage in Proverbs speaks of Wisdom, but Abaye was hardly guilty of some unconscionable liberty when he applied the words to the Torah itself, in which tradition-minded Jews find the locus of God's wisdom in articulate form. The verse Abaye cites is applied liturgically to the Torah, along with the ones that precede and follow it: *Length of days is in her right hand, prosperity and honor in her left* and *A tree of life is she to those who hold fast to her, and fortunate are those who uphold her* (Proverbs 3:16, 18).

Clearly, it is with verses like these in mind that Maimonides boldly states that human knowledge of good and evil and the capacity to choose between them make it possible for one to reach out his arm and take fruit from the tree of life and eat, as it were, and live forever.[170] Indeed, the staves of Torah scrolls are called *trees of life*. So it is not unnatural for a modern halakhist, Aharon Lichtenstein, citing these and similar texts, to hold that the Jewish tradition clearly assumes a "natural morality"[171] and to find in the Mishnah rabbinic endorsement for the interdependence of human ethics and Halakha, in the well-known words of Eleazar ben Azariah: "Without Torah there is no ethics [*derekh eretz*], and without ethics, there is no Torah" (M. Avot 3.17).[172]

That thought is no invention of the Rabbis. It's the Torah's own self-appraisal, echoed brilliantly in the lyric idiom of the psalms. For it's the linkage of God's Law with justice and truth that the psalmist intends in the words *By thy light do we see light* (Psalms 36:10), as the context makes crystal clear. After reflecting on the hateful motives and self-deceiving rationalizations of the wrongdoer, the poet addresses God (36:6–9), acknowledging the immensity of his steadfast love (*ḥasdeikha*) and justice (*mishpatekha*), which span the loftiest mountains and plumb the depths of the sea, preserving man and beast but granting precious favor to humankind, letting God's human flock graze, as it were, on his own lawn (*deshen beitekha*) and watering them at his Edenic stream (*naḥal ʿadanekha*). Resolving its own pastoral imagery, the psalm names the source of that stream in a second image, calling it light and specifying that this means the life-giving wisdom of God's Law: *For with Thee is the fount of life. By thy light do we see light.*[173]

Michael Harris, surveying the texts of the tradition with a keen eye, takes exception to the categorical and universal character of Roth's description of the canon and argues in extenso that Sagi and Statman have oversimplified. He finds their hermeneutic "substantially flawed" and the canon far more problematic than they allow: "The truth of the matter," he writes, "is that both the biblical text as it stands and later Jewish tradition contain both a good deal that accords with our modern Western moral sensibilities and a good deal that does not."[174] That is true, of course, and Harris's description of the experience of a modern reader's moral "roller coaster" ride on encountering these varied texts is no doubt confirmed in many readers' experience, as they are "jolted" and "jarred" from the edifying to the shocking and back again. But I think we need to distinguish three rather different sorts of hermeneutic in our reading of the canon if we are to make sense of the disagreement between Harris and, say, Roth or Sagi and Statman.

A reader who approaches these texts with purely historical interests might harbor an analytic or even alienated intent, perhaps sharpened to a fine point by concerns about some very specific agenda. An apologist, on the other hand, might seek to whitewash what seems unpleasant or unwelcome to prevailing sensibilities. Between these two extremes lies a wide range of possibilities for critical appropriation. That sort of approach is clearly most appropriate for those who read the canon in search of norms rather than targets of cynical dismissal or effusive chauvinism. And critical appropriation, modulated by varying sensibilities, is in fact well attested by the frequent reappraisals that have gone on within the tradition throughout its long history.

The Torah, Maimonides writes, should be read not as a book of history or poetry but as "a guide to all men, from the earliest to the last."[175] If we read normatively, as judges read a constitution and not as archeologists read a palimpsest, we'll likely read the Torah, and the rabbinic literature with it, not as a dead letter but as a living organism, a growing body of norms, that human beings can appropriate and live by. That, I think, is what Deuteronomy does with the earlier books of the Pentateuch. It's what the Mishnah does with the Mosaic Law, what the Gemara does with the Mishnah, and what the Tosefta and Responsa do with the received body Halakha down to the present day. It's also what Genesis invites one to do when it prefigures norms of the Law in the epochal events of cosmic beginnings and patriarchal history.

But when I speak of critical appropriation and the work of finding a mean at a remove from slavish apologetics and alienated distance, I'm not assuming that we should merely privilege what Harris calls modern ethical sensibilities. Those sensibilities are as fallible as any that reach us from the past; and their bias may be much harder for us to detect. That's why I speak of chimneying and think of the middle ground we'd like to clear as a project to be worked on, not a simple given. Here again, I see precedents among the architects of the normative tradition throughout its life.

So what about legal positivism and even theistic subjectivism in the tradition?

Well, as Harris shows, the tradition is a mixed bag. It helps somewhat to parse what is to be found there. Sagi and Statman distinguish "strong dependence" (there would be no moral obligations without divine commands) from "weak" (we would not know our obligations, or at least not the full extent of them, without God's guidance). Harris lays out a far more elaborate typology of options, a fine-tooth comb for appraising the varied positions he describes. But, just using Sagi and Statman's relatively simple disjunction, we find that the general tenor of the tradition is pretty clear: The moral roots run strong and deep. God's goodness is a central axiom. So it's not surprising that little support turns up for "strong dependence." There is, however, ample testimony for what these authors class as the weaker view.

Halakhists typically warrant the specific practices mandated in the Law by appeal to biblical or rabbinic norms. But that, of course, as Sagi and Statman note, does not exclude the axiological soundness of the norms. Indeed, halakhic appeals are typically underwritten by the tacit or explicit assumption that God is just and generous in ways that we humans can readily identify. The Rabbis will affirm that God cares, say, about the cost and convenience of a chicken for the table; Rabbi Akiva refutes the dismissal of a suit protesting an indignity to a woman by arguing that dignity is God given and not proportioned to social standing.[176]

Searching for texts that seem to predicate moral norms in a more positive way on divine commands, Sagi and Statman cite Obadiah of Bertinoro, who comments on the famous opening words of Mishnah Avot, which trace the provenance of the Oral Law. These words, Rabbi Obadiah writes, are prefaced to the moral precepts of Avot to teach that, although "the sages of the world have also written books where they invented rules to guide human beings in their behavior," the Mishnah wants to make it clear that the ethical precepts assembled here "were not a fabrication of the Mishnaic sages, but they too come from Sinai."[177] That is, they have divine authority. The remark does not imply that the precepts of Avot would have no normative standing otherwise.[178] The intent, plainly, is to privilege the Mishnaic text: It is inspired, not invented. But that is to claim a higher objectivity for it than what might be found in, say, secular works on ethics. God's guidance, Obadiah suggests, takes us closer to moral truth than do merely human insights. The comment does not reject the objectivity of morality but presumes it, although qualifying human claims with an implied caution as to human fallibility.

Rabbi Tzvi Hirsch Levin, commenting on the same passage in Avot, seems at first blush to advance a strong dependence thesis: "we have neither morality nor virtue unless a divine religion can be presumed to exist."[179] Levin instances strikingly counterintuitive biblical prescriptions like the command, in effect, to "bear a grudge" against Amalek. But he goes on to insist that God's prescriptions embody a higher wisdom and are only apparently contrary to moral principle. So Levin does see potential conflicts between biblical prescriptions and familiar moral values. But, as Sagi and Statman argue, he does not deny or discard reason but seeks to show that, if adequately informed, we would see the wisdom in God's commands.

S. Safrai sees quite another theme at the start of Avot: "The first saying of the men of the Great Assembly," he writes, "sets down the requirement that the administration of justice be humanized," as indicated by the words "be cautious in judgment." The next, he continues, "states that the world is established on three pillars: Tora study, worship, and the doing of good deeds." The third is the precept of Antigonos of Socho, urging service without a view to gaining a reward. Rather, we must act "for the sake of heaven"—which in rabbinic parlance means doing what is right and good for its own sake and not for some extrinsic reason or ulterior motive. "None of these views and conceptions," Safrai continues "are found in the Bible." All "are innovations of the Sages." Not that the teachings are alien to the Torah's themes. On the contrary, they are new ways of articulating those very themes, and the confidence with which these new wings are built onto the ancient mansion is clearly indicative of the Rabbis' deep understanding of the biblical ethos and their deep commitment to its moral concerns.[180]

The Ḥazon Ish says that Halakha determines morality. But, in making his point, he reveals just how laden Halakha is with appeals *to* moral concerns: Teachers, he rules, are exempt from the usual restrictions on unfair competition, since "The jealousy of scribes increaseth wisdom" (B. Bava Batra 22a). That is, the value of learning, which is enhanced by competition, trumps the usual halakhic protectiveness toward an established enterprise.

Arguing in more general terms, the Ḥazon Ish urges his readers to rely on Halakha when seeking to determine, in cases of human conflict, "who is the oppressor and who the oppressed"[181]—that is, who is in the right and who is in the wrong. So the Ḥazon Ish assumes a halakhic intent to find in favor of the meritorious cause, a core axiom of morals. Halakha, he proposes, gives guidance essential in determining just who *is* in the right and who is in the wrong. Far from making some arbitrary fiat the basis of morality, he argues (like any committed jurist) the law gives us the gauge we need in making such a judgment. So, even as he affirms the dependence of morals on Halakha, he appeals to values that he expects to resonate morally. Indeed, he presumes the precedence of such values and presses his case for Halakha in part by showing the centrality of moral values in the halakhic constellation.

Samson Raphael Hirsch is at home enough in the idioms of European thought to give a familiar name to the motives the Ḥazon Ish invokes: "A general conception of Right, of what man owes his fellow man, is planted in the conscience of every uncorrupted human being, and this general consciousness of Right is also the Voice of God."[182] Needless to say, such appeals to conscience do not void the authority of Halakha in this revered rabbi's teaching. But the notion of a conflict between historic revelation as passed down in text and tradition and the inner revelation of the still, small voice is utterly alien to his thinking.

In a precious volume of sermons hidden and preserved in the Warsaw Ghetto, Rabbi Kalonymus Shapira, the last rabbi of that Ghetto, argued against what he called the Gentile view that truth (or right) "is a thing in itself" commanded by God because it is true. Israel, he wrote, has no truth but God; all truth and justice depend on his will. Had God commanded Abraham to go through with the sacrifice of Isaac, that would have been right.

Shapira's is the only traditional source that Sagi and Statman found that explicitly affirms a strong version of divine command morality. Shapira sees no conflict between morality and faith, since for him morals is entirely an expression of faith.[183] Yet, as Sagi and Statman note, Shapira elsewhere turns to "more traditional conceptions of theodicy," incompatible with strong dependence—that is, incompatible with the asseveration that God acts arbitrarily. Shapira takes up the rabbinic idea that humanity is tested or purged by suffering, perhaps in preparation for the coming of the Messiah. That gives God's actions a clear, if troubling, purpose. Elsewhere he argues that God's purposes are beyond our comprehension.

Plainly, Rabbi Shapira was a tortured witness. Unlike Fox and Twersky, who struggle to maintain the ritual practices of a community whose lives they fear may have become all too comfortable, Shapira confronts the enormity of history's horror. His struggle, in the face of the Shoah, is to maintain his trust in God and God's justice. Understandably, his conceptual grid buckles under the inhuman pressure. As Maimonides says of the corresponding view best known to him from work of the Muslim theologians of the Ashᶜarite school, those who reached conclusions of this kind cannot be blamed for adopting such views: They were torn between conflicting demands—unwilling to renounce God's justice but also unwilling to concede that God does not immediately control every event and pass judgment in every fortuity (*Guide* III 17).

You mention the Ashᶜarites in Islam. Isn't theirs a legitimate position, natural and appropriate for religious people? Calvin, too, identified what is right with God's will and insisted that nothing is more acceptable to God than acceptance of that will.[184] *Luther thinks in much the same way. Aren't these views of theirs the real religious outlook, recognizing that we creatures are as feeble in our judgments, including our moral judgments, as we are in our physical powers?*

Well, I don't think the outlook you're describing makes for the best theology, if theology means what Plato says it does, saying what is worthy of the divine.[185]

I'm concerned about what happens to our idea of God if we equate what's right with God's will but fail to identify God's will with what is right. The Ash'arite theologians did hold a strong version of the dependence of moral values on God's command, for just the sort of reasons that Maimonides mentions, the cross pressures between the divine ideal and our human experience—especially of the suffering of innocents. But, as Maimonides explained, the Ash'arites paid a heavy price for sundering the nexus between God and our moral knowledge. Their insistence on God's justice became sheerly nominal. They could say that God is just, but not in the sense that we human beings normally use.

Rudolf Otto, writing as a kind of natural historian of religious experience, felt that he had discovered the core of piety in that very disconnect between human reason and the divine. To his sensibilities, fed on fin de siècle romanticism and chastised by the witness of the Great War, religious authenticity seemed to find its heart in the idea that God himself is paradox. It was with this thought in mind that Otto quotes Luther as calling God "more terrible than the Devil" and goes on to equate Luther's sense of horror with the biblical idea of the holy. Otto contrasts Luther's terror with "the small change of popular edification, that soothes itself with the thought that God's ways are too high for us men." What seems to him most real in Luther and in the sort of piety that burns in Luther's writings are the moments "in which he lays hold of some startling paradox . . . that God is 'beyond tracking out in His mysteries and His judgments.' . . . His essence hidden away from all reason, knows no measure, law, or aim, and is verified in paradox."[186]

Luther's intent in announcing God's unknowability and irrefragability, Otto writes, "is not simply to note this as an inconceivable paradox, to acknowledge it and bow before it but to recognize that such a paradox is essential to the nature of God and even its distinguishing characteristic." Implicit in this thought is the pointed claim that bred it: "good is good because God wills it"—even if, as Otto adds, that means "attributing to God a fortuitous will, which would in fact turn Him into a 'capricious despot.'" Otto slips into the subjunctive, standing back a bit from that explosive thought. And then, as if in recoil at its report: "These doctrines are especially prominent in the theology of Islam."[187]

Yet, Luther appeals also to moral terms, to the idea of retribution specifically, to warrant his sense of dread and situate his evocation of Israel's vision of God at Sinai as *a consuming fire* (Exodus 24:17). That theophany, however, viewed in context, is not punitive but revelatory, not "*exlex*" (in Otto's phrase) but the very prelude to Moses' ascent to receive the Law!

Fixated on paradox, Otto marvels that the same Luther who "endeavors to put the whole of Christianity into a confiding faith" made "violent onslaughts upon the 'whore Reason.'" What matters in Luther, as indeed (with lesser intensity) in the Gospels as Otto reads them, is the mystery of the unapproachable/approachable, an idea that finds "only very dubious expression in the subsequent one-sided doctrine of the schools," where God's wrath is muted, in the name of goodness, into a mere expression of divine justice. This last, of course, is what the Rabbis call *middat ha-Din*, the inseparable counterpart of God's mercy and compassion, *middat ha-Raḥamim*. Both of these attributes, on the rabbinic view, are expressed in the acts of creation and revelation. But, according to Rav, founder of the Babylonian Academy of Sura and a member of the first generation of Amora'im (the rabbis of the Mishnah), whose authority was so great that he was counted as a Tanna (Mishnaic authority), God himself prays, "May it be my will that my compassion overcome my wrath and prevail over all my attributes, so that I treat my children mercifully and show them charity beyond the strict sentence of the Law" (B. B^{e}rakhot 7a).

With Rav's homily held clearly in mind, I want to wave a caution sign for those who find themselves drawn toward theistic subjectivism. More is at stake in making God's judgments arbitrary than just admitting that our moral views are fallible and our character too readily suborned. If God indeed is arbitrary, we can no longer find our way to him through the recognition of value in the world: Saints and martyrs no longer point the way, since they and their acts are merely human. Truth and beauty no longer point toward God. The divine becomes a sheer, if absolute, cipher. What ensues places those who think out the consequences of their views gravely at risk of reducing their God to some simulacrum of dogma or authority. Such a deity is no longer the good Creator or the faithful Source of revelation but a creature, the reflex of what the offending hermeneutic presumes to be the scriptural message. We can no longer say, with the psalmist, *By Thy light do we see light*; in place of God's authority, the nominal recipient of our moral and intellectual surrender, we face an unbending positivity—which, if we can descry its face, looks suspiciously like the projected image of a fear of freedom or demand for control.

The Ash'arite experience is instructive here, and not just for the predicament these theologians faced (and its parallel in some Christian theologians). We can also study how the great Muslim theologian al-Ghazālī dealt with these issues. He was himself a rather penetrating Ash'arite. His ability to respond to a panoply of concerns can make him seem prescient at times, even, like Maimonides, timeless in certain ways.

Ghazālī treats Ash'arite theistic subjectivism not as gateway to orthodoxy but as a trap door to heresy. In his classic ethical work *Mizān al-'Amal* (The Scale of Action), he adopts and adapts the Aristotelian doctrine of the mean.

Addressing the work of the Neoplatonic and Aristotelian thinkers whom he called simply the Philosophers (using the transliterated Greek term, to emphasize the exotic origin of their texts), he argued in his spiritual autobiography that the ethical teachings of this school

> are simply taken from the teachings of the Sufis, who constantly sought God in meditation, battled the passions and pursued the path to Him by shunning worldly delights. Through their struggle, the soul's traits and weaknesses were laid bare to them, and they candidly spelled out the flaws in human practice. The Philosophers took over these insights and mingled them with their own theories, to pretty up their rubbish for the market—although there was a body of godly men in theirs as in every age (of whom God never leaves the world bereft), tent posts of the earth.[188]

The idea of the mean was among the sound ideas that Ghazālī found mingled with the "rubbish" of the Philosophers. Avoidance of extremes, he urges, is the safest path. Even an ant placed in a heated iron ring will seek the midpoint. A human being, in just this way, ringed by desires, must avoid both the rash and the cowardly, extravagance and stinginess alike. The ant may die, but even then it will die where the ring is coolest. And the man who finds refuge from the passions that beset him has found a bridge, as it were, an optimum, not just a middle. This is the straight way so prominent in the Qur'ān (e.g., 1:6). Slipping off that narrow bridge lands the soul in hellfire. But if one keeps to the middle, the soul, on death, can leave the body cleanly.[189]

Ghazālī here practices just the kind of hybridizing that he charges against the Philosophers: He takes up Aristotle's reflections on the mean and Plato's thoughts of winning immortality by cutting the cords that bind the soul to matter. By spiritualizing immortality, he de-emphasizes the Qur'ānic visions of physical resurrection.[190] But he overlays the naturalistic appeal of Aristotle's model of the mean with Qur'ānic imagery and Sufi pietism.[191] Pressing beyond sheer asceticism, Ghazālī affirms Plato's view that the liberated soul will float free of the body. Still, every human being will spend at least part of eternity in hellfire. And it is God, as the Qur'ān so often insists,[192] who guides one to the straight path. Grace and election, not merit, lead the way: No one can find the proper mean without God's guidance, through revelation, and, indeed, the mentorship of a *Pir* or *Shaykh*, a spiritual guide and master.[193]

The early Muslim theologians of the Muʿtazilite school were objectivists in ethics and voluntarists about human choices.[194] God, they reasoned, being just, must give us fair warning of his expectations, or reward and punishment would be unjust. The revelation of the Qur'ān thus becomes a moral necessity, to which God did, of course, respond. Human freedom, to accede to God's commands or bear the onus if we do not, must also be a given, or God's requital of our choices once again would be unjust. Muʿtazilism became the dominant Islamic school by the ninth century and won favor among the early ʿAbassid caliphs.[195] But that favor and the rationalist turn of Muʿtazilite exegesis put the school in bad odor with rivals, who voiced their opposition in the name of tradition.

A powerful reaction took hold toward the end of the ninth century, and in 912/13 a former Muʿtazilite, Abū ʾl-Ḥasan al-Ashʿarī, broke away from his Muʿtazilite mentor to found a school of his own. Ashʿarism became the mainstay of Sunni orthodoxy—although Muʿtazilite ideas live on in Shīʿite thought. The motives of Ashʿarī's conversion are captured in the story that he dreamed of a soul modestly placed in paradise but complaining that another was ranked higher. "You did not have his works," came the reply. "I did not have his years," the disappointed soul responded. "I cut short your years lest you turn to evil ways." At which, a soul cried out from the depths of Hell: "Lord of the universe, why did you not cut short my years before I turned to evil ways!"

God's ways, as Ashʿarī came to see it, are unanswerable, his power absolute. God owes nothing to his creatures but rules their every thought and act, choosing whom He will for salvation or damnation. Action does require capacities (for it did seem paradoxical to claim that one could act without the capacity to do so). But each capacity for an action, Ashʿarī held, was God's instant creation, pertaining only to that very act and no alternative, and there was no precedence of capacity to action. For man was not the creator of his acts. Shifting the boundaries of usage, the Ashʿarites dubbed their adversaries *Qadariyya*, fatalists, for seeming, in effect, to tie God's hands. It was they, the Ashʿarites, who were voluntarists. For they maintained God's absolute freedom.

It did not help the Muʿtazilites that, as the once regnant school, they had instituted tests of spiritual sincerity, the *Miḥna*, a kind of inquisition. That smacked of the notorious violence of the Kharijite rebels, who deemed all grave sinners (including all who accepted the established Muslim state) insincere and therefore apostates, liable to the death penalty in this world and damnation in the next. The Muʿtazilites did not go that far. They held to what they called a middle ground, leaving the fate of grave sinners in the hands of God. Even so, their interest in sincerity and free choice seemed to link them with the *takfīrī*s, those who damned their adversaries. Reaction against such views pushed the Ashʿarites into a kind of behaviorism still visible in Ghazālī's affirmation that one cannot pry open a man's heart to test his faith. Lip service alone, the mere outer husk of the precious kernel of faith, is enough to save the neck of any professing individual.[196]

Although an Ashʿarite, Ghazālī was no slavish follower of the school. A champion (and definer) of orthodoxy, he channeled a sober form of Sufism into the mainstream tradition he was forging, stripping from ecstatic mysticism its immanentist and antinomian tendencies. He struck hard in polemics against the Ismāʿīlī Shīʿites and against the Neoplatonic Aristotelian philosophers of Islam. But his prominence as an Ashʿarite culture champion made his independent-mindedness all the more troubling to more conventional thinkers. He jettisoned the ad hoc hypothetical logic of the *kalām* in favor of the Aristotelian syllogistic of his philosopher adversaries. He abandoned *kalām* occasionalism, which had atomized time and, in deference to the doctrine that God's is the only power, had sundered the causal nexus. Rather than constitute a world of instantly evanescent, dimensionless atoms, Ghazālī based his critique of causal necessity on the *logical* independence of one event from another. That shift allowed him to preserve miracles and divine creation alongside his own versions of Neoplatonic emanation and Aristotelian essentialism. So the natural order could still be seen as an outpouring of God's wisdom.[197] Ghazālī even declared that no world could possibly have been more marvelous than this, the world God created.

That uninhibited celebration of God's handiwork left other Ashʿarites to worry and wonder for centuries how the great Proof of Islam, as Ghazālī was called, could limit God's power (to have created a better world) and hemmed in his will (within merely human standards of value). How could he have written so affirmatively of a world whose defects they scored in their polemics? For Ashʿarites typically maintained that God could have made a better world, had He so chosen. Surely, as one Ashʿarite put it, the air over Damascus would never have been so foul as it is were ours indeed the best of all possible worlds![198]

Ever the independent spirit, Ghazālī does not simply hew to the Ashʿarite dogma of theistic subjectivism. His *Iqtiṣād fī 'l-Iʿtiqād* (The Golden Mean in Faith)[199] is, as Richard Frank explains, "by no means an ordinary manual of traditional Ashʿarite theology." Often it "modifies or sets aside the traditional teaching of the school."[200] Ghazālī's troubles with the Ashʿarite outlook here begin with the view, taught by his master al-Juwaynī, that every competent man (from puberty on) has a duty to establish God's reality. For the able, this would mean reasoning one's way to a natural theology. For others, it might betoken an obligation to hearken to God's prophet, a demand pressed in the Qur'ān, with "dire threats," as Frank puts it, from God, via Muḥammad, "against those who do not accept his message as being from God and as requiring obedience."[201] Ghazālī sees a logical snag here: If one does not yet know God, what reason has one to heed his messenger?

Ghazālī responds, as Frank explains, by arguing that it is only prudent, given the warnings, "to look seriously into the possibility that the prophet's claim may be true, since to neglect doing so might entail untold harm."[202] The imperative can only be prudential. For, *per hypothesi*, the real roots of moral obligation are not yet known. Ordinary men rely on notional evidence (*adilla wahmiyya*).[203] The ignorant and the unwashed, in any case, are not receptive to rigorous arguments and presumably would not respond to them. They are caught up in scriptural anthropomorphisms. So they will have to take it on authority that there is a higher sense in sacred writ, a sense that is beyond their ken.[204]

Ghazālī here might seem to make the promises and threats of the Qur'ān mere accommodations to the limited understanding of the common folk, as proposed in the Platonic line of exegesis developed by al-Fārābī, a leading figure in the Islamic philosophical school whose teachings Ghazālī criticized. Still, the metaphysics and the method of the Philosophers remain off limits—above all, their project of constructing a vision of the world and the good life by sheer use of reason. Even as he trusts reason to shape his own doctrine and his critique of rivals, Ghazālī remains adamant that the ultimate human good is unknown to reason or experience. For it involves the next life and thus is known only by revelation (*bi-nūri 'l-nubuwwa*, by the light of prophecy).[205] Without revelation, we are without a moral compass.

But notice the shift, couched in the language of orthodoxy: Just as he moderates *kalām* occasionalism, leaving room for miracles and creation but also for natural kinds, essences, and emanation, Ghazālī rolls back the absolute claims of Ash'arite theistic subjectivism, arguing *not* for the strong view that there *is* no right or wrong apart from God's dictum but for the lesser claim that we are powerless to *find* the straight path without God's guidance. He quietly shifts the thesis from strong to weak dependence: It's not that there would *be* no morality without God's command but rather that its dicta would be unknown to us—or, milder still, that the fine tuning of our moral responses, our search for the mean, would be impossible without God's guidance. Now, is that true?

People do sometimes say that without God there is no morality. Often, I think, they're seeking leverage for theism, suggesting that we'd lose all moral knowledge if we didn't know God's commands. One elderly rabbi I know is fond of saying that without the Torah we'd have no way of distinguishing Mother Theresa from Adolph Hitler. But I think we have plenty of morally relevant ways of making that kind of distinction. That does not call for quite so discriminating a moral capacity as what we need for locating the mean—where cultural cues and, yes, laws and traditions, are more than merely helpful. My rabbi friend in fact *presumes* on just the sort of knowledge that he wants to problematize. He knows that we find Hitler abhorrent and Mother Theresa saintly—even though the full catalogue of the *mitzvot,* as he knows them, were not uppermost in her mind as she pursued her saintly life. Dialectically, his argument gets what purchase it has just because we *do* have moral standards that do not lean on the norms he wants to treat as our only source of moral knowledge.

But the risk, with any kind of leverage, physical or fiscal, is that the torques are readily reversed. There are plenty of people who take the dictum 'If God is dead, everything is permitted' not as a Dostoevskian appeal to morality in support of faith but as a Nietzschean cry of liberation from all confinement and constraint, even *or especially* the constraints of conscience. There's no sharper instance of the philosopher's saw that one man's *modus ponens* is another's *modus tollens.* With that kind of turnabout in mind, I prefer to move a little closer to the center of the seesaw and say that the linkage of morality to God, working at its best, informs both morals and theology without making either of them arbitrary or suppositious. After all, there are plenty of upright people who don't think much of God. It's not fair to brand them out of hand as immoral, and it's not responsible or even nice (especially if they're young people) to try to shake or shove them into theism by convincing them that moral claims have no basis without a prior pledge to God that many may find alien or distracting.

It's true that pegging morality to theism has long appealed to the pious. It seems to show why revelation is indispensable. But, in practical terms, it's unhelpful: When moral standards are in doubt, there's little that religion can do to sustain them. God and the good are too closely mapped on each other. The devout may find heightened definition for their norms in the tenets of their chosen or received tradition. But miscreants, as we have noted, cast aside religious claims as freely as moral ones.

Humanists of secular conviction tend to see the claim that we are lost without a divinely given moral guide as invidious and suppositious, trading on ungrounded and contested commitments. The moral skeptic swiftly turns the tables: If moral knowledge needs God's help, then we have no moral knowledge. One could trip up such skeptical dogmatism, of course. For, if there are no real values, it seems odd (in the name of truth or candor?) to proclaim it. But setting aside the moral skeptic's plaints, one still must deal with the ardent secularist's charge—James Rachels's well-known argument, say, that theism is impossible, since it asks us to worship a being who demands that we give up our morality, a demand that Rachels takes to be both necessary in religion and unworthy in an object of veneration. Our answer is straightforward: It's theistic subjectivism, not theism, that asks us to poke out our moral lights.

But, once again, isn't a theist someone who believes that God is the source of all values?

Well, I do think that God is the source of all values, but not directly of all our *thoughts* about value. Lots of things can intervene between real values and those thoughts, filtering or distorting how we judge and what we think we see. That's what Maimonides is saying in his reading of the story of Adam and Eve: that the real consequence of the emblematic first couple's choice (and the real character of the human condition made vivid in that story) is the compromising of moral objectivity: Adam and Eve, before they disobeyed, were in free and open converse with God. But the access to the Truth they once enjoyed is now displaced by a kind of self-serving that sets them on all fours with the beasts and then stitches or pastes their moral judgments to social conventions. That outcome (lest we be tempted to take Genesis too literally and thus break its impact) is not a historical event whose effects we now confront, although we took no part in it. Rather it's a poetic painting of the condition in which all of us now stand. Yes, we have reason and the power to choose. But we have to reach out our hand to grasp the fruits of the tree of life; only with difficulty do our choices break free of our animal nature and rise above a narrow, conventional perspective. The Torah, as Maimonides puts it, conveys insights of this sort with the utmost economy and without counting on abstract words like 'subjectivity' or conceptual terms like 'nature.' That, in his view, is a clear sign that its dramatic poesy is inspired.[206]

So, judging from what you're saying about Maimonides and the biblical story of Adam and Eve, I guess you don't believe in original sin?

I don't think the idea of inherited guilt is a very Jewish idea, and I don't think it's what the Torah wants us to learn from that narrative. Genesis does present Adam and Eve as figures of humanity. It makes their disobedience a parable of the human condition. But with biblical poetry we always need to unpack the tropes, whether the ideas to be grasped are couched in the language of myth, as they are in the opening chapters of Genesis, or in internal dialogue, as in Ecclesiastes, or in fable, as in the Book of Jonah, court romance, as in the Book of Esther, dream revery, as in the Song of Songs, apothegm, as in Proverbs, or hymn and lyric, as in the Psalms. The Talmud relates that at the moment when a child is conceived, an angel called Night asks God whether this person will be rich or poor, strong or weak, but when the angel asks if the babe will become virtuous or vicious, God holds his peace. For each human being holds that portion of destiny in his own hands.[207]

We humans do have moral weaknesses. That's why we need moral counsels, and not just guidelines but laws and commandments. The ego is a source of moral distortion. But I don't think we're so morally impoverished as to be incapable of sound judgment, even in our own case—although it's wise to recognize that setting oneself up as the sole and sufficient arbiter of one's own case does not yield the freedom Nietzsche thought it promised. It's more likely destructive to self and society, as the Torah warns (Judges 21:25). Saadiah believes that Job can know himself—not through complacency, of course, but through self-scrutiny. So Job—another archetype of humanity, like Adam and Noah—can know his own innocence. Without that possibility, I think there's no space for moral judgment and thus no morals at all. I agree with Saadiah that the authenticity of our existence, the genuineness of God's creative gift, rests on the imparting of reason and responsibility that we see in the human condition, in the demand our situation makes to find our own way morally. That's where I see an ember of truth in Korsgaard's claims, even if I'm not entirely sure that she and I mean quite the same thing by 'reason.'

The notion that we can't know the good before God proclaims it is a special case of the broader claim that we mortals cannot *do* what is right as long as we are mortals. The notion that all human moral thinking is radically inadequate is part of a larger sense of human inadequacy, a lingering shadow of the idea of original sin. The old Adam of Christian homily still seems to have his apple caught in his craw. But that catch in the throat, as I see it, is symptomatic of a logical malaise. John Bunyan opens *Pilgrim's Progress* by making Christian realize that the weight of sin he carries is beyond his strength. Seeing sin as an unexorcisable incubus turns him toward Christ's grace. The pieces fit so nicely that it's hard to see which was shaped to fit the other—the mystery of vicarious atonement or the dogma of inherited sin, the *felix culpa*, whose wound is healed only by Christ's sacrifice.[208] The salve of the familiar makes Christ's death and resurrection (to be followed by a rebirth of our own) not just an archetype of popular imagination but an anchor of apologetics. Still, the price to be paid is the bracketing of all worth in a life that seems otherwise worthy of celebration and that is (at other moments) taken to be an emblem of God's grace.

Medieval iconography carves the Church as a fair and winning maid. The synagogue is the broken crone surmounting the left cathedral door—provincial, parochial, particularistic, where Christian comity is for all.[209] But does it make universal sense to suspend truth and moral adequacy from tales of inherited sin and vicarious atonement? Do we see God best when we paint his world as worthless and the life He gave (not by dying but by breathing of his spirit into lifeless clay) as valueless if it does not lead on to another, like it in many ways but stripped of any categories or conditions that might prick or sting?

Fideists like to invoke moral skepticism as a kind of pry bar to dislodge our human hopes of moral knowledge, expecting divine authority to fill its place. But that does not always happen, and what offers itself as a divine mandate is not always worthy of the name. So I find it more fruitful to take reason and tradition not as enemies but as allies whose strengths can complement and support one another. Deference to any authority, be it God or conscience, scripture or the call of pleasure or interest, still relies on some appraisal of the values we confront. Plumping for any of these without thinking of the rest and how they might fit together in a life seems to me to be backing into morals, rather than backing it up. It means deferring to a value presumptively, whereas, in fact, a moral claim is often best established with the aid of experience, personal or communal, historical or even fictive—for literature and the arts, even music, can broaden our experience and deepen, as well as intensify, our sensibilities.

It's with such thoughts in mind that I've argued against the renaissance and romantic vision of the human moral situation as that of an isolated figure in an existential crisis. That Faustian image, the mental iconography of, say, Luther's "Here I stand," stiffened by Kant's distaste for the idea of historic revelation (which he too readily pictures as momentary rather than transgenerational)[210] neglects or ignores the far more typical locus of the ethical in our daily interactions and the far more poignant moral pedagogy of custom and example.

So, when you ask about original sin, I have to say I don't believe that imputable evil is inherited. The Rabbis do speak of a *yetzer ha-ra*ʿ, often called the "evil inclination" in traditional texts. But, more strictly speaking, *ra*ʿ in Hebrew just means bad, not evil; and the human *yetzer* is our forming, that is, the way God made us. So I've translated it as our "bent." Bible readers are well familiar with God's judgment that *the bent of man's heart is bad from his youth* (*ki yetzer lev ha-'adam ra*ʿ *mi-ne*ʿ*urav*, Genesis 8:21)—*from his youth*, not from birth. In Genesis, God's recognition of this fact is his reason for not intervening to disrupt human wrongdoing by destroying the world: God knows our weaknesses. It was He who determined that lesser beings than He would have life—and lesser beings than we, as well. But creation, in the human case, gives us freedom, including the freedom to err. The *yetzer* does not utterly exonerate, but it does explain, and original sin is not the Jewish explanation.

In popular Jewish parlance, the *yetzer ha-ra'* does play a role similar to the one that original sin plays for Christians. But, taking their text from Genesis (4:7), *sin coucheth at the door,* the Rabbis argue midrashically that our penchant for wrongdoing is with us from birth but not from conception (B. Sanhedrin 91b). Otherwise, they say, the fetus would be far too restless to be carried. Ill tendencies, they say, do not manifest themselves actually until puberty, the age at which one becomes responsible for one's acts (*Avot de-R. Nathan* 16). By then, as Maimonides explains, the inclination toward goodness has also begun to take its mature form. For that inclination needs to be fostered, trained up, and developed.[211]

Although often given voice medievally in fictive internal dialogues, the *yetzer ha-ra'* is typically tacit and very much within us. It's not a personality in fact but wrongdoing, dramatically personified.[212] And it's not all bad: Its existence is not a bad thing. For, as the Rabbis argue, on the creation of man, the Torah tells us, *God saw all that He had made, and lo it was very good* (Genesis 1:31). That appraisal, they infer, must include our penchant for wrongdoing. They see a hint of that in the odd spelling of the verb *va-yyitzer,* where the Torah records that God *formed* Adam from the dust of the ground (Genesis 2:7). The doubling of the letter *yod,* they tell us, signals not just of the duality of human nature, which anyone can observe, but the fact that this duality was itself part of God's creative act. For isn't a double *yod* one way of writing God's ineffable name? Can our penchant for wrongdoing, then, be counted among God's acts of grace? The Rabbis answer by reference to the phenomenology of human motivation: "Were it not for the *yetzer ha-ra'*," they say, "no one would build a house, or marry, or beget children, or undertake any business!" (Genesis Rabbah 9.7).

That midrash might help us understand the Jewish view, where nature is God's work and not his antithesis. Hare invokes divine help in overcoming original sin, our tendency to serve our own impulses rather than answer the call of duty. I agree that we need God's help in all things, not least in rising above selfishness. But when Hare argues that, without *Christ*'s help, we cannot overcome our penchant for giving precedence to impulse over duty, he loses me a little. Christ's sacrifice does not seem to make its beneficiaries morally better than they were—even if the image or example of Jesus might for many. The main function of redemption, on Hare's account, seems to be to make sinners more acceptable to God. Hare's discussions of justification, atonement, and sanctification, mediated by the Son, the Father, and the Holy Ghost, accordingly, seem more directly to address a sense of guilt than to aid us in responding to the moral problems that we face: Christ, Hare urges, atones for human sinfulness through his sacrifice, by binding others to him, as if by adoption. So God, in judging us, views us not just as we are but as we are becoming, ultimately and ideally cleansed and united with Christ.

I think the Torah's approach is more firmly grounded in our moral condition. It treats both our generous and our selfish inclinations as facets of our creation, and it seeks to aid us in improving our character, as Maimonides teaches. We have a will to aid others and also a centeredness that can become exaggerated into self-centeredness. But there would be no self to undertake acts of altruism without some centering of identity and efficacious agency. Only God's agency is universal, recognizing particularity in ways that do not focus on one being to the exclusion of another. We do owe much to others, as their due. We owe them recognition of their deserts. But neither they nor we would exist or act at all without the being of *selves*. This too is part of what we can draw from Genesis. It's also a presumption in all Kantian talk of moral agency and personhood. I don't think our existence as subjects is something to feel guilty about or burdened by. Biblically, the soul—which is the centering of an identity—is a gift. Guilt feelings over the very normal centeredness of our subjecthood are unhelpful. Yet they can grow to paralyzing magnitude, even in highly secularized contexts.

Utilitarians, to give just one example, are sometimes driven into paradox by charges that one can never succeed in according all others their due—if we are bound to assign no interest greater weight than any other. That seems to leave one no reason at all to prefer, say, parents or a spouse to strangers. Indeed, if Bentham is right that pleasure is the only good and pain the only evil, and if he's right again in agreeing with Epicurus that all pains and pleasures are of a type and can be plotted on a single scale, there are no grounds to prefer humans to any animal. So Peter Singer professes that one should devote the lion's share of one's pay to those less fortunate. He assigns rights to animals while denying (along with Bentham) that the notion of rights has more than a rhetorical sway—even as he campaigns for recognition of a right to infanticide. The fact is, there's not much to say for utility unless there are objects of value; and there's not much to say for the equality of deserts unless there are subjects, that is, persons, as well as merely sentient (and barely sentient) beings to whom deference is due.

Hare takes a calmer tack than Singer. He sees the nexus between Kantian universalizability and the biblical commandment to love one another as we love ourselves. He puts the matter rather starkly, though, in terms of removing the "singular reference" from our maxims—that is, cutting clear of particularites—although he does recognize that this might decontextualize moral imperatives and force an artificial formalism onto our norms, just the sort of thing he labored to avoid when arguing with the medieval nominalists like Duns Scotus that not every moral imperative takes the form of a rule.[213] For Hare, "the most significant exclusion" of particularity in the moral law is the exclusion of oneself.[214] But the biblical *Love thy neighbor as thyself,* as we've observed, avoids that level of abstraction. For, to treat you lovingly, I must know something of your strengths and needs. And it makes no moral sense to speak of putting myself in your shoes if I cannot presume some sort of positive attitude toward myself. Here the Torah's explicitness about love (and not just formal symmetry) is vital: Our charge is not to treat others as we are willing to be treated but to treat them lovingly. How lovingly? Well, in general terms, as lovingly as a person with a strong sense of self, a hardy love of life, and a healthy demand for happiness would wish to be treated.

When the categorical imperative takes material form and abandons the posture of strict formalism, calling on us to treat others, and ourselves as well, as ends and never merely as means, it opens up a ready alternative to the seeming conundrum of Utilitarianism and to the apparent paradoxes generosity as self-immolation. Treating others as ends should mean recognizing them as moral agents, not robbing them of agency. So it excludes slavery and other forms of invidious exploitation, including meretricious self-exploitation. But it also means not robbing oneself of the means of action. That entailment sets Kantian ethics squarely in the liberal tradition: Each of us, as a moral agent, has responsibilities. But the notion that we can fulfill our obligations only by depleting, even exhausting and morally undermining the very powers through which any duty can be met dismantles the idea of responsibility, robbing it of efficacy and ultimately, even of motive. That kind of strategy is not just impractical, it's foolish. It irresponsibly ignores the strengths that accrue to our actions through cooperation and fails to see that collaboration is not a zero-sum game. But the tactic of self-abnegation, if it's more than mere rhetoric and moralistic posturing, is also illogical and immoral: illogical because it makes maximal demands of the very resources it sets out to sap, and immoral because it validates and valorizes self-exploitation.

If every human being is an end and not just a means, each of us has responsibilities to aid in the fulfillment of all human beings—and not least ourselves. So self-discovery and self-creation are prime moral tasks, not in the self-indulgent sense sometimes linked with adolescence or that second adolescence of midlife but in the sense of self-cultivation, the refinement of character and building of understanding. It's here that individual and collaborative agency can be most effective. The work of self-development, properly pursued, will not yield atomic or alienated social isolates. We do have responsibilities to others, and our moral adequacy is in great part in the measure of our responsiveness to such duties. But even these are most effectively fulfilled toward those we know and care for, and best met by fostering *their* subjecthood.

Toward a wider circle, where intimacy recedes, our capabilities and our rights to a say fall away steeply. Material help is feasible, often obligatory. But our powers are limited de facto, and our control de jure. Typically, the best we can do for strangers is help them to their feet with food, clothing, shelter, and protection from disease, enslavement, torture, and oppression. We cannot and should not direct others in how to live or what to think or where or when or whether to worship, even if we think their welfare in this world and beyond hangs in the balance. We *can* provide for others' education. But that works best within some common social structure or network of cultural commitments. Even then, our task is not to mold or shape but to empower, by which I mean not instilling false pride or chauvinism cloaked in the name of self-esteem but imparting tools of thought and action, skills not just of work but of thought, communication, and discovery and material knowledge of history, science, philosophy and literature, geography, anthropology, hygiene, and, yes, moral regard for our planet and its denizens. These tools will enable those we hope to educate to make of themselves more effectual human beings, capable of contributing to human welfare and the welfare of the world.

All this is a tall enough order for personal and communal undertaking, an agenda to be shared sensitively by public and private agency. But it cannot be tackled in the absence of all agency, where decentering has sped so far and fast that the very idea of organism, let alone subjecthood, is negated by false and guilty scruples. For such responses to the human condition and the attendant sense of powerlessness in the face of hunger, illness, pain, and oppression yield only paralysis when confronting the enormity of the human task.

How widely do our duties spread? It's easy to see them as global. The divine purview (not a perspective at all in our human sense!) does that; this is an outlook we are called upon to emulate. Indeed, we pursue a universal view when we act ethically, even as regards uniqueness and particularity. That purview is preserved even in the utilitarian recognition that pain and pleasure, or joy and sorrow (if we prefer Spinoza's words), weigh no less in others than in ourselves. But such vital moral facts are not, insofar as they are moral, the sort of facts that rightly burden us beyond our bearing. Hence the relevance of Rabbi Tarfon's words, once again: "It's not your charge to complete the task, but you are not free to give it up!" (M. Avot 2.21–22). Freedom, as Kant saw, imparts responsibility; duty, for that very reason, does not set the self aside.

Facing the claim of human moral inadequacy, whether it arises as a counterpart of vicarious atonement or in a secular sigh of guilt or moral despond,

I think we can reject both its pious and its profane offspring—not because all human needs have suddenly, magically been met but because there is no structural barrier against our turning to address them, cooperatively or emulatively, or in both ways together. For all great undertakings demand integration of these two kinds of motive. They exist independently only by abstraction.

What aids us in shouldering our responsibilities is not a moral myth but engagement in community, sharing the human burden and enlisting even our beneficiaries. For human beings are rarely utterly helpless and almost never utterly isolated. Normatively and prudentially, we must bear in mind Spinoza's counsel that nothing is more valuable to man than man. Granted, as Spinoza also teaches, neither our sympathies nor our means are broad enough for any one of us to take on the human burden single-handed. But part of our charge is to enlist others in the task. There are many communal and corporate models for this, and many openings and opportunities for service. I would not be as swift as Hare is to dismiss market means among them. For, to cite Spinoza once again, perceived self-interest is among the steadiest draws in recruiting human energies toward a common goal. By attracting individuals to labor in one another's interest as if it were their own, money, the notorious root of evil, can become a powerful catalyst of the common weal, allowing and encouraging us to treat others' interests as our own. The liquidity of money may make it the readiest vehicle in shifting and diffusing interests. But other infamous externals—honor, fame, pride, and emulation—can also serve common good, even though all of these are modulations of the so-called *yetzer ha-ra'*.

Over the long haul of history and the broad sweep of social diversity, morals gains its firmest purchase and greatest leverage by enlisting ego. That works best, as Plato saw, when reason steps forward to assume its proper place as our regnant identity. For only reason can weigh incommensurables, and only reason can recognize the parity of another person's interests with one's own. It was the power of the conatus, acting under the guidance of reason, that led Spinoza to anchor service to the common good in the idea of self-interest, even as he recognized that identities are elastic and capable of enlargement—invidiously in ambition, but lovingly in *humanitas*, as he called it, which he linked with *pietas* through the synonymy of both with *ḥesed*.

Recognizing that the public interest is impoverished when sequestered from the private, Bentham urged, rhetorically and categorically, but not hyperbolically, that

> Every system of management which has disinterestedness pretended or real for its foundation is rotten at the root, susceptible of mo-

> mentary prosperity at the outset, but sure to perish in the long run. That principle of action is most to be depended upon whose influence is most constant, most uniform, most lasting and most general among mankind. Personal interest is that principle and a system of economy built on any other foundation is built upon quicksand.[215]

Bentham's appeal was to what is often called realism. But his conclusion also follows on strictly moral grounds. For to try to enlist others in a common scheme without consulting *their* interests is the height of exploitation and illiberal usurpation. And to view one's beneficiaries only in terms of their need and not in terms of their active agency, talents, and potential contributions is to treat them only as objects and not as subjects at all.

It is with such thoughts in mind that the great moral teachers of humankind have sought consistently to build moral bonds among human beings that foster a broad, social sense of identity. Such an identity finds personal and communal fulfillment in generous acts. It sees others as second selves whose interests are not only congruent but complementary. When the great moral teachers engaged in social or political activity—as Moses, or Lincoln, or Gandhi did—they sought to build bonds of sodality and communities (from the level of the family all the way to society and humanity at large) in which individual interest is readily seen and shown and proved to be maximized through cooperative enterprise and collaborative endeavor. An underlying goal in all such projects, be they intellectual and spiritual or economic and political, is to foster a conception of enlightened self-interest in which duty and inclination do not diverge but strengthen each other.

The great weakness in all ideas of enlightened self-interest, as Kant saw clearly, is the risk of self-deception. The alignment of duty with interest makes it frighteningly easy for self-serving to masquerade as merit, breeding a complacency that is often more disturbing than sheer hypocrisy. For hypocrisy, at least, has a guilty conscience. But complacency is pure self-righteousness. The solution to that problem comes not from moral theory but from the forging of a culture and the forming of an ethos that foster the self-scrutiny that ethical authenticity demands. That kind of culture and ethos open up an edge where self-criticism can slip its scalpel between the folds of moral fat and remove a few layers. In preparation for that kind of surgery, of course, we need a thorough examination, one that would, as Bobby Burns put it, allow us, if all went well, to see ourselves as others see us.

The Torah, with its admonitions to love God with all our hearts and to express that love in acts of *ḥesed*, seeks to build such a culture and ethos through its rules of practice. Its moral code is not alone in that. But it is ancient, effective, and respected, highly elaborated and influential. The work it cuts out for us remains unfinished, as Rabbi Tarfon says. But one does not press that work toward consummation by dismissive talk about slavery to the Law or by endorsing the Pauline polemical view that, since the Law sets down demands that distinguish right from wrong, the law is somehow the *creator* of sin and sinfulness.

The Gifford lectures take natural theology as their theme, that is, ideas about God and how He calls on us to live that are grounded not in scripture or any instituted tradition of thought or practice but in human reason. That, I think, makes the present occasion an important opportunity for collaborative work, allowing all of us, from different traditions, theistic or humanistic, to come together in a waking moment and converse about our dreams—to interpret and compare, triangulate from one another's standpoints, and see if that collaborative activity can't help us to determine which of our dreams are veridical and worthy of our lives, which are compatible, which are parochial or particular—which are better forgotten or locked up in the reliquary of history, and which are worthy of new or continued sustenance, whether for their intrinsic beauty or for the life they guide us to and the lives that we in turn can model for all those whose lives we touch.

Appendix

Authors Cited

Aaron Halevi of Barcelona (13th century). Probable author of the *Sefer ha-Ḥinnukh.*

Abba Saul (2nd century). Tanna (Mishnaic authority) of the third generation. He urged those who would pray to prepare their hearts and ears—that is, to ensure that their prayers came from the heart.

Abravanel, Isaac (1437–1508). Spanish statesman, philosopher, and exegete. As treasurer of Alfonso V of Portugal, he was falsely accused of conspiracy and fled to Toledo, where he then served Ferdinand and Isabella. Unable to persuade them to rescind their edict of expulsion, he led Spanish Jewry into exile in 1492, settled in Naples, and continued his diplomacy. He was a Maimonidean rationalist and is the author, inter alia, of the *Rosh Amanah.* His son Judah Abravanel, known as Leone Ebreo (ca. 1460–ca. 1535), wrote the classic *Dialoghi di Amore.*

Akiva (ca. 40–135). Tanna of the third generation. He is among the most celebrated and revered of Talmudic authorities and was martyred by Rome for his support of the Bar Kokhva rebellion.

al-Ashʿarī, Abū ʾl-Ḥasan (873/4–935/6). Founder of the Ashʿarite school of Islamic theology.

Avtalyon (1st century B.C.E.). A rabbinic leader of pre-Mishnaic period. He was maliciously said to be of pagan ancestry and lived in Alexandria during Alexander Yannai's persecution of the Pharisees. He and Shemaya founded the rabbinic mode of hermeneutics. They are the first exegetes and decisors to be cited in later aggadic and halakhic readings of the Jewish canon. Hillel, his disciple, formalized his exegetical midrashic methods.

Baal Shem Tov (1700–1760). Founder of Hasidic movement, modern Jewish pietism, which is known for its interest in joyous, even ecstatic worship, its allegorical exegetical approach, and its openness to mystical trends rooted in Kabbalah.

Badad, Joseph (1800–1875). Halakhist and exegete.

Baḥya ben Asher (ca. 1260–1340). An exegete and mystic of Saragossa and pupil of Solomon ben Abraham Adret. He wrote a commentary on M. Avot and a wide ranging ethical work, the *Kad ha-Qemaḥ* ("The Flour Jar"). His commentary on the Pentateuch interweaves philosophical and kabbalistic themes. It was the first kabbalistic work to appear in print (1492).

Baḥya ibn Paquda (11th century). Andalusian philosopher. His *Book of Guidance to the Duties of the Heart,* a systematic exposition of pietist Jewish philosophy, appeared in Arabic in 1080 and was translated into Hebrew in 1161 by Judah Ibn Tibbon.

Ben-Azzai (2nd century). Among the scholars who gathered with Yoḥanan ben Zakkai at Yavneh. Like Ben-Zoma, he is said to have delved into mysteries, to ill effect. He argued successfully for including the Song of Songs in the biblical canon. He and Ben-Zoma did not live to gain the title Rabbi, although both were distinguished decisors.

Ben-Zoma (2nd century). Tanna of the third generation. He was a celebrated exegete whose mystical or philosophical explorations are traditionally said to have gone too far. Of the "four who entered" that "Garden" (*pardes*), only Akiva is said to have emerged unscathed.

Bentham, Jeremy (1748–1832). British philosopher, jurist, and social theorist. A founder of Utilitarianism and pioneer of modern penal theory.

Blauser, Yitzḥaq (1837–1907).

Chasman, Yehudah Loeb (1869–1935).

Cohen, Hermann (1842–1914). Neo-Kantian philosopher. Son of a cantor and son-in-law of the great liturgical composer Louis Lewandowski, Cohen was the first unbaptized Jew to hold a major chair in philosophy at a Prussian university. His students included Boris Pasternak, José Ortega y Gasset, Ernst Cassirer, Nicolai Hartmann, Hans-Georg Gadamer, and August Stadler, the professor who taught Einstein his Kant in Zurich in 1900.

David ben Zimra (called Radvaz, ca. 1479–1573). Born in Spain, he studied in Safed with Joseph Saragossi, and then in Egypt, where he was a major rabbinical authority. He had a splendid library of manuscripts, kept an open house, composed quarrels, supported scholars, and disputed actively with learned Muslims and Karaite sectarians. Highly critical of the exegesis of Abraham Ibn Ezra and Joseph Kimḥi, he rejected the idea of creeds, regarding all *mitzvot* as equally holy. Aggadah too was holy in his view. He believed in demons but opposed magic, because it was pagan. He was known as a humane and scientific reader of scripture.

Ehrenfeld, Shmuel (1805–1883). Called the Ḥatan Sofer. He was the grandson of the Ḥatam Sofer.

Eleazar ben Azariah (1st century C.E.). A Tanna of the second/third generation. Wealthy and well born, he traced his roots to Ezra the Scribe. While still young he became president of the Academy at Yavneh, his premature white hair taken as a sign from heaven of the respect he was due. He attracted throngs of students and pioneered in the use of parataxis in scriptural exegesis. Among his glosses: From the exhortation "On that day . . . shall ye cleanse yourselves of all your sins before the Lord" (Leviticus 16:30) he inferred that we must seek forgiveness of affronts to our human fellows before our spiritual relations with God can be adequately restored. Among his teachings: the interdependence of Torah (rabbinic learning) with ethics, of piety with wisdom, of knowledge with understanding, and of practicality ("flour") with Torah, that is, theory with practice (M. Avot 3.21).

Elijah ben Solomon (called the Vilna Gaon or the Gra, 1720–1797). A major talmudist and kabbalist, and the author of some seventy books, chiefly commentaries on biblical and rabbinic texts. He encouraged mathematical and scientific studies and prompted one disciple to translate Euclid into Hebrew. An ardent foe of Hasidism for its popularization of Kabbalistic ideas and its seeming substitution of levity and simple tales for gravitas and serious scholarly endeavor, he sparked a revival of biblical and talmudic studies through his writings and teachings. Following his urgings, his disciples left Europe for the land of Israel about ten years after his death. Desires, he said, should be purified, not effaced.

Ephraim Shelomo ben Ḥayyim of Luntshitz (1550–1619). Known as Ephraim of Luntshitz (Leczyca in Polish) or by the title of his book, the *K^eli Yaqar* (The Precious Vessel), he was a poet and celebrated preacher. After having studied with Solomon Luria he became president of the Prague rabbinical court. He railed against the wealthy who shirked caring for the poor, but also chided the poor for adopting a posture of dependency. He was similarly critical of scholars who substituted logic chopping for the quest for truth.

Fārābī (d. 950). Muslim philosopher with special interests in logic, language, political philosophy, and social philosophy.

Rabban Gamaliel II (d. before 132). President of the Sanhedrin that formalized the scriptural canon. A grandfather of Judah the Prince, he journeyed often to Rome in behalf of his fellow Jews. He standarized the forms of prayer and extended the standards of priestly purity to the Israelite laity.

Gamaliel III (3rd century). Son of Judah the Prince. He helped complete the Mishnah. His precept that Torah study must be complemented with worldly work (*derekh eretz*) was traditionally read as calling for scholars to practice a trade and not live as idlers. But it was later read as calling for a synthesis of sacred with secular studies.

R. Gamaliel cautioned against involvement with the powers that be, given their self-serving agendas: all public and communal work should be "for the sake of heaven"—undertaken for its intrinsic merit, without ulterior aim. (M. Avot 2.2–4).

Gershom ben Yehudah of Mainz (called Me'or ha-Golah, the Light of the Exile, ca. 965–ca. 1028). Talmudist and halakhist, celebrated for his *taqqanah* or rabbinic decree mandating monogamy. Rabbenu Gershom, "our teacher Gershom," also decreed that a woman must agree if she is to be divorced. He declared it a major sin to read another person's mail and forbade shaming those who returned to Judaism after forced conversions to Christianity.

Ghazālī (1058–1111). Muslim theologian, philosopher, and jurist. Author of *The Incoherence of the Philosophers,* a systematic critique of the Islamic Neoplatonic Aristotelians, chiefly, al-Fārābī and Avicenna; and *Iḥyā ʿUlūm al-Dīn* (Reviving the Religious Sciences), an elaboration of Islamic spirituality and ritual. His *Al-Munqidh min al-Ḍalāl* retraces his path from skepticism to piety.

Ginzburg, Asher (Aḥad Ha-ʿAm, literally, "One of the People," 1856–1927). An essayist and early Zionist. He broke with political Zionism, deeming it premature to build a Jewish state before adequate cultural foundations had been laid. He championed revival of the Hebrew language and reported in detail on the problems returning Jews faced in the first Yishuv. A realist about those issues, he was less sensitive than his friend Leon Pinsker had been to the risks of the Diaspora. He never envisioned the horrors that would overtake European Jewry in the Holocaust.

Ḥafetz Ḥayyim (Rabbi Israel Meir Kagan, 1838–1933). Under the name he adopted from the Psalms (34:13—*Who is the man who loveth life*), he is best known for his efforts to curb malicious speech. He was the founder of a celebrated yeshiva and wrote the *Mishnah B^e^rurah,* a six-volume commentary on the *Orakh Ḥayyim,* the ritual section of Joseph Karo's *Shulḥan Arukh.*

Ḥatam Sofer (Rabbi Moshe Schreiber, 1762–1839). Like many rabbinic authors, he is best known by the title of his widely read book. He was born in Frankfurt and recognized as a genius in his youth. He founded a yeshiva at Pressburg (Bratislava). Many of his students became rabbis in Hungary. An ardent traditionalist, he pronounced novelty biblically forbidden.

Ḥazon Ish (Rabbi Abraham Isaiah Karelitz, 1878–1953). Famed for his 1911 commentary on the *Shulḥan Arukh,* he became known by its title "The Man of vision." He left Vilna for Israel in 1933 and settled in B^e^nei B^e^rak. He is said to have been well versed in the sciences. He lived extremely modestly, supported by his wife, and was widely regarded as a holy and learned scholar. Supportive of Zionism, he was consulted by David Ben Gurion about women's military service.

Hero of Alexandria (fl. ca. 62 C.E.). Greek mathematician, engineer, and geometer. Among his inventions was a suspended glass globe that spun when water inside was heated, allowing steam to escape through jets in its sides.

Hertz, Joseph H. (1872–1946). Author of widely used commentaries on the Pentateuch, the Hebrew prayer book, and M. Avot. Born in Austro-Hungary but educated at City College in New York and Columbia University, he was the first graduate of the Jewish Theological Seminary of America. After service as a rabbi in Syracuse he took a pulpit in Johannesburg, where the South African president Paul Kruger tried to have him dismissed in reaction to his pro-British sympathies. Named Chief Rabbi of the British Empire in 1913, he won over many who thought him insufficiently orthodox by appointing a traditionalist to head the London Rabbinical Court—although others were put off by his outspoken Zionism. In the 1920s he led a successful effort to block the League of Nations' attempt to institute a "World Calendar" that would force the days of the week to fall on the same calendar date each year, since the necessary intercalary "world days" would have put sabbaths out of phase with the official days of the work week.

Hillel (ca. 70 B.C.E.–10 C.E.). Born in Babylonia, he traveled to Jerusalem, overcame great hardship to study, and became one of the most revered halakhic authorities. Hillel and his school generally rule less stringently than their counterpart, the school of Shammai. His most famous reform, the Prosbul, was a device to sidestep cancellation of loans in the Sabbatical year. By freeing up the flow of capital in an increasingly monetary economy, the Prosbul protected the needy, who faced a denial of credit as the seventh year approached. Among Hillel's ethical teachings: the admonition not to break with the community, not to be too trusting in oneself, not to judge others until one had stood in their position, not to speak obscurely or ambiguously, not to defer studying for a leisure that might never arrive. "A boor," he said "cannot be godfearing; an ignoramus cannot be saintly. The shamefaced cannot learn, the irascible cannot teach, and success in business does not make one wise. Where there are no men, strive to be a man" (M. Avot 2.5–6).

Hirsch, Samson Raphael (1808–1888). A founder of Jewish neo-orthodoxy. He voiced a fierce commitment to tradition in the language of European humanism, beginning with the publication of his *Nineteen Letters,* written in 1830 when he was chief rabbi of Oldenburg. He became chief rabbi of Aurich and Osnabrück in 1841, and of Moravia and Austrian Silesia from 1847 until 1851. He led the "Israelitish Religious Society" of Frankfurt-am-Main until his death.

al-Hujwīrī, Alī b. ʿUthmān (d. ca. 1070). Afghan scholar and Sufi, author of the first Persian treatise on Sufism.

Ibn Ezra, Abraham (1092–1167). Born in Toledo, he settled in Cordova, where he was known as a poet, exegete, and philosopher. He knew Joseph ibn Zaddik and Judah Halevi. He left Spain around 1140, probably after his son Isaac embraced Islam. Traveling widely in Europe, he introduced many European Jews to the Arabo-Judaic literature of Andalusia.

Jakobovits, Immanuel (1921–1999). Born in Germany, he escaped the Holocaust with his family and became Chief Rabbi of Ireland in 1949. He held the pulpit of the

Fifth Avenue Synagogue in New York from its founding in 1958 until he was named Chief Rabbi of the British Commonwealth in 1967. Admired by Queen Elizabeth, he was knighted and made a life peer. He was the first Jew to receive a Lambeth Doctorate of Divinity from the Archbishop of Canterbury. His chief contributions to philosophy lie in medical ethics.

Jonah ben Abraham Gerondi (1200–1263). A cousin of Naḥmanides, he was a student of Solomon of Montpellier, a leading anti-Maimonist. He was also a signer of the 1233 ban on the *Guide* and the *Book of Knowledge,* the first volume of Maimonides' Code. His student Hillel of Verona reports that Jonah later regretted this act, which led to the burning of those books by Christian authorities (for Jonah lived to see wagonloads of Talmuds burned at the same location). He is said to have repented of his anti-Maimonideanism as well. He was an active exegete and is chiefly remembered as a moralist and for such works as *The Gates of Repentance* (*Sha'arei T*^{e}*shuvah*).

José ben Ḥalafta (2nd century). A Tanna of the fourth generation. He was a distinguished disciple of Rabbi Akiva and the father of R. Ishmael, who succeeded him. He is cited over three hundred times in the Mishnah. The Romans executed Rabbi Judah ben Bava for ordaining him and others in defiance of a ban issued during the Bar Kokhva revolt; but R. José returned from exile to teach in the ruins of Tzippori, the city destroyed in the same reprisal. He is known for his love of compromise and hatred of contention, and he is quoted as saying that he would almost violate a clear ritual law if that were the ruling of his colleagues. A matron is said to have asked him what God had been doing since the creation. He answered that God was pairing up couples. Anyone can do that, she answered: I can match up my servants. That may be easy for you, he replied, but for God it is as hard as it was to split the Red Sea. After a brief and highly unsuccessful experiment in forced matchmaking, the matron returned to tell R. José how right he was.

Judah ben Simon Pazzi (3rd century). An Amora of the third and fourth generation known for his strict proceduralism in behalf of the presumption of innocence. Of priestly birth, he served as *dayyan,* halakhic judge of Lod in the land of Israel. He was said to have found the meaning of the Torah summed up not in the words, *Thou shalt love thy neighbor as thyself,* nor even in the affirmation of monotheism, *Hear, O Israel, the Lord thy God, the Lord is one,* but in a single detail of the sacrificial cult—for it enshrined the practices of the lost Temple.

Judah the Prince (135–219 C.E.). Said to have been born on the day of Akiva's martyrdom, he was broadly educated by his father, Simon b. Gamaliel II, and reportedly well-versed in Greek. After learning at the feet of many of Akiva's prominent students, he succeeded his father as leader of the Jews of the land of Israel and moved the academy to Bet She'arim. Both Talmuds ascribe the redaction of the Mishnah to him, but the work was completed by his son and successor, Gamaliel III. In the Mishnah he is named simply Rabbi. He is known for his sensitivity, and he is said often to have been moved to tears at the thought of Jewish martyrs and exemplars of piety.

Juwaynī (1028–1085). Ash'arite theologian and teacher of Ghazālī. He was called Imām al-Ḥaramayn, the spiritual guide of Mecca and Medina.

Karo, Joseph (1488–1575). Exiled from Spain, his family fled to Turkey, and he settled in Safed in 1535, where he won wide renown as a halakhic decisor. His monumental *Shulḥan Arukh* remains an authoritative and comprehensive halakhic code, although Karo himself saw it as a guide for young students unable to follow the complexities of his more technical works.

Levin, Tzvi Hirsch (also known as Hirschel Levin, 1721–1800,). Born in Galicia, he became Chief rabbi in London and later Berlin. He studied philosophy, the sciences, poetry, and other secular subjects, and as a young man distinguished himself as a Talmudist. He was a close friend of Moses Mendelssohn and gave rabbinic approval to Mendelssohn's German translation of the Pentateuch. He asked Mendelssohn to prepare a summary of Jewish civil laws pertaining to the family, at the instance of the German government, since his own fluency in German was not up to the task. Mendelssohn's book, prepared under Hirsch's oversight, appeared in 1778.

Aharon Lichtenstein (1933–). Born in France but raised in the United States and educated at Yeshiva University and Harvard, where he earned a Ph.D. in English literature. He made aliyah to Israel in 1971 and is known for his innovative traditionalism in the tradition of his teacher and father-in-law, Joseph Soloveichik.

Lipkin, Israel (Israel Salanter, 1810–1883). Founder of the Mussar movement, a traditionalist approach to Jewish ethics. Stressing practical application of Jewish values, he extolled the virtues of manual labor and prompted the reprinting at Vilna of ethical classics by Moses Luzzatto and Solomon Ibn Gabirol.

Luzzatto, Samuel David (1800–1865). A keen linguist in his youth, as a teen, Luzzatto argued in a pamphlet that the *Zohar* must be dated much later than the Talmudic period. In 1829, he became a professor at the rabbinical college in Padua. He is noted for his critical reading of scripture; he objected to philosophy in general and to Ibn Ezra, Maimonides, and Spinoza in particular.

Marvell, Andrew (1621–1678). English metaphysical poet, tutor to Oliver Cromwell's ward, William Dutton, and assistant to John Milton. Even after the Restoration, he remained active in politics as a member of Parliament.

Maimonides (Moses ben Maimon, known as the Rambam, 1138–1204). Philosopher, halakhist, and physician. Born in Cordova, he left with his family in the wake of the Almohad persecutions and forced conversions, ultimately settling in Cairo. His code of Jewish law, the *Mishneh Torah,* remains an authoritative reference and object of study. His *Guide to the Perplexed* has had a lasting impact on Jewish, Muslim, and Christian thinkers.

Makkī (d. 998). Muslim scholar, jurist, and Sufi.

Miller, Avigdor (1908–2001). Born in Baltimore, he traveled to Lithuania in 1932 to study at the famous Slabodka Yeshiva, and he escaped to the United States with his newly formed family on the eve of the Holocaust. He served as a rabbi in Brooklyn and wrote extensively, often in an anti-Zionist mode.

Muḥāsibī (d. 857). Sufi and theologian.

Naḥmanides (Moses ben Naḥman Gerondi, 1194–1270). Philosopher, kabbalist, physician, and exegete. A respectful critic of Maimonides' philosophy and philosophical exegesis. He did not join the anti-Maimonists but sought, unsuccessfully, to work out a compromise between them and their adversaries, suggesting the ban be lifted from the *Book of Knowledge* but strengthened against the *Guide*. Naḥmanides prevailed in defending Judaism against Christian polemics in a forced disputation held at Barcelona in the presence of King James of Aragon. Although assured that he might speak freely, he was exiled at the instance of the Church after publishing an account of the debate. He ended his days in the land of Israel.

Obadiah of Bertinoro (ca. 1450–before 1516). Author of the most widely used commentary on the Mishnah, printed at Venice in 1548–1549. The work makes ample use of both Maimonides and Rashi. He preached extensively in Italy but declined to become a rabbi. Known as a peace maker, he gathered funds for the poor and became the leader of the Jews of Jerusalem. He followed up on Hillel's precept by seeking lucidity and immediate clarity in his writing.

Or ha-Ḥayyim (Ḥayyim ben Moses Attar, 1696–1743). Born in Morocco, he hoped to emigrate to Palestine, but the Jews of Leghorn (Livorno) established a yeshiva for him and he reached Jerusalem only a year before his death. The book by which he is known, the *Light of Life*, is a multi-leveled commentary on the Pentateuch.

Rabad (Rabbi Abraham ben David of Posquieres, 1120–1198). A Provençal Talmudist. He generously supported poor scholars and students, although his wealth also brought him into conflict with the local lord, until Count Roger II of Carcassonne intervened on his behalf. A severe critic of Maimonides' Code, Rabad objected to the Maimonidean articles of belief and to the very project of a readily accessible handbook of Halakha.

Rashi (Rabbi Simon ben Isaac, 1040–1105). Leaving his native Troyes only once at any length, to study in the Rhineland, Rashi founded a school on his return that won wide fame and attracted many students. His commentaries, printed in standard texts of the Talmud and Hebrew Bible, are still closely studied and have attracted many supercommentaries. His glosses often anthologize bits of rabbinic midrash, but they can also pursue a simple sense in the text. At times naively homiletical, they shift effortlessly to subtle psychological and linguistic insights.

Rav (R. Abba bar Aivu, ca. 175–247). Babylonian Amora of the first generation, cited hundreds of times in the Babylonian and Jerusalem Talmuds. As tradition has it, he was ordained by Judah the Prince, he knew the later Tannaim, and he was called Rav since he was seen as the teacher of all the Diaspora. Valuing Torah study even above restoration of the Temple, he saw the refinement of character as the purpose of the *mitzvot*. Blessed with a good voice, Rav created several liturgical works that are still in use. He is said to have spoken always truthfully but never idly. In all matters calling for generosity of spirit, he went beyond the letter of the Law. He valued tact and opposed asceticism and reportedly counseled a disciple to make the most of life since there is no pleasure in the grave. In a famous and much discussed dictum, he said that in the World to Come there is no eating or drinking or procreation; instead, the righteous sit with their crowns on and feast on the divine glory.

Resh Lakish (Rabbi Shimon ben Lakish, ca. 200–275). An Amora in the land of Israel. Driven by debt to sell himself as a gladiator in his youth, he was known for his integrity and his immense strength. A formidable debater, he married the sister of his mentor, who confessed his brilliance and compared his own teachings without the disciple's expositions to the clapping of one hand. He boldly ruled that even the rabbinical president must not accept gifts, saying, "Do you think fear would stop me from teaching God's Torah?" Anger, he said, banishes the wisdom from a sage and inspiration from a prophet.

Saadiah Gaon (882–942). Born in the Fayyum region of Egypt, Saadiah became head of the ancient rabbinic academy of Sura, which, by his time, was located in Baghdad. His *Book of Critically Chosen Beliefs and Convictions* was the first systematic work of Jewish philosophy. A founding figure in every discipline of Jewish learning, he wrote the pioneering works of Hebrew grammar, lexicography, and liturgy. His Arabic translations with commentary on books of the Hebrew Bible avoid midrashic excursions. They are noted for their thematic introductions, their sophisticated use of philosophical and philological reasoning, and their openness to current knowledge of astronomy, physiology, and mathematics.

Sforno, Ovadiah (ca. 1470–ca. 1550). Italian exegete, philosopher, linguist, and physician. He studied medicine in Rome and argued against various views of Aristotle.

Shemaya (1st century B.C.E.). A rabbinic leader of the pre-Mishnaic period, Shemaya came from Alexandria and presided over the Sanhedrin before and during Herod's reign. When the king was called before the Sanhedrin to be cited for unilaterally executing the leader of the national party in Galilee. Shemaya was said to be the only member bold enough to speak out against him.

Shimon bar Yoḥai (2nd century). A Tanna of the fourth generation. He was born in the Galilee and was a leading disciple of Rabbi Akiva. His father had enjoyed Roman favor, but Hadrian's persecution turned the son against Rome, and Shimon went into hiding to escape execution. Halakhot in his name appear throughout the Talmud, and the medieval authors of the Zohar ascribed the work to him.

Simon ben Eleazar. A Tanna of the fifth generation. He lived in Tiberias. Among his ethical precepts were admonitions of tact: Do not try to please a friend when he is angry or console him when his loved one's corpse is still laid out before him. Do not ask questions when he's making a vow or press to see him when he's in disgrace (M. Avot 4.18). "A man," he said, "should be soft as a reed, not rigid like a cedar" (*Avot d^e-R. Nathan* 41, B. Ta'anit 20ab).

Simeon ben Shetaḥ (ca. 80–50 B.C.E.). President of the Sanhedrin and active during the reigns of Alexander Yannai and his wife Alexandra. He was the brother of the queen and enjoyed royal tolerance. When he joined the Sanhedrin, most of its members were Sadducees, for the king himself was of priestly birth and the Sadducees were the priestly party. The ascendancy of the Pharisees is largely credited to Simeon's efforts. When the Pharisees fell from favor and were forced to flee, the queen persuaded the king to allow her brother to return to the court; and when she succeeded her husband, Simeon was able to reestablish Pharisaic authority.

Joseph Soloveitchik (1903–1993). Scion of an eminent rabbinic lineage, he studied liberal arts, economics, and political science in Europe and wrote his Ph.D. thesis on Hermann Cohen's philosophy. He founded the Maimonides School in Boston in 1937 and succeeded his father, Moses, as head of Yeshiva University's rabbinical seminary in 1941. His writings include *Halakhic Man* and *The Lonely Man of Faith.*

Susskind, Alexander ben Moses of Grodno (d. 1793). Author of *Y^{e}sod Ve-Shoresh ha-'Avodah* (The Essence and Root of Worship). He was a kabbalist, exegete, and supercommentator on Rashi.

Tacitus (ca. 55–ca. 117). Roman senator and historian and author of the *Annals* and the *Histories,* which cover Roman history for most of the first century C.E. Book V of the *Histories* tells of the Jews and Titus' handling of the Jewish Revolt.

Rabbi Tarfon (fl. ca. 100). A Tanna of third generation. He was of priestly birth and served in the Temple before its destruction by Titus. He followed the school of Shammai but ruled against it when he found its rulings too severe.

Tyndale, William (ca. 1494–1535). English Protestant translator of the Bible, martyred in the reign of Henry VIII.

Worringer, Wilhelm (1881–1965). German art historian.

Yoḥanan ben Zakkai (first century C.E.). A Tanna of the first generation. He founded the academy at Yavneh after the destruction of the Temple in 70 C.E The rabbinic traditions that took root as a result enshrined the Temple cult in memory but built more largely on the heritage of the biblical prophets, sublimating the rituals of purity long associated with the Temple into vehicles of spiritual and moral piety. Hillel, who was his teacher, is said to have called Yoḥanan, his youngest student, "the father of wisdom" and "the father of coming generations."

Notes

CHAPTER I

1. See Vernon Lee (pen name of Violet Paget), "Beauty and Ugliness" (1893), reprinted in V. Lee and C. Anstruther-Thomson, *Beauty and Ugliness*; Theodore Lipps, *Archiv für gesamte Psychologie* 1 (1903), expanding on his work of 1893–97, which Paget learned of in 1899; Wilhelm Worringer, *Abstraction and Empathy*; Melvin Rader, *A Modern Book of Aesthetics*, 370–91. For the psychology of empathy, Edward B. Tichener, *Lectures on the Experimental Psychology of the Thought-Processes*; Robert Vischer, *Über das optische Formgefühl*; Hermann Lotze, *Mikrokosmos*. The ideas of projection and identification have ancient roots in Aristotle's account of friendship and Stoic thoughts of *sympatheia*, the interconnectedness of all things. Modern accounts of empathy in aesthetics rely on Keats's idea of negative capability and Herder's thought that "the beauty of a line is movement, and the beauty of movement, expression." Recent work by Marco Iacoboni of UCLA and other neuroscientists suggests that specific areas in the brain map and mirror movements and sensations perceived in the external world, laying a neurological basis for empathy and engagement. But ethically, of course, with empathy as with affront, the ethical issue lies in our appropriation of the underlying impulse, not in its sheer presence.

2. See Spinoza, *Ethics* (1677) Part 3, Propositions 11–35.

3. See Lucretius, *De Rerum Natura*, II 1– 2.

4. See Cicero, *De Finibus*, III 16–17.

5. David Hume, *A Treatise of Human Nature* (1739), 414–17, 457–58, 463–69.

6. Hume, *Treatise*, 316–17.

7. Hume, *Enquiries Concerning Human Understanding and Concerning the Principles of Morals* (1772/1777), 184, 224–29.

8. Hume, *Treatise*, 357–62.

9. Hume, *Enquiries*, 23–33; *Treatise*, 252, 469–70.

10. Hume, *Enquiries*, 172.

11. Hume, *Enquiries*, 173; cf. *Treatise* 417, 439.

12. See Hume, *Enquiries*, 13.

13. See Cicero, *De Finibus*, III 17–18, 20–25.

14. See Darwin, *The Descent of Man*, Chapter 5.

15. See Wilson, *Sociobiology*, 562.

16. Wilson, *Sociobiology*, 562.

17. Some thinkers, in pursuit of naturalism in ethics, have sought to construct an evolutionary ethics, often seeking foundations in sociobiology. I see three problems here. The first arises from heteronomy—If ethics is an artifact of evolution, it is not ours. Our moral choices are not our own, our appropriation or failure to appropriate ethical counsels is not of our own doing but simply a dictate of our history—or prehistory. Differences in ethical style or even intent become matters of genetics, neural action, or hormonal balance. Gandhi, then, will differ from Idi Amin only in temperament. Moral judgments dissolve into biochemistry. Second, and closely related, is the price evolutionary ethics pays for its naturalism in the coin of deference to determinism. If ethics becomes a snarl of heritable traits, personal agency vanishes, and, with it, moral responsibility and accountability. Morality becomes a reflex, not amenable to personal or social betterment or decline, let alone praise or blame, punishment, or reward. There will then be facts and even necessities but no real choices or deliberations. Third, and perhaps most damaging pragmatically, some of the tendencies (real or imagined) that are ascribed to human evolutionary history are highly undesirable. They include extreme versions of kin preference and the displacement of ethical ideals by notions of altruism that reduce that ethical motive to a self-serving (or gene-serving) mechanism. The ethos that evolution is thought to foster thus seems to reduce to the mentality once summed up by F. M. Cornford in the motto "You scratch my back, I'll scratch yours—and if not I'll scratch your eyes out." From there the repertoire of evolutionary cynics may extend to rationales for racism and xenophobia (by appeal to the purportedly general and heritable human penchant for love of the ingroup and hatred of outsiders) to the alleged male penchants for rape and promiscuity and the alleged female penchants for infanticide and for docile, submissive, and meretricious behavior. See Lionel Tiger, *Men in Groups*, 32–40; Lionel Tiger and Robin Fox, *The Imperial Animal*, 31–36; Steven Goldberg, *The Inevitability of Patriarchy*, 93, and its updated edition, *Why Men Rule*; C. R. Austin and R. V. Short, *Human Sexuality*, 2, 8–10, 131–33, and *Reproductive Fitness*; A. Keith, *A New Theory of Human Evolution*, 234–35, 252–54. See also David Buss, *The Adapted Mind*; John H. Beckstrom, *Sociobiology and the Law*. For a critique of the biological pretensions underlying such theses, see L. E. Goodman and M. J. Goodman, " 'Particularly Amongst the Sunburnt Nations'–The Persistence of Sexual Stereotypes of Race in Bio-Science." But my nisus here is ethical: If nor-

mative ethics is left to sociobiology, we become powerless to distinguish wholesome from unwholesome, morally desirable from morally repugnant impulses.

18. Alī b. Uthman al-Hujwīrī, *Kashf al-Maḥjūb*, 200.

19. Baḥya Ibn Paqudah, *K. al-Hidāya ilā Farā'iḍ al-Qulūb*, ed. Yahuda, 5.5, p. 232; tr. Mansoor, 277.

20. See Deuteronomy 13; cf. Hobbes, *De Cive*, Chapter 16 § 11; *Leviathan*, III 32; and Chapter 2.

21. See Qur'ān 7:20, 20:120, 50:16, 114:4–5.

22. Baḥya, *Farā'iḍ al-Qulūb*, ed. Yahuda 231, *ll.* 10–17; the translation here is my own. See also tr. Mansoor, 276. The passage is a subtle phenomenological gloss of Genesis 4:7, *Sin coucheth at the door*, imaging sin as a beast of prey, lying in wait for an opening: *La-petaḥ ḥatat rovetz*. Baḥya envisions a false friend offering specious advice in the inner counsels of the heart. For the *yetzer ha-ra'* as an internal enemy, see Resh Lakish and R. Ḥuna, B. Sukkah 52b.

23. Tomás Kulka, *Art and Kitsch*, understands kitsch as a pretension to art that fails to enlarge or heighten our sensibilities but merely plays upon presumed responses. Kitsch is thus manipulative. Its counterpart in argument is flattery or playing to the biases of an audience, the massaging of familiar expectations that masquerade as reasoning.

24. Melville's marvelous riposte to romantic Schwarmerei about *unio mystica* has Ishmael in the crow's nest almost swooning into the empty air, until his body, his adrenalin, we might say, startles him awake and he grabs hold of ihe rail and finds himself not ready quite yet or quite so materially ready to merge into the All.

25. J. Ḥagiga 2:1. For the formulaic invocation of the World to Come, see Goodman, *On Justice*, Chapter 6.

26. See Goodman, *On Justice*, 24–26, etc.

27. Joseph Karo, *Shulḥan 'Arukh, Yoreh De'ah* 157:1.

28. Naḥmanides, at Leviticus 19:18.

29. Naḥmanides thus cites Jonathan's love of David (1 Samuel 20:17, 20:30–31, 23:17) as the epitome of such love, since the young prince, to his father's dismay and disgust, was willing to cede his claims to the kingdom to his friend; see Goodman, *In Defense of Truth*, 137–38.

30. The *Sefer ha-Ḥinnukh*, first printed in 1523, is ascribed to a Rabbi Aaron, identified in 1549 as Aaron Halevi, a well-known Spanish tamudist. See Gersion Appel's commentary, *A Philosophy of Mitzvot*. Cited here is the discussion at commandment 243.

31. Spinoza, *Ethics*, Part 3, Proposition 29, scholium; "Definitions of the Emotions' 43–44, ed. Gebhardt 2.162, 202.

32. William Tyndale made the first English translation of fourteen books of the Hebrew Bible, laying the basis for the language and conception of the King James version of 1611. Falling foul of the ban on such work in the still-Catholic England of Henry VIII, he worked in exile on the Continent, publishing his Pentateuch in 1530. He was betrayed at Antwerp, jailed, strangled, and burnt at the stake for blasphemy. His books too were burnt, but Henry's Protestant turn not long afterward

opened the door to their use by the King James translators. See David Daniel, ed., *Tyndale's Old Testament.*

33. James A. H. Murray, ed., *The Oxford English Dictionary*—s.v. neighbour. Murray cites the echo of the Torah's commandment at Luke 10:27, as if that were the prime text for the biblical obligation—which for many it has become. Most of Chaucer's *Canterbury Tales,* unfinished at the author's death in 1400, was written after 1387.

34. See Genesis 11:3, Exodus 11:2, 18:16, 21:18, 22:6, 9, etc.; cf. Leviticus 26:37; Exodus 26:3, 5, 17.

35. See Ernest Klein, *A Comprehensive Etymological Dictionary of the Hebrew Language,* 621–22, svv. *reʿa*[i] and *reʿah*[i-ii].

36. See Solomon Mandelkern, *Veteris Testamenti Concordantiae,* 1098.

37. See Hermann Cohen, *Religion of Reason out of the Sources of Judaism,* Chapter 8, "The Discovery of Man as Fellowman."

38. See, e.g. Deuteronomy 17:15, Leviticus 22:10, 12, 13.

39. Leviticus 19:33–34, as cited by Cohen, *Religion of Reason,* 127. Strangers, Cohen notes, citing Numbers 15:14–16 and 1 Kings 8:41–43, may offer sacrifices at God's Temple, and King Solomon will offer prayers for them.

40. Use of the singular here and in Leviticus 19:18 shows that the commandment is addressed to each individual and must be taken to heart individually. Any collective or social appropriation of its obligations rests on the ethos nurtured in the hearts of individuals and expressed in their actions and intentions toward one another.

41. We see a similar dynamic and expansive usage in the pragmatics of many a traditional logic—in the Mohist idea, for example, that *x* isn't always or just *x* and in the Confucian rectification of names ('If you are a brother, *be* a brother.'). Biblical usage, characteristically, expands the idea of purity dynamically, layering moral and spiritual meanings onto the physical and hygienic base concept. See Goodman, *God of Abraham,* 215–19. Similarly, expressions like 'holy of holies' and 'vanity of vanities' dynamically intensify the original (never wholly neutral) sense of a term. The Havdalah liturgy that marks the division between Sabbaths and holy days blesses God for distinguishing not, as usual, between the holy and the day-to-day but between the holy and the holy. Here the iridescent terms are parsed explicitly, resolving the verbal paradox: "who distinguishes holy from holy—the sanctity of the Sabbath day from holiday sanctity."

42. Justinian's Code opens by defining justice as "the steady, unwavering intent to give each his own." In fairness, this should be glossed, as some translate: To give each his due.

43. Ḥafetz Ḥayyim (Israel Meir Kagan), *Ahavat Ḥesed,* Introduction and Chapter 12.

44. Cf. Aristotle, *Nicomachaean Ethics,* IV 2: "A magnificent man is like an artist. For he sees what is fitting and can spend large sums tastefully. . . . Magnificence involves expenditures deemed laudable, as on worship of the gods—votive offerings, buildings, sacrifices, or . . . all enterprises that are proper objects of public-spirited

ambition, as when people think they ought to equip a chorus or a trireme, or entertain the city brilliantly. In all such cases, as we've said, we must keep in mind who the agent is and what his resources are. For the expense must be in keeping with his means.... Of private occasions the most suitable are those that happen only once—a wedding or the like.... A magnificent man will furnish his house as befits his means (for even a house is a sort of public ornament), and will spend by preference on things that are lasting (since they are the finest). And on every class of things he will spend appropriately. For the same things are not fit for gods and men, and what suits a temple does not suit a tomb.... A lovely ball or bottle is magnificent as a gift to a child, although the price is small and hardly extravagant" (1122a 33, 1122b 19–25, translating after Ostwald and after Urmson's revision of W. D. Ross, in Barnes, 2.1771–72).

45. Maimonides, *MT* VIII iv, Things Prohibited for the Altar, 7.11. According to the Midrash, Cain's offering was orts from his own meal of roasted grain and flax seeds. No wonder it was rejected. See *Pirkei d*[e]*-R. Eliezer*, ed. G. Friedlander, 153. In the same text, on the next page, Joshua ben Korḥah is quoted as explaining the biblical ban on linsey-woolsey (*sha'atnez*) as a reminder against mixing up Cain's offering with Abel's.

46. Exodus 21:33–35, Deuteronomy 22:8; Maimonides, *MT* XI, Book of Torts; Karo, *Shulḥan Arukh, Ḥoshen Mishpat* 389:1, 410:1, 20, 22; 415.

47. Exodus 23:4; Karo, *Shulḥan Arukh, Ḥoshen Mishpat* 259.

48. Maimonides, *MT* VII ii, Gifts to the Poor, 10.7, citing Leviticus 25:35: *If thy brother who dwelleth with thee grow poor and his means fail thou shalt uphold him, though he be a client or sojourner, that he may live with thee.* The verse is read in several ways, but the present reading is consistent with the norms rabbinic law draws from it.

49. *Midrash Tanḥuma* (echoed by Rashi at Genesis 3:6) teaches that the tree Eve and Adam ate from is unnamed in the Torah, since God was loath to bring grief to any of his creations—lest people say, "This is the tree that brought sorrow into the world."

50. See Maimonides, *MT* I ii, Ethical Laws, 6.3. Rabbi Israel Lipkin, known as Israel Salanter, reading that the ancient sage R. Ḥanokh kept his mind on higher things even while plying his trade as a shoemaker, took the rabbi's elevated thoughts as addressed not to supernal mysteries but to intense concentration on making each stitch perfect and each shoe as comfortable as he could so as not to shortchange the wearers. His work thus became a sacred service to his fellows. See Eliyahu Dessler, *Mikhtav Mei-Eliyahu* 1.34–35. Rabbi Avigdor Miller sees Jacob's care for Laban's flocks as exemplary of concern for another's goods (*Any torn by beasts I did not bring to you; I myself made up the loss*... Genesis 31:39).

51. Cf. the Ḥafetz Ḥayyim, *Ahavat Ḥesed*, 2.2.

52. Thus Alexander Susskind, *Y*[e]*sod v*[e]*-Shoresh ha-'Avodah*, 1.7–8.

53. The Ḥafetz Ḥayyim sees Joseph's concern for Pharaoh's downcast servants, even when himself imprisoned (Genesis 40:6–7), as exemplary of the concern we owe others. *Ḥovat ha-Sh*[e]*mirah* (Warsaw, 1920). Even sufferers, the Ḥatam Sofer stresses, must show sympathy for another's trouble.

54. Naḥmanides, at Leviticus 19:17.

55. God, the Midrash notes, did not cut short Abraham's pleas for the Cities of the Plain. He knew that Sodom and Gomorrah had not even the handful of innocents that would warrant saving the cities. Yet he heard out each stage of Abraham's plea (*Avot d^e-Rabbi Nathan* 37.12 on Genesis 18:33).

56. Maimonides, *MT* I v, Laws of Repentance, 3.14; I II, Ethical Laws, 6.3; Karo, *Shulḥan Arukh, Ḥoshen Mishpat* 228:4.

57. M^ekhilta, cited by Rashi at Exodus 21:1.

58. Ḥafetz Ḥayyim, *Ahavat Ḥesed*, Part 2, Chapter 2. The Talmud (B. Y^evamot 79a) treats Deuteronomy 13:18, which speaks of God's bestowal of mercy, not just as a showing of mercy but as an *imparting* of mercy—an even greater gift.

59. See Deuteronomy 7:12, 15:7–8, J. Kiddushin 1:1, and B. Y^evamot 79a. Maimonides, *MT* VII II, Gifts for the Poor, 10.1, relies on the traditional Hebraic equation of charity with justice:

> We must use more care in observing the commandments concerning charity than about any other affirmative *mitzvot*. For charity (*tz^edakah*) is the mark of the righteous (*tzaddik*) scion of Abraham our Forefather, as it is written: *I have known him that he may command his offspring and his house after him (to keep the way of the Lord), by doing charity and justice* (*tz^edakkah u-mishpat*, Genesis 18:19). Israel's sovereignty cannot be regained or the true faith upheld without charity. As it is written: *By charity* (*tz^edakah*) *shalt thou be established* (Isaiah 54:14). And Israel will be redeemed only by righteousness (*tz^edakah*), as it is written: *Zion will be redeemed through justice, and her returning exiles, through charity.* (Isaiah 1:27)

60. See Goodman, *God of Abraham*, 90–99; cf. Goodman, *On Justice*, 87–88, 99–103, 203; and see the Q&A section of this book.

61. See Goodman, *God of Abraham*, Chapter 1.

62. Rashi offers a midrash at Numbers 24:5 arguing that the overwhelming realization that led Balaam to change his curse to a blessing, voiced in his words, *How goodly are thy tents, O Jacob*—came when he saw that the Israelites' tent doors did not face one another, thus affording privacy to those within.

63. See Deuteronomy 23:18 and Goodman, *God of Abraham*, Chapters 5–6.

64. *M^esikhta Derekh Eretz Zuta*, Chapter 3, advises that one should practice confessing one's ignorance, since discomfort with doing so makes lying more likely. Lying is seen as an affront to God (cf. Psalms 101:7). But, like the warrant, the limits are not Kantian. One may lie to save a life or prevent an injury, to avoid being cheated or robbed, to avoid committing slander, to maintain one's humility, avoiding boasting or vainglory, and (as a last resort) to make peace between persons who have quarreled.

65. *Sifre* reasons: If it is forbidden to curse the deaf, a fortiori is it wrong to curse the hearing. The former are unwitting victims of vitriol, but the latter suffer in hearing themselves abused.

66. J. H. Hertz, at Leviticus 19:14, in *The Pentateuch*, 500. See B. P^{e}saḥim 22b; B. Mo'ed Katan 5a, 17a; B. Kiddushin 32a,b; B. N^{e}darim 62b; B. Bava M^{e}tzia 75b; B. Ḥullin 7b; B. Avodah Zarah 14a; Sifra *K^{e}doshim*. Maimonides, *MT* XI v, Laws of Murder and Preservation of Life, 12.12–14. Glossing Leviticus 19:14 as Negative Commandment 299, *Against giving misleading advice*, Maimonides writes: "Sifra (ad loc.) says: 'If one is "blind" about a certain matter and asks you for advice, do not give him advice unsuited to him'" (ed., Chavel, 2.278). The Sages generalize the prohibition to cover causing or abetting another's sin, enabling one who is blinded by passion to consummate a wrong, or giving him means to achieve it. The plain sense of the commandment still stands, of course. But Maimonides explains: We must give sincere and helpful advice when asked and not misleading or deceptive advice or ill-suited counsel. He heeds the *mitzvah* himself by veiling his intent in the *Guide to the Perplexed*, making its counsels accessible to those who will profit from them but obscure to the ill prepared, who have not seriously pondered the issues of biblical theology, philosophy and science.

67. Karo, *Shulḥan Arukh, Ḥoshen Mishpat* 70:1; Yitzḥaq Blauser, *P^{e}ri Yitzḥaq*, vol. 1, article 48; Shmuel Ehrenfeld, *Ḥatan Sofer* 138b.

68. Moshe Zalman Zaturenski, *'Eqev Anava: b^{e}-Birur Halakhot Ga'avah v^{e}-'Anavah*, 9.

69. B. Avodah Zarah 15b.

70. The Rabbis treat reproof as a form of consideration. Rabbi Akiva welcomed it in much the way that Socrates welcomed intellectual correction. False tact impedes execution of this generous if delicate responsibility; see B. Arakhin 16b.

71. Ibn Ezra and other traditional exegetes, noting that the prohibition against tale bearing is paired in the same verse with that against standing idly by at a scene of bloodshed, take the commandment to demand protection of others not just from bloodshed but from slander. For character assassination, too, is a grievous injury.

72. See Maimonides, *Book of the Commandments*, Positive Commandment 247, Negative Commandment 297, citing Deuteronomy 25:11–12; Maimonides, *MT* XI v, Laws of Murder and the Preservation of Life, 1.6–8, 1.10–16; B. Bava Kamma 26a, B. Sanhedrin 72b-73a, M. Bava Kamma 8.3, *Sifre Ki Tetzei*, and *K^{e}doshim*.

73. Deuteronomy 25:12. Maimonides asks why the permission to slay a would-be murderer does not extend to the preemption of idolatry or desecration of the Sabbath. His answer: murder is irreparable, but the idolater or Sabbath breaker may yet repent. See *Guide* III 40, ed. Munk, 3.87b.

74. The Rabbis derive the provisos of tact and privacy from the linkage of the biblical obligation to reprove one's neighbor with the further stipulation that one must not "bear sin on his account" (B. Arakhin 16b; Sifra to Leviticus 19:17). See Maimonides, *MT* I 11, Ethical Laws, 6.7; *Book of the Commandments*, Negative Commandment 303. Reproof itself is Positive Commandment 205: "We are commanded to reprove anyone committing a sin or so disposed. . . . One may not say, 'I am not going to sin; and if someone else does, that's between him and God.' That attitude is repugnant to the Torah." The obligation of reproof does not expire even when

prior admonitions have gone unheeded; one must persist, gently but firmly, "even a hundred times" (B. Bava M^etzia 31a). The Ḥafetz Ḥayyim glosses the story of Abraham's admonishing Avimelech about the well his servants had taken over (Genesis 21:25), explaining that it was the wrong, not the injury, that prompted the reproof. The motive was not a stinging reproach but correction of a wrong. Avimelech was the beneficiary. Hence Abraham's face-saving allowance that Avimelech's servants were at fault. He ought to have overseen them more closely, but room is left for his excuse: that the affront was unknown to him. The ethical message is the need to extinguish ego in reproof. Similarly, in the more intimate context of Isaac's admonition to Jacob not to marry a Canaanite woman, the Ḥafetz Ḥayyim notes that a blessing precedes the admonition, softening the sense of reproach. For the exercise of tact, see Elijah ben Shlomo Zalman, the Vilna Gaon, on Proverbs 10:20.

75. One is forbidden to shame another, even in private. Maimonides, *MT* I 11, Ethical Laws, 6.8. Even a stare or gesture or an allusion to the disgrace of another's relative is forbidden. It is not enough to avoid only acts that would embarrass oneself. The standard set by *love thy neighbor as thyself* is avoidance of anything that would embarrass the other. Further, one must not shame even a child who is old enough to experience embarrassment, and one's own spouse and child are included among those one may not embarrass. Y^evamot 8.3 explains that the sin offering and general burnt offering were slaughtered in the same place in the Temple to avoid shaming those who brought the former. Similarly, the core daily prayers are recited silently so as not to shame those who confess their sins before God in prayer (B. Soṭah 32b).

76. Sin is normally called slipping or stumbling in Hebrew. Thus, in Lamentations 1:8–9: *Jerusalem hath stumbled badly. That is why she is mocked. Having seen her exposed, her admirers all now scorn her, and she can only sigh and shrink back, filth in her skirts.* Cf. Sifra to Leviticus 26:37; B. Sanhedrin 27b.

77. See R. H. Charles, *A Critical and Exegetical Commentary on the Book of Daniel*, citing Morris Jastrow, "*Ro'eh* and *ḥozeh* in the Old Testament." Compare Muḥammad's protest that he was not a *kāhin*—a finder of lost camels.

78. The Qur'ānic obligation to ordain what is right and prohibit what is wrong springs from similar moral sensibilities. Its channelization in the diverse Islamic *madhāhib* has not begun to exhaust its moral relevance. See Michael Cook, *Commanding Right and Forbidding Wrong in Islamic Thought*; and Goodman, *Islamic Humanism*, 92–96.

79. See Eugene Garver, *Aristotle's* Rhetoric, and *For the Sake of Argument.*

80. See Ezekiel 17:2, 24:3 1 Kings 5:12; cf. Maimonides, *Guide*, Introduction.

81. Numbers 23:7, 18, 24:3, 15, 20, 21, 23; Micah 2:4; Isaiah 14:4. At Habakkuk 2:6–8 the arrogant and insatiable are put on notice: *Won't all take up their poesy (mashal) against him, a riddling bitingly against him, saying "O you who are amassing what is not yours—how long!—piling up the burden of your debt! Your creditors will arise soon enough, waking and rousting you. You'll be despoiled by them, just as you despoiled many nations"*; cf. Proverbs 1:6. Prophetic voices warn against becoming

a proverb or parable (*mashal*)—an object lesson and a byword; see Deuteronomy 28:37, 1 Kings 9:7.

82. Richard Wilbur, *Collected Poems 1943–2004*, 120–21.

83. In *William Rush and his Model* (1908, Honolulu Academy of Art), Eakins recasts a theme long essayed in his earlier works and brought to fruition in *William Rush Carving his Allegorical Figure of the Schuylkill River* (also 1908).

84. See Lenn Goodman, *Judaism, Human Rights and Human Values*, 110–18.

85. See L. E. Goodman, "Naked in the Public Square," forthcoming.

86. See Thomas Hobbes, *De Cive*, Chapter 12 § 6:

> It is a common doctrine, that faith and holiness are not acquired by study and natural reason, but are always supernaturally infused, and inspired into men. Which, if it were true, I understand not why we should be commanded to give an account of our faith; or why any man, who is truly a Christian should not be a prophet; or lastly, why every man should not judge what is fit for him to do, what to avoid, rather out of his own inspiration, than by the precepts of his superiors or right reason. A return therefore must be made to the private knowledge of good and evil; which cannot be granted without the ruin of all governments. This opinion hath spread itself so largely through the whole Christian world, that the number of apostates from natural reason is almost become infinite. And it sprang from sick-brained men, who having gotten good store of holy words by frequent reading of the Scriptures, made such a connexion of them usually in their preaching, that their sermons, signifying just nothing, yet to unlearned men seemed most divine; for he whose nonsense appears to be a divine speech must necessarily seem to be inspired from above.

Cf. *Leviathan* Part II, Chapters 29, 36, where Hobbes lists among the doctrines poisonous to a commonwealth the "seditious" opinion that "every private man is judge of good and evil actions" and that "whatever a man does against his conscience is sin," that "he that hath sovereign power is subject to the civil laws," "that every private man has an absolute propriety in his goods" to the exclusion of the sovereign, "that the sovereign power may be divided." Hobbes here inveighs against every principle of natural right, popular sovereignty, checks and balances, limited authority, the safeguards of private property, and, above all, private conscience. He pillories his adversaries by assigning to them an extreme and categorical affirmation of the rights and powers of conscience and conscientiousness, as if everyone who spoke out of conscience or inspiration were at once a pretended prophet and a rebel. The caricature leaves little room for real prophets, let alone loyal, conscientious, principled, or natural dissent.

87. See John Rawls, *Political Liberalism*. Rawls urges that all arguments that appeal to "comprehensive doctrines"—religious or metaphysically grounded claims about genuine right or wrong—are out of place in public policy discourse—a markedly pickwickian notion of liberalism.

88. Amos calls them *cows of Bashan that exploit the poor* (*ʿosqot dallim*) *and crush the needy* (4:1), parodying the self-praise of men who fancy themselves bulls, stags, rams, or stallions, as Francis Andersen and David Noel Freedman note in the Anchor Bible, ad loc. Amos inveighs against the ruinous taxation of the penurious (5:11) and contrasts the ivoried beds and elaborate palaces of the thoughtless oppressors (6:1–6), who devour and annihilate the helpless and can hardly wait for sabbaths or new moons to end so that they can resume selling grain *with a skant ephah and fat shekel* (8:4–7). No single study can exhaust the ethical issues raised by the idea of exploitation, but Alan Wertheimer, *Exploitation* invokes several key principles. From David Gauthier's *Morals by Agreement*, 145, he quotes the following: "no one can expect any other rational person to be willing to make a concession if he would not be willing to make a similar concession." This dictum sheathes its moral force in the language of rational expectations; taken prescriptively, it displays a key facet of our obligation to love one another as we love ourselves. Even so, the formula remains tepid, since it neglects the affirmative obligations of love, or charity, or social responsibility. Social negligence can itself be a form of exploitation. Wertheimer supplements Gauthier by appeal to intuitions about fairness and the values of openness and friendship—parallel to the claims of *reʿut*. He opens up these envelopes to address matters of need, exigency, risk, and the capital and opportunity costs of reliably meeting needs and sharing risks in a community.

89. Gates, biblically, are public squares; see Genesis 19:1, 22:17, Ruth 4:1–2, Proverbs 31:31. People in ancient times often lived well beyond the city walls, withdrawing within them in time of siege. So the gates, by metonymy, were public places, the city's agoras.

90. *Shivʿah mitzvot bᵉnei Noʼaḥ*. For the rabbinic concept of the seven commandments applicable to all descendants of Noah, see David Novak, *The Image of the Non-Jew in Judaism*; *Natural Law in Judaism*, Chapter 6; and Nahum Rakover, *Law and the Noahides*.

91. See Goodman, *God of Abraham*, 119.

92. See Goodman, *God of Abraham*, 97; *On Justice*, 110, with 46, 52–55, 58, 104.

93. Babies do not have, and tyrants do not use, moral sensibilities of much subtlety or stability. But babes are eager to learn. Tyrants reject moral learning. They devour lands, goods, and persons, testing the limits of tolerance not in the interest of accommodation but in the service of violent and oppressive domination. They chew up and spit out the norms they encounter, exploiting, deforming, and distorting them. If a tyrant is one who seeks to shape the world around his demands and to conform all things to his own passions, the Nietzschean hero, as a re-maker of values, fails by the old Socratic test of pursuing aims not critically examined. The tyrannical person has not asked, quite specifically, how human flourishing comports with moral isolation.

94. The Talmud (B. Bava Batra 60b, B. Bava Mᵉtzia 107b) admonishes us to correct ourselves before correcting others. But that caution against priggishness does not void the obligation of reproof—or rendering aid—nor does a failure of introspection render a rebuke invalid. Still, correction does begin at home. In a homiletic

gloss, Bunim of Parshischo reads *My teaching shall drop as rain, my speech distill like the dew* (Deuteronomy 32:2) as a hint that reproof does not always yield an immediate change of course but works subtly and over time.

95. Maimonides argues that worldly gains and losses are ultimately inconsequential and not worth a retaliatory response (*MT* I ii, Ethical Laws, 7.7).

96. Naḥmanides, at Leviticus 19:17.

97. Halakhically, one who so much as raises his hand against his fellow is disqualified from serving as a witness in court; Karo, *Shulḥan Arukh, Ḥoshen Mishpat* 34:4.

98. Kant, *Groundwork*, 13.

99. Kant, *Groundwork*, 10.

100. Kant, *Groundwork*, 11.

101. Kant, *Groundwork*, 11.

102. See Goodman, *On Justice*, esp. Chapter 1.

103. Cf. the more prudentially phrased advice of Proverbs 25:21–22.

104. Maimonides, *Eight Chapters*, 4, ed. Gorfinkle, 26–27 in the Hebrew, 65 in the English).

105. See Maimonides, *Eight Chapters*, 4.

106. Psalm 19:8, as glossed by Maimonides at *Eight Chapters*, 4.

107. The halakhists note that one who has made use of fallen grains, for example, say by baking bread from their flour, owes compensation to the poor. Isaac Abravanel accounts the *mitzvah* of assigning forgotten sheaves and fruit to the poor and dependent as a mark of freedom, liberality of spirit, and confidence in God's provision for our needs. Baḥya ben Asher notes that this *mitzvah* highlights the importance of anonymous charity.

108. Widows and orphans are accorded special protections via the biblical proviso against ill-treating them (Exodus 22:21). As Rashi notes (ad loc., citing the *M^ekhilta*), no one, of course, is to be mistreated. But these vulnerable persons are due special consideration—even if wealthy. They must, as Maimonides explains, be treated kindly and respectfully, not overtaxed with work or hard words, let alone cursed or struck; one must protect their property more carefully than one's own (*MT* I ii, Ethical Laws, 6.10). Does that last proviso make the special treatment of widows and orphans a freestanding commandment rather than a corollary of *love thy neighbor as thyself*? On the contrary, like the other demands of charity and special regard, it is a direct implication of the recognition that anyone is vulnerable to loss or disadvantage. The reasoning is not prudential: Not 'I will look after others in hopes that others would look after me in similar circumstances.' Rather, the consideration is strictly moral, based on the recognition that all are entitled to the same consideration that one would hope for in a comparable plight.

109. Joseph Karo, *Yoreh De'ah* 250:1.

110. Maimonides, *MT* XIV iv, Laws of Mourning, 14.1, citing M. Pe'ah 1.1 and B. Shabbat 127a.

111. See Exodus Rabbah 26.2, citing Micah 7:18; Leviticus Rabbah at 19:2. Spinoza reflects the moral outlook of these ancient texts when he argues (*Ethics*, Part 4,

Proposition 46): "He who lives by the guidance of reason strives, insofar as he is able, to repay another's hatred, anger, contempt, and the rest, with love and generosity." The Book of Proverbs takes a mildly cynical tone, urging: *When thine enemy falleth, do not rejoice; let not thy heart be glad if he stumble, lest the Lord see and it displease Him and He turn his wrath away from him* (Proverbs 24:17). Again: *If thine enemy be hungry, give him bread, and if he be thirsty, give him water to drink. For that will heap brands upon his head, and the Lord will requite thee* (Proverbs 25:21). Such counsels play to a presumption of spite. But they place God above our petty enmities: God requites the generous act, even when it was undertaken in the wrong spirit.

The cynic is reminded, however, that God might well favor the underdog. So the attitude that passes for worldliness is meant to find itself wanting. The acts of kindness that the text recommends may help to dissolve the cyncism it presumes.

112. Imperfect obligations are traditionally defined as duties that create no rights, duties whose violation is not unjust. But that seems a bit paradoxical. More coherently, I would say, an imperfect obligation is one that creates no *specific* rights. Thus, I have an obligation to develop my talents. It does not oblige me to take voice lessons. But it is wrong for me to neglect every talent I have. An imperfect obligation entails a more general perfect obligation: I do have an obligation to cultivate my talents prudently and appropriately, even though that does not tell me just how it should be done. For knowing that I have an obligation does not define its scope and character, tenor and tone. I have an obligation to provide charitable aid. My means and sympathies will modulate its fulfillment. So will the charitable acts and choices of others. If I give no charity, I am culpable and remiss, and worthy recipients (on the Mosaic account) *are* deprived of what is theirs by right. My general obligation does not specify the recipients or modalities of my giving. But even these are not wholly arbitrary. Unmet needs as well as my own capabilities must modulate my choices; considerations of tact and anonymity, self-sufficiency and dependency, and the likelihood of lasting benefit are among the factors I must consider. An imperfect obligation is no less real and no more appropriately halfhearted than a perfect obligation. It lacks only the specificity of a perfect obligation.

113. See Plato, *Laws* 719E, where laws with a preface setting out their reasons are deemed the proper treatment of free and rational citizens.

114. Hillel compared his frequenting the baths to the work of the custodians who washed the emperor's statues: Our bodies are God's icons. Even an executed criminal's corpse may not be exposed overnight but must be taken down and buried; Deuteronomy 21:22–23, B. Y^{e}vamot 79a, B. Sanhedrin 38b, 45b–47a, B. Bava Kamma 82b, B. Shabbat 30b; M. Kiddushin 4.1, M. Nazir 7.1; *Sifre*, Ki Tetze; Maimonides, *MT* XIV I, Sanhedrin, 15, and *MT* XIV IV, Mourning, 14; *The Commandments*, Positive Commandments 230–31, Negative Commandment 66.

CHAPTER 2

1. J. N^{e}darim 9:4, 41c; Sifra K^{e}doshim 4.12, and Genesis Rabbah 24.7. The two *tanna'im* were contemporaries. Akiva was martyred by the Romans after supporting

the Bar Kokhva Rebellion. Ben-Azzai died young, unmarried, and unordained, his early death linked by tradition with his mystical explorations.

2. The Rabbis find this sense in the parataxis of the blessing with the mention of Seth's being begotten in Adam's image, which was God's image, of course, as Ibn Ezra and Naḥmanides remind us, ad loc.

3. See Nahum Sarna, *The JPS Commentary* Genesis, 12.

4. Sarna, *The JPS Commentary* Genesis, 12.

5. On Genesis 1:26–27, see Sarna, *The JPS Commentary* Genesis, 12–13.

6. B. Sanhedrin 38a. The same passage combats infection of our morals by genetic determinism—lest the wicked, as the Rabbis put it, seek exoneration or the righteous find complacency in their lineage.

7. Naḥmanides ad Gen. 5:3.

8. Shmuel Sambursky was fond of contrasting the preciousness of the unique in Hebraic texts with the prizing of the universal among Greek writers, and their corresponding tendency to problematize the particular under the notions of idiosyncrasy, materiality, and the accidental as distinguished from the essential. Human uniqueness is, of course, one way in which we humans reflect the divine image, since God too is unique. Spinoza is much in tune with the Judaic sources when he transforms the Aristotelian and ultimately Platonic idea of essences, making all essences unique and dynamic, rather than static and universal.

9. Thus Pope in the *Anchor Bible: Job*, 288, 295.

10. Baḥya ibn Paquda, *Kitāb al-Hidāya ilā Farā'iḍ al-Qulūb*, 2.4, trans. Mansoor, 158. I translate from the Arabic, ed. Yahuda, 103.

11. The would-be architects of artificial languages try to ban all ambiguity, failing to see that ambiguity is not only a source of nuance in poetry and prose but an inevitable feature of every linguistic utterance. The ambiguities so prominent in natural languages reflect and protect the privacy of the mind, preserving the distinction of inner from outer, what is thought from what is spoken. See Goodman, *In Defense of Truth*, Chapter 4. Privacy is safeguarded prescriptively, by demands for discretion. Thus, halakhically, one has no right to repeat what another has said unless the source has explicitly authorized one to do so or made it public himself (B. Yoma 4b; cf. B. Sanhedrin 31a).

12. Thus Genesis 1:27, and the *Alphabet of Akiva*, 59; see Louis Ginzburg, *Legends of the Jews*, 2.4 and 5.63, note 3.

13. See Menachem Kellner, *Must a Jew Believe Anything?*

14. See Hermann Cohen, *Religion of Reason out of the Sources of Judaism*. Cohen himself was no reductionist, but he sublimated the idea of God in an ethical direction by following Kant in making God the guarantor of the everlasting progress that Kant had adapted from Moses Mendelssohn's vision of immortality. For Cohen, that progress in turn was interpreted in socialist terms. His words: "man's hope is translated into faith when he no longer thinks of himself alone, that is, of his salvation in the here and now, or of his eternal salvation (the latter, if I may say so, with calculating sanctimoniousness). Hope is translated into faith when man associates the future with the emergence of a community whose concerns will reach

beyond its everyday concrete reality. Such a community will not be composed merely of man's immediate circle of friends or family nor will it include only those who share his own cherished beliefs; indeed it will even cut across the borders of his own country because it will represent the community of mankind." Translated from Hermann Cohen's *Jüdische Schriften* by Eva Jospe, in *Reason and Hope*, 123–24. For my own attempt to situate the messianic ideal between reform and apocalypse, see Goodman, *On Justice*, Chapter 5. On Cohen's achievement, see Ernst Cassirer, "Hermann Cohen"; Michael Zank, *Reconciling Judaism and Cultural Consciousness* and *The Idea of Atonement in the Philosophy of Hermann Cohen*. For Mendelssohn's vision of immortality and its appropriation by Kant, see Mendelssohn, *Phaedon*, and Alexander Altmann, *Moses Mendelssohn: A Biographical Study*.

15. Cf. Rabbi Simeon in M. Avot 2.18: "In prayer, do not make your prayer a chore but a plea for grace (*taḥanun*) before the All-inclusive—as it is said, *He is gracious (ḥanun) and compassionate, long suffering, abundant in love (ḥesed), and relenting of ill* (Joel 2:13)—and do not think of yourself as wicked." For devotion and intent are not synonymous with a sense of guilt. Reflecting on sin and self-respect, Joseph Hertz comments on that last by citing Maimonides on the dangers of giving up on oneself and quotes Aḥad Ha-ʿAm (Asher Ginzburg): "Nothing is more dangerous for a nation or an individual than to plead guilty to imaginary sins. Where the sin is real—by honest endeavor the sinner can purify himself. But when a man has been persuaded to suspect himself unjustly—what *can* he do? Our greatest need is emancipation from self-contempt, from this idea that we are really worse than all the world." *Sayings of the Fathers*, ed. Hertz, 42.

16. See Baḥya, *K. al-Hidāya ilā Farā'iḍ al-Qulūb*, Introduction, and Part I; tr. Mansoor, 85–121.

17. Gordon Kaufman, *God the Problem*.

18. See Ikhwān al-Safā', *The Case of the Animals vs. Man before the King of the Jinn*, 193–96.

19. That, as I have argued, and no notion of blind faith is the core message of the biblical story of the binding of Isaac; see Goodman, *God of Abraham*, Chapter 1.

20. Ḥafetz Ḥayyim, *Ahavat Ḥesed*, Part 2, Chapter 2.

21. Confronting the death of a loved one, we call God *Dayyan 'emet*, the true Judge: not that God's judgment concocts the truth arbitrarily or simply declares true what creatures must therefore accept but because God's judgment *is* true, that is, just, fair, truthful and trustworthy, intrinsically.

22. The Talmud (B. Bava M^etzia 32b) calls the ban on causing needless suffering to animals biblical, but authorities differ as to its textual basis. Rashi (ad B. Shabbat 128b) cites Deuteronomy 22:4, commanding aid to another in righting his fallen beast of burden. Maimonides (*Guide* III 17) looks to the rebuke of Balaam for beating his ass when it balked at the sight of the angel blocking his way (Numbers 22:32). Others cite the Noahidic prohibition against consuming a limb torn from a living beast, which reflects the dietary ban on blood that is linked in turn with the permission to Noah's descendants to eat animal flesh (Genesis 9:3–4). Still others cite *walk in God's ways* (Deuteronomy 13:5, 28:9), which the Rabbis take to

call for emulation of God's mercy. See B. Soṭah 14a, B. Shabbat 133b; Leviticus Rabbah 24; *Sifre* to Deuteronomy 10:12; *Guide* I 54; cf. "Eight Chapters," 5, 7. Most often cited in aggadot protective of animals is *His mercies are on all His works* (Psalms 145:9)—including insects and reptiles, as *ᶜEtz Yosef* adds (at Genesis Rabbah 33.3).

23. The broad imperative against wanton destruction, *bal tashḥit* (B. Kiddushin 32a), rests on the protection of fruit trees (in peace as well as in war). It is understood to forbid killing animals for convenience (B. Ḥullin 7b), wasting fuel (B. Shabbat 67b), and eating extravagant foods when simpler ones are available (B. Shabbat 140b). The ban on destructive behavior extends to the protection of household goods, articles of clothing, foodstuffs, buildings, and springs. See Maimonides, *MT* XIV v, Laws of Kings and Wars, 6.8–10. At *MT* XIV iv, Laws of Mourning, 14.24, we read: "A person should be taught not to be wasteful and not to ruin or spoil garments—better to give them to the poor and not just leave them to the worms and maggots. So anyone who goes to excess in clothing the dead violates the commandment *bal tashḥit*."

24. Maimonides, *MT* XIV v, Laws of Kings and Wars, 6.7.

25. See Rashi, citing *Sifre* ad loc.

26. Maimonides, *MT* XIV v, Laws of Kings and Wars, 7.15, citing Jeremiah 48:10.

27. The ordinance of the Sabbath at Exodus 31:16–17 closes with the unusual form *va-yinaffash*, usually translated "and He rested"—or perhaps more properly, "refreshed Himself" (cf. 2 Samuel 16:14). Thus:

> *The children of Israel shall keep the Sabbath, observing the Sabbath throughout their generations as an eternal covenant. Between Me and the children of Israel it is an everlasting sign that in six days the Lord made heaven and earth and on the seventh day ceased* (shabbat) *and refreshed Himself.*

Etymologically, the verb looks like it should mean "took a breather." But, midrashically, the verses, chanted in the Sabbath liturgy and in the Kiddush prayer that sanctifies each Shabbat, the idea that the Eternal was fatigued by the work of creation is eschewed, and the word is taken not reflexively, as signifying that God rested, but causatively, as its grammatical form seems to require, yielding the sense that God infused an added breath of life and spirit into his human handiwork.

28. See Tacitus, *Complete Works*, 657–66. Even Aristotle was not prepared to reject the institution of slavery, since he could not conceive of the liberation of the human mind and spirit for anyone unless some were exploited as slaves. Leisure is necessary if human life is to be fully and truly human; and slaves, Aristotle argues, make leisure possible (see Aristotle, *Politics* II 9, VII 3, 14, 15). If we had automata to take care of our drudgery, things might be different, he reasons; but since we do not, slavery and the institutions that support it, including imperial warfare, remain necessary. Calling a slave a living tool, Aristotle writes:

> Tools are of varied sorts; some living and some lifeless. In the rudder a ship's pilot has a lifeless instrument; in the lookout, a living one. The servant too is an instrument of his instruments. For if every tool could do its own work,

> obeying or anticipating the will of others like the statues of Daedelus or the tripods of Hephaestus, of which the poet says 'of their own accord they entered the assembly of the gods' (*Iliad* 18.369), and in like manner if the shuttle wove and the plectrum touched the lyre, master craftsmen would not need workers, nor masters slaves. (*Politics* I 4, 1253b 27–1254a 1)

Aristotle finds it easier to conceive magical automata eliminating the need for slavery than to propose a universal day of rest or to project reciprocity of the sort that Gandhi instituted at his ashram, where even the Untouchables received massages from those of higher caste and even the latter took their turns at cleaning the latrines. For Aristotle's description of automata, see *De Motu Animalium* 7, 701b 1–14. The ingenious Hero might have sparked quite an ancient industrial revolution, since many devices that might have eased human labors were feasible within the parameters of technology available, say, in the Hellenistic age. But the most cunning devices were relegated to use as toys or in religious or theatrical spectacles. They might have been used to lighten human burdens, but slave labor was too readily and too cheaply available to make an alternative economically attractive. Here the circularity of Aristotle's line of rationalization becomes evident, as does the price to be paid when economic rather than moral values are made paramount.

29. See Genesis 38, Deuteronomy 25:5–10, and Y^{e}vamot. For the weight of the levirate obligation in patriarchal times, see Jon Levenson, *Resurrection and the Restoration of Israel*, 116–120. As he concludes that discussion: "the continuation of the family constitutes the biblical expectation of survival. . . . in the stories of Abraham and Judah, of Ruth and Job, death indeed threatens . . . the family itself. . . . evoking the terror that later generations (including our own) feel in the face of their personal death. . . . despite a long tradition of viewing the sin of Adam and Eve (and the mortality thought to go with it) as the most memorable event in Genesis, the great enemy in that book is not death as we think of it at all (still less is it sin) but death in the twin forms of barrenness and the loss of children" (119–20).

30. For the procedural protections of rabbnic law, see Mishnah Sanhedrin.

31. Jeremy Bentham, *Anarchical Fallacies* (1791–95).

32. There is no truth unless some truths are categorical. Making all truths only probable generates an infinite regress of probabilities: 'It's probable that it's probable that it's probable. . . .' In the same way, there are no imperatives unless some are categorical. If all imperatives are hypothetical, all norms become contingent. And if all imperatives are hypothetical, none has purchase; all are toothless. It never becomes simply obligatory to do as we ought, even if the stipulated conditions are met—for (on the incoherent assumption that all imperatives are hypothetical) even then there is no categorical obligation: If I must earn the right to what I've earned, I'll never get my pay. In the same way, crucially, there are no rights at all unless some rights are inviolable. My right to defend my rights, for example, cannot be bargained away without sapping all the rights it protects. That's one way of seeing that slavery is always wrong.

33. Utilitarians and pragmatists often see themselves and present themselves as guardians of rights; they do have certain favorites, like freedom of expression.

In the interest of those favorites, they will even (quietly) cheat on their favored metaphysic: In criticizing the death penalty, they may deny its deterrent impact, or, in defending pornography under the rubric of free expression, they may deny that invasive or demeaning images pose any risk or harm to women. They prefer to contest the facts rather than argue the moral merits of the case that a degraded or demeaning image holds the threat of more material harm. But the adamant stance such would-be liberals take acquires an a priori aura. Counterevidence from unhelpful studies is dismissed. And that suggests an underlying commitment not derivable on utilitarian grounds. Spelled out, the assumption would be that capital punishment is wrong regardless of its putative effects or that pornography, or lap dancing, deserves protection regardless of its impact on society at large or on the image, roles, and dignity of women in particular. Such arguments deserve to be contested. But that's hard to do when principled differences are draped in disputed facts. See Goodman, *Judaism, Human Rights and Human Values,* Chapter 4.

34. See Goodman, *On Justice,* esp. Chapter 1.

35. The example is not fanciful. Under Frequently Asked Questions on Animals and Morality (*www.animal-rights.com/arpage.htm*), we find Question 20: "A house is on fire and a dog and a baby are inside. Which do you save first?" Answers: "The one I save first tells us nothing about the ethical decisions we face. I might decide to save my child before I saved yours, but this certainly does not mean that I should be able to experiment on your child or exploit your child in some other way....—LK." Or again: "Like anyone else in this situation, I would probably save the one to which I am emotionally more attached. Most likely that would be the child. Someone might prefer to save his own beloved dog before saving the baby of a stranger. However, as LK states above, this tells us nothing about any ethical principles. DVH."

36. See Goodman, *On Justice,* 13–23.

37. See Goodman, *Judaism, Human Rights and Human Values,* 49–60.

38. Some here might think of fideistic, christological, or even Kierkegaardian readings of the binding of Isaac. But, as I've stressed already and apparently cannot stress too often, what the biblical narrative speaks of when it announces that on that mountain God revealed Himself (Genesis 22:14) is the true nature of God: that it is not the case, as so many have thought and still think, that the absolute God demands the absolute sacrifice, not just of all that we love but of all that we hold sacred and inviolable. On the contrary, God's demand is for love and trust, uprightness and justice. God does not become powerful through violence—or holy through any teleological suspension of the ethical. See Goodman, *God of Abraham,* Chapter 1.

39. My friend and colleague Amy-Jill Levine paints a marvelous picture of herself at the Pearly Gates, overhearing a man with a "red-letter Bible" protesting about her presence: "Jesus says here, in red letters, that he is the way. I've seen this woman on television.... She's not Christian; she's not baptized—she shouldn't be here!" A few minutes later, "a man about five foot three with dark hair and eyes" and disturbing "holes in his wrists" hears the complaint: "didn't you say that no one comes to the Father except through you?" Jesus answers: "if you flip back to the

Gospel of Matthew, which does come first in the canon, you'll notice in chapter 25, at the judgment of the sheep and the goats, that I'm not interested in those who say 'Lord, Lord,' but in those who do their best to live a righteous life, feeding the hungry, visiting people in prison"—which I can testify that Amy does. The red-letter man sputters: "But, but, that's *works righteousness.* You're saying she's earned her way into heaven?" Jesus answers, "I *am* not saying that at all. I *am* saying that *I am* the way, not you, not your church, not your reading of John's Gospel, and not the claim of any individual Christian or any particular congregation. *I am* making the determination, and it is by my grace that anyone gets in, including you. Do you want to argue?" Amy-Jill Levine, *The Misunderstood Jew*, 92–93.

40. Cf. Philip Quinn, *Divine Commands and Moral Requirements*, especially Chapter 1, for its response to Rachels, "God and Human Attitudes."

41. Ḥafetz Ḥayyim, *Ahavat Ḥesed*, Chapter 10; cf. Philo, *De Specialibus Legibus* I 23–27. In *De Decalogo* 108–10, Philo writes that those who serve only God or only man reach only the halfway mark of virtue. God Himself is a lover of mankind, so only those who serve man *and* God consummate the love of God. God is not fed by sacrifices, Philo insists. Rather, He is nourished by lives of piety and virtue; *Questions on Genesis* IV 9.

42. This was Aristotle's objection to Plato's appeal to our inner knowledge of pure Goodness: Such universal intuitions, even if we possess them, will not inform us about the specific doable good; *Nicomachaean Ethics* I 6, 1096b 15–25, 1097a 20–23. Aristotle answers his own question by treating the term 'good' as *pros hen* equivocal when applied to the widely diverse ends that are sought as goods. In the language of monotheism, the same idea would be articulated by saying that all good things are expressions of God's creative work and grace: Each manifests some particular or specific facet of God's infinite goodness. God Himself remains transcendent. Compare Maimonides' idea that the world of matter and form (that is, bodies, minds, and the rational principles that give order to bodies and make them intelligible to minds) is where the effects of God's work are seen; it is thus the realm where finite minds encounter what *we* call God's attributes. Compare, in turn, Spinoza's calling thought and extension attributes expressive of God's infinite reality. See *Ethics* Part 1, Definition 4, and Propositions 8–11; Goodman, "Matter and Form as Attributes of God in Maimonides' Philosophy"; Goodman, "What Does Spinoza Contribute to Jewish Philosophy," 34–38, 63–66; Goodman, "God and the Good Life."

43. John Quincy Adams hated slavery but could not conceive a way of ending it without violating the property rights of slaveholders. Nor did his vision extend so far as to recognize the wrongs wrought upon native Americans by the western spread of the civilization he loved. These outsiders to the American covenant seemed mere savages; and the lands they inhabited, mere waste, before their appropriation by the new commonwealth.

44. Cf. Genesis 1:27, 2:18–23. The ideal wife of Proverbs 31 is, of course, also the sole wife of her husband. Isaiah (8:3) refers to his wife in the language of monogamy, calling her *ha-nevi'ah.* Hosea (2:18) looks forward to a day when his

wife will no longer call him *ba'alī*, my lord, but simply *ishī*, my man or husband. Ezekiel (24:15–19) speaks poignantly of his wife's death and God's instructions as to his mourning for her. Citing these passages and Isaiah 54:6, *Can one give up the wife of his youth?*, Salo Baron argues: "Apparently marriage with more than one wife was never widespread in ancient Israel." Malachi (2:14), as Baron notes, treats it as an abomination to spurn one's lawful wife, the friend and bride of one's youth. The rabbinic effort to protect women from arbitrary divorce "reached its climax in the Shammaite school's restriction of divorce to cases of a wife's sexual infidelity (M. Gittin 9.10) and the analogous divorce laws of early Christianity." Baron, *A Social and Religious History of the Jews*, 1.112, 114.

45. Mishnah Yoma requires monogamy of the High Priest, and the Taqqanah of Rabbi Gershom ben Yehudah of Mainz, called M^{e}'or ha-Golah, the Light of the Exile, decreed monogamy for all Ashkenazi Jews in about the year 1000, making mandatory what had long been established practice. Rabbi Gershom also banned nonconsensual divorce. Polygamy was practiced, albeit rarely, by Jews in Muslim lands until fairly recent times. It died out as Sephardi Jews made their way to Israel.

46. See Hertz at Deuteronomy 23:16–17; cf. Leviticus 25:39–54. Commenting on the latter passage, Hertz remarks that rabbinic law forbids a master to give his Hebrew bondservants food or accommodation inferior to his own. He notes that Leviticus uses the same language as Exodus 1:13 when it forbids ruling over servants *with rigor*, and he explains that the accompaniment of that demand with the alternative *but thou shalt fear the Lord* is the Torah's way of underscoring the requirements of what Sifra calls "heart religion," which is, "part of natural piety and fundamental humanity in dealing with our fellowmen." The Rabbis apply the standard of manumission for an injured slave to non-Israelites; for Israelite slaves the rule is compensation, be they slaves or free; see at Exodus 21:20–21. Hertz notes that Hammurabi's Code penalizes those who injure *another's* slave, apparently taking it for granted that one would not normally harm one's own property and that if one did, the injury could only have been accidental or deserved. Capping the barbarities of the pagan classical world—exposure of ill slaves, extermination of redundant ones, condign punishment for those who sought escape—Hertz, in commenting on M. Avot, relates of ancient Rome: "Tacitus records that as late as the Empire the 400 slaves of one household were all put to death because they had been under their master's roof when he was murdered."

47. See McFayden, *A Guide to the Understanding of the Old Testament.*

48. See Goodman, *In Defense of Truth*, Chapter 9, and *On Justice*, Chapter 5.

49. Paraphrasing Elihu at Job 34:18, Saadiah argues: "munificence means bestowing more than is deserved. One does not call a giver lavish if he retains anything that ought rightfully to have been given. Munificence begins where fairness leaves off. Hence, since it is established that His bounty surpasses the lesser level, it goes without saying that He is fair." Again addressing Elihu's theodicy and in a similar vein, Saadiah writes: "the king deserves to rule only for his justice. So it is absurd that He be a rightful king and yet be vicious. Such a thing could occur only among humans through a struggle for power." In a third interpretive paraphrase

at the same juncture, Saadiah writes: "the doings of the Creator cannot be impugned and His judgment overruled by some denier. For it is absurd to impugn Truth itself." *The Book of Theodicy*, tr. Goodman, 360. Saadiah's argument rests on the Hebraic equation of truth with justice and on a Platonic conception of God as Truth. In both cases, the underlying assumption excludes regarding God's will as arbitrary or his acts as capricious.

50. Following Samuel David Luzzatto, Jeffrey Tigay notes in the JPS Deuteronomy, ad loc., "Proclaiming God's name means declaring His qualities, recounting His deeds. See Exodus 33:19, and especially 34:5: 'The Lord . . . proclaimed the name Lord . . . a God compassionate and gracious'; and Psalms 105:1–2: 'Proclaim His name, Proclaim His deeds . . . speak of all His wondrous acts.' Proclaiming God's qualities is a major theme of *Ha'azinu*, The Song of Moses at Deuteronomy 32:1–43. God's justice is epitomized in verse 4 and explicated throughout the poem."

51. Cf. the poem of Andrew Marvell, "On a Drop of Dew."

52. God's worship is unsullied by violence or decadence, so it can transcend epochal change, its core holding steady throughout history.

53. Philip Quinn rightly distinguishes questions about the grounding of objective values from questions about our sources of knowledge as to those values. Addressing the case of a moral thinker who believes that our sole access to knowledge of God's will in moral matters is "through moral inquiry of the usual sort," he argues: "If I have only a ruler, then the only way I can find out whether a certain triangular object is approximately equiangular may be first to measure its sides to determine whether it is approximately equilateral. But this restriction on my epistemic access to geometrical facts does nothing to falsify or undermine the necessary truth that something is an equilateral triangle if and only if it is an equiangular triangle." For similar reasons, Quinn argues, "it seems unreasonable to suppose" that the limitations on our access to knowledge of God's will render that will any the less prescriptive for us. *Divine Commands and Moral Requirements*, 44–45. Similarly, I would argue, a theist who regards God's commands as our sole reliable source of moral knowledge need not for that reason deem moral claims upon us any the less objective. Against James Rachels's notion that only an extreme theistic subjectivism is properly worshipful (and is thus incoherent, since it takes as worthy of worship a God whose arbitrariness and demands for surrender of our moral judgment makes that God manifestly unworthy of worship), Quinn responds: "Surely theists need only be committed to obeying God's commands because they are morally legitimate themselves; they need not be committed to obeying them simply because they are the decrees of a superior power. What could be more natural, then, than using reflective moral judgements as touchstones for determining which claims to moral authority might plausibly be regarded as divine? Doubtless many theists do in fact surrender their moral autonomy to human institutions and authorities, but then so do many non-theists. What seems clear is that a theist is not required by logic to suspend his moral judgement in the face of any human authority. Of course, a theist may be committed to the view that if God commands then he should obey, but he may not be able to justify the belief that God has

commanded a certain action without having good moral reasons to think that he ought to do what has been commanded." Quinn, *Divine Commandments,* 9.

54. See Jonah ben Abraham Gerondi, *Sha^carei T^eshuvah, The Gates of Repentance.* The Ḥafetz Ḥayyim lists truthfulness thirteenth among the Torah's affirmative commandments.

55. The parallelism in the Hebrew suggests that falsehood is wicked and truthfulness obligatory. I translate the verses in keeping with Saadiah's Arabic rendering.

56. Kant insists that a lie is dehumanizing even when internal, that is, even when one is lying to oneself:

> In the doctrine of Right an intentional untruth is called a lie only if it violates another's right; but in ethics, where no authorization is derived from harmlessness, it is clear of itself that no intentional untruth in the expression of one's thoughts can refuse this harsh name. For the dishonor (being an object of contempt) that accompanies a lie also accompanies a liar like his shadow. A lie can be an external lie (*mendacium externum*) or also an internal lie. By an external lie a man makes himself an object of contempt in the eyes of others; by an internal lie he does what is still worse: He makes himself contemptible in his own eyes and violates the dignity of humanity in his own person . . . annihilates his dignity as a man. A man who does not himself believe what he tells another (even if the other is a merely ideal person) has even less worth than if he were a mere thing; for a thing, because it is something real and given, has the property of being serviceable so that another can put it to some use. But communication of one's thoughts to someone through words that yet (intentionally) contain the contrary of what the speaker thinks on the subject is an end that is directly opposed to the natural purposiveness of the speaker's capacity to communicate his thoughts, and is thus a renunciation by the speaker of his personality, and such a speaker is a mere deceptive appearance of a man, not a man himself.
> (*The Metaphysics of Morals,* tr. Gregor, 225–26)

57. Saadiah, *ED* Introductory Treatise 5, tr. Rosenblatt, 19.

58. See Saadiah, *ED* III 2, ed. Kafih 119–20, tr. Rosenblatt 141–42; cf. *The Book of Theodicy,* tr. Goodman, 178–79.

59. At Genesis 27:12 Jacob fears a curse rather than a blessing if he deceives his father. Sanhedrin 92a endorses that fear and underscores it with a reference to Jeremiah 10:15, where idols are called a vain deceit. The rabbis, homiletically, make the equation commutative: lies are tantamount to idolatry. Citing Psalms 101:7, *He who speaks lies shall not be established before Mine eyes,* Sotah 42a warns that liars lose access to God's immanent presence in their lives.

60. Saadiah, *ED* V 7, citing Proverbs 28:6 and 2 Samuel 12:4, argues that honesty is dearest in the poor and deception gravest in the wealthy. Incentives and motives matter here; consequences come second.

61. At Job 18:4, as Saadiah reads the text, Bildad "hurls" at Job the epithet "self-savager." In defending his own innocence, Bildad reasons, Job has impugned

God's justice, in effect trying to shift the world to suit his preferences. The real outcome, Bildad argues, is that Job has condemned himself out of his own mouth—as any subjectivist must do. For to lie or (like a subjectivist) to try to construct the world around one's preferences and prejudices is to reject the very idea of truth and thus to condemn and deny whatever one claims, even as one claims it. Bildad errs, Saadiah argues, in assuming that only the guilty and never the innocent suffer, but Bildad is right, on Saadiah's account, in seeing subjectivism and special pleading as affronts to God. See *The Book of Theodicy*, tr. Goodman, 282 and *ED* I 3, tr. Rosenblatt, 80.

62. Cf. Goodman, *God of Abraham*, 97–98, 183–84.

63. My student Greg Caramenico sees a distinctively Jewish outlook here, very different from the thought of some Christians, that reason is corrupted by the fall, and different too from the Ash^{c}arite idea that right is right only because God makes it so. I confess here to that degree of optimism about reason; I think my student's labeling is roughly accurate, although not comprehensive, since many Christians, Muslims, and others share my views, and some Jews do not. There are Jewish legal positivists and even theistic subjectivists. So the division is not strictly confessional. But my aim is not an empirical doxology, a natural history of Jewish thinking and experience. Rather, I seek a philosophically grounded view, coherent in itself and in harmony with the best that I can find in Jewish and philosophical sources. A crucial premise of my argument: that we humans have some moral knowledge—not infallible or ineligible for outside help but capable of telling right from wrong reliably, at least some of the time, and thus judging what kind of norms are worthy of the divine. To predicate all obligations on revelation falsely assumes that we know in advance what to treat as revelation and leaves the scriptural fideist knotted in circularity. These issues rise to the surface for fuller discussion in the Q&A section that follows the body of these lectures.

64. For the urgency of the need for an heir in a biblical society where one's project and fulfillment were conceived in those terms, see Levenson, *Resurrection and the Restoration of Israel*, 109–21, where, as we have noted, the ancient laws and customs of levirate marriage are explained in the same terms.

65. Cf. Deuteronomy 25:3: corporal punishment is abated, *lest thy brother be disgraced before your eyes*; B. Makkot 23a. Rashi's source is Shimon Ḥasida or Shimon bar Yoḥai, B. B^{e}rakhot 43b, B. K^{e}tuvot 67b, B. Soṭah 101b.

66. Judah's reluctance to leave Joseph to die and his politic compromise in proposing his sale to a passing caravan of Ishmaelites (Genesis 37:26–27) do not make him a moral paragon, but they do reveal a flicker of conscience. What, then, of his peremptory command just three months after the encounter with Tamar, which had itself occurred *at about the same time that Judah left his brothers* (Genesis 38:1), condemning his pregnant daughter-in-law: *take her out to be burnt* (Genesis 38:24)? Some Hebrew commentators seek to rationalize Judah's harsh order, but the others contextualize that command to its barbarous moment. The celebrated challenge of Jesus *Let him who is without sin cast the first stone* (John 8:9) revisits the bias toward mercy that the Torah brings to Tamar's story. Severe toward the judgmental

but compassionate toward the offending woman, his posture, brilliantly limned by Rembrandt, has rabbinic precedent: The Torah, drawn in conflicting directions by its demand for two witnesses in a capital case and its abhorrence for adultery as a devastating breach of trust, in the instance of a woman charged with adultery on insufficient evidence allowed into its code the alien notion of trial by ordeal (Numbers 5:12–27). But the Mishnah so hems this law about as to make it inoperative, declaring in the end that ancient accusers might have been presumed innocent, but since that presumption was no longer safe, no one any longer had the standing to demand the ordeal. See Goodman, *God of Abraham*, 137–38, 298 n. 77.

67. See Genesis Rabbah 35.1, 6, 8–10. W. Gunter Plaut writes: "Why was the Tamar story included in the Jacob-Joseph cycle and why was it preserved with such careful attention to detail? Perhaps the intriguing nature of the incident played a role, but the major reason does not lie in historical, literary, or dramatic factors. The chief figures are Tamar and Judah, and Judah is the ultimate preserver of the house of Israel. From the union of the tribal progenitor and his daughter-in-law, Perez is born, and from him will descend the person and the house of David. The Tamar tale thus became an important part of the David saga, just as the Book of Ruth did in later days. We are told that Ruth and Boaz would be forebears of the king, and that Boaz traced his line to Perez, son of Tamar and Judah (Ruth 4:12–22)." *The Torah: A Modern Commentary*, 253. Biblical interest is clearly aroused by an ultimately messianic genealogy. But Rashi's concern is moral. The Midrash conflates the genealogical and moral issues, coloring the character of the protagonists with expectations as to their descendants; cf. Genesis Rabbah 35.2, 7 on the purity of Tamar's motive. As Patriarchs and Matriarchs, the figures are cleansed morally in the Midrash. But it is for the sake of moral edification that they are cast as paragons.

68. Cf. Maimonides, *Guide* I 2. The story of Tamar, as read by the rabbinic Midrash, dramatizes the primacy of the ethical over ancient patriarchal norms in much the way that the narrative of the binding of Isaac dramatizes the centrality of the ethical over ancient cultic norms regarding God.

69. A. C. Grayling, *The Meaning of Things*, 100.

70. Cf. Goodman, *On Justice*, 203; and see the Q&A section.

71. See Rawls, *Political Liberalism*, and Goodman, "Naked in the Public Square."

72. Cf. R. Yehudah Loeb Chasman, *Or Yaḥel*, vol. 2, ad Exod. 1:17.

73. See Sifra ad loc.; Maimonides, *Book of the Commandments*, Positive Commandment 9.

74. Maimonides, *MT* I i, Foundations of the Torah, 5.11.

75. Ben-Zoma's query and his response are part of the famous series, all at M. Avot 4.1: "Who is wise? One who learns from all men? Who is a hero? One who masters his bent. Who is rich? One who is delighted with what he has. Who deserves honor? One who honors God's creatures."

76. Joseph Hertz, in his translation of *Pirkei Avot, Sayings of the Fathers*, at M. Avot 1.12.

77. B. B^{e}rakhot 58a.

78. Quoted by Hertz, ad M. Avot 4.1. The passage in full:

> Ben Zoma said, Who is wise? He who learns from all men; as it is said, *From all my teachers I have gotten understanding* [Psalms 119:99; Ben-Zoma plays on the psalmist's words, *mi-kol m^e^lam^e^dai hiskalti*, where context might seem to require: *more than all my teachers have I gained insight*]. Who is mighty? He who subdues his passions [literally, his *yetzer*, or "bent"]; as it is said, *He that is slow to anger is better than the mighty, and he that ruleth over his spirit than he that taketh a city* [Proverbs 16:32; "Another noble definition of 'mighty,' given by the Rabbis," Hertz notes, "is 'he who turns his enemy into a friend."] Who is rich? He who delights in his portion; as it is said, *When thou eatest the labour of thine hands, happy art thou, and it shall be well with thee* [Psalms 128:2. Hertz quotes the Hasidic Rabbi Elimelech here: "Whatever a man's occupation, the wares in which he deals, or the work he performs; so long as he respects his wares, honours his calling and is happy in his work–they will be a source of sanctification to him, and of usefulness to his fellow-men."]: *happy art thou*—in this world; *and it shall be well with thee*—in the hereafter. Who is worthy of honour? He who honors his fellow-men; as it is said, *For them that honor me I will honor, and they that despise me shall be held in contempt* (1 Samuel 2:30)."

The inference is that one shows honor to God by honoring his creatures.

79. The *Ḥinnukh* offers a prudential rationale.

80. Naḥmanides refers to B. Bava Kamma 100a, where the supererogatory is called *lifnim mi-shurat ha-din*, beyond the sentence of the law. Often cited to the same effect: *that thou mayest walk in the way of the good and keep to the course of the righteous* (Proverbs 2:20); see B. Bava M^e^tzia 30b. For supererogation in Jewish law, see Shilo, "Lifnim Mishurat Hadin"; Goodman, *God of Abraham*, 106, 157, 192.

81. Naḥmanides at Deuteronomy 6:18.

82. Baḥya ibn Paquda, *Ḥovot* 2.2, citing Isaiah 5:12, B. Shabbat 75a.

83. Novak, *The Theology of Naḥmanides Systematically Presented*, 112.

84. My reading of the story is enriched by my colleague Jack Sasson's recounting of the narrative, since his vast erudition in the manners and customs of the ancient Near East reveals the markings of royal matchmaking in the tale, as well as portents for posterity. See Jack M. Sasson, "Wooing Rebecca: How Isaac Got a Wife" (University of North Carolina, Charlotte, Loy H. Witherspoon Lecture, April 21, 2005).

85. The aggadic elaborations of the Midrash often embroider on a text and may go off on tangents. So the intent of Genesis in the telling of any tale will hardly exhaust the ingenuity of later readers in glossing it. But thematically, midrashic flights of fancy typically hew closely to the authentic spiritual and ethical themes of scripture.

86. Yoḥanan ben Zakkai, a disciple of Hillel's, founded the rabbinic academy at Yavneh. Among his achievements was the abolition of the ordeal of the suspected adulteress.

87. On Exodus 20:22, *M^e^khilta d^e^-Rabbi Ishmael*, 2.290. For the tools, see Maimonides, *MT* VIII i, Temple Service, 1.15. Likewise with the ramp: "The stones of the altar have no sense of what is proper or improper. Yet God said that you should not treat them disrespectfully. It is therefore only logical that you must refrain from treating another person with disrespect. For he is made in the image of Him who spoke and brought the world into being" (*M^e^khilta*, 2.291–92).

88. *Avot d^e^-R. Nathan*, version 1, 3.14; cf. *M^e^khilta*, Amalek, ed. Lauterbach, 2.189–90. See Urbach, *The Sages*, 1.566, 575, 592.

89. See the Q&A, where this claim is taken up.

90. See B. Bava Kamma 92a.

91. At M. Avot 1.6, Joshua ben Peraḥyah is cited for the dictum "Judge everyone favorably," or, more literally: tilt the balance of judgment in favor of all. Maimonides, *MT* I v, Laws of Repentance, 4.4, notes that thinking ill of others is one of five commandments that people rarely repent of breaking—imagining that such thoughts have done no harm and not realizing that even suspicion of the innocent is an inherent wrong.

92. See Goodman, *God of Abraham*, Chapter 6.

93. In keeping with the Hebrew usage, Spinoza equates *pietas* with *humanitas*, the desire to act to the benefit of one's fellows. As we have noted, he distinguishes it sharply from *ambitio*, the desire to act so as to please others or simply win their praise. See *Ethics* Part 3 Proposition 29 Scholium, and Definitions of the Emotions 43–44.

94. Plato's parallel to the command in Leviticus 19:2, *You shall be holy, for I the Lord thy God am holy*, is found in the *Theaetetus* (176), where Socrates tells Theodorus: "Evils, Theodorus, can never be done away with, for the good must always have its contrary; nor have they any place in the divine world; but they must needs haunt this region of our moral nature. That is why we should make all speed to take flight from this world to the other; and that means becoming divine as far as we can, and that again is to become righteous with the help of wisdom." The Mosaic Torah does not conceive the task of becoming as like to God as humanly possible in terms of flight to another world. But it shares with Plato in describing our human calling as that of becoming righteous with the help of wisdom, and like Plato it calls that a likening to God.

95. Philo, *De Specialibus Legibus* IV 187–88; tr. Colson, 8.122–25.

96. Cf. Deuteronomy 5:33, 8:6, 10:12, 11:22, 19:9, 26:17, 28:9, 30:16 and Genesis 17:1.

97. Philo, *De Opificio Mundi* 144.

98. *Ḥinnukh*, commandment 89.

99. Kagan, *Ahavat Ḥesed*, Part II, Chapter 2.

100. Sifra on Leviticus 19:2, echoed by Rashi ad loc.

101. The Ḥatam Sofer, *Otzer Ḥayyim*, 3.114

102. *M^e^khilta* to Exodus 15:2; ed. Lauterbach 2.25.

103. B. Shabbat 133b, drawing on Exodus 34:6 and Psalms 111:4.

104. *M^e^khilta* to Exodus 15:2, ed. Lauterbach, 2.28–29, citing Joshua 2:10–11, 5:1 and Ezekiel 36:20–23.

105. Cf. Deuteronomy 13; cf. Moses Mendelssohn, *Nacherinnerung zur "Antwort" Lavaters*, in *Gesammelte Schriften*, 3.65; and Nehama Leibowitz, *Studies in Devarim*, Re'eh, ad loc.

CHAPTER 3

1. Cf. Korsgaard, *Sources of Normativity*, 30.

2. Korsgaard, *Sources of Normativity*, 18.

3. The key texts from Luther and Calvin and background passages from Ockham and Scotus that anchor the divine command theory of more recent authors are gathered and discussed in Michael Harris, *Divine Command Ethics*, 27–31. See Marilyn McCord Adams, "The Structure of Ockham's Moral Theory"; Gene Outka and John P. Reeder, eds., *Religion and Morality*, which includes Robert M. Adams's essay; William E. Mann, "Modality, Morality and God"; Mark C. Murphy, "Divine Command, Divine Will and Moral Obligation"; Philip Quinn, *Divine Commands and Moral Requirements*; James Rachels, "God and Human Attitudes," reprinted in Paul Helm, ed., *Divine Commands and Morality*; Paul Rooney, *Divine Command Morality*; Avi Sagi and Daniel Statman, *Religion and Morality*. See also Heiko Obermann, *The Harvest of Medieval Theology*.

4. For the domains of the Olympian gods as emblems of a moral order, see F. M. Cornford, *From Religion to Philosophy*; and see E. R. Dodds, *The Greeks and the Irrational*.

5. E. R. Dodds elegantly traces the moral and spiritual shift from the heroic (Homeric) age to that of Hesiod, say, in the anthropologists' distinction of an honor/shame culture from a merit/guilt culture—*The Greeks and the Irrational*, 28–63. No culture, to be sure, speaks with a single voice. But moral and religious ideals continue to map each other even as individuals vary.

6. See Goodman, *God of Abraham*, Chapter 1.

7. Alexander Bickel, *The Morality of Consent*.

8. *And the Lord smelled the sweet savor, and the Lord said in his heart, "I will not again curse the earth on man's account. For the bent of man's heart is bad from his youth. And I will not again smite all living things, as I have done. As long as the earth endureth seedtime and harvest, cold and heat, summer and winter, day and night will not cease"* (Genesis 8:21–22).

9. Cf. J. L. Mackie, *Ethics: Inventing Right and Wrong*.

10. See Goodman, *On Justice*, esp. Chapter 1.

11. See Goodman, "Respect for Nature in the Jewish Tradition."

12. Korsgaard, *Sources of Normativity*, 19.

13. See, e.g., Alan Goldman, *Moral Knowledge*, 53–61.

14. Korsgaard, *Sources of Normativity*, 50.

15. Ibid., 51.

16. See Goodman, "Some Moral Minima."

17. Korsgaard, *Sources of Normativity*, 2–4. She herself waxes teleological when she treats responses to pain as "the *unreflective* rejection of a threat to your identity" (150).

18. Korsgaard, *Sources of Normativity*, 91.

19. Ibid, 93.

20. Ibid, 92–94.

21. Ibid, 97.

22. Ibid, 113.

23. Ibid,113.

24. Ibid, 113.

25. Ibid, 117.

26. Ibid, 121.

27. Cf. Ibid, 160–61: "My account does not depend on the existence of supernatural beings or non-natural facts, and it is consistent with although not part of the Scientific World View. In that sense, it is a form of naturalism. But in another sense it is not. . . . The fact of value isn't value itself—it is merely a fact. But it is a fact of life. In fact, it is *the* fact of life. It is the natural condition of living things to be valuers, and that is why value exists."

28. Ibid, 122–23.

29. Korsgaard writes: "Although we are not supposed to do our duty out of fear of punishment or the hope of a reward, no one who cannot impose sanctions on us is in a position to *require* anything of us . . . a person's own mind does indeed impose sanctions on her . . . we punish ourselves by guilt and regret and repentance and remorse" (151). Well, sometimes we do, and reward ourselves too, and not always in proportion to the merit or the offense. But sometimes we do no such thing. Korsgaard here equivocates on 'require,' italicizing the word as if to mark it as the pivot of her argument. Is the demand she speaks of here coercive or monitory, making her inference trivial? Or is it moral? If so, her implication melts into a mere assertion. Clearly, when a parent or a friend asks for a favor or imposes an obligation, the operative spring of normativity in the request is actuated not by threats of punishment or promises of reward but simply by the relationship. And Plato argues in the *Crito* that the laws work the same way: They command us in virtue of past and present benefits received and in virtue of our dependence on one another as members of a society or community. If promises and threats were the issue, our obligations would lapse as those sanctions became less pressing or less prominent. But of course they do not. Penalties become relevant, I would argue, for those who fail to accept the obligations imposed by some imperative, be it legal or moral. And, of course, sanctions have other functions as well—deterrence and retribution in the case of punishments, the expression of gratitude and honor, inter alia, in the case of rewards. Bear in mind that most of the Torah's *mitzvot* bear no sanction. Their legislation is seen not as a burden but as a blessing; and the opportunity to fulfill them is a privilege, the very basis of the much maligned conception of Israel's chosenness.

30. Ibid, 129.

31. James Grady finds the choicest sentence in Korsgaard's book in a *Q.E.D.*: "It follows from this argument that human beings are valuable" (123). What sort of argument is needed to prove that? What sort of conversation partner who needs that to be proved would find any proof of it cogent? The argument: "Since you

are human you *must* take something to be normative, that is, some conception of practical identity must be normative for you. If you had no normative conception of your identity, you could have no reasons for action, and because your consciousness is reflective, you could not then act at all. Since you cannot act without reasons and your humanity is the source of your reasons, you must value your own humanity if you are to act at all." Yet people find all sorts of grounds for action, not all of them consistent with the rest and, regrettably, not all of them admirable.

32. Korsgaard, *Sources of Normativity*, 164–65.

33. Ibid, 165.

34. The hiddenness of autonomy was something of a rhetorical fiction on Kant's part. Both the Stoics and the Epicureans thought that the key to ethics lay in discovery of one's true identity. So, for that matter, did Plato, Aristotle, and the Cynics. But all of these philosophers had their own ideas of the locus of that identity: The Stoics found it in the willing, ruling *hegemonikon*, the Epicureans in the hedonic will, Plato in the divine rational soul, Aristotle in the individual, intellectual human essence, the Cynics in the snarling voice of candor that throws off the trammels of convention. For Kant, of course, the real self was the pure rational will that both lays down and reverentially accepts the moral law.

35. See Kant, *Groundwork*, 432.

36. Goodman, *On Justice*, 118.

37. See Goodman, *God of Abraham*, 226.

38. Hare, *The Moral Gap*, 12.

39. By picturing the state as the individual "writ large," Plato's *Republic* steals a march on the Sophists' insistence that discussions of justice and the like are empty if we don't know *to whom* and *for whom* such goods are intended. Rawls's veil of ignorance serves the same purpose. See Goodman, *On Justice*; *God of Abraham*; and *Judaism, Human Rights and Human Values*.

40. Michael J. Harris, *Divine Command Ethics*, 47–48, wonders if my work is consistent in saying that God is the source of all values but rejecting the notion that values just are what God determines them to be. He finds me not guilty of inconsistency when I identify God's will with the right, since I do not make that relationship asymmetrical. Indeed, symmetry is what I'm counting on when I speak of a dialectic and of chimneying and say that our values are constitutive in our idea of God. Harris does think I'm inconsistent in declaring God to be the Source of all values. Perhaps it would help to recall that I think of values in objective rather than subjective terms: God is the source of all that is real and of all the beauty, dynamism, and truth that are the marks of his handiwork, the values that elicit our respect aesthetically and intellectually and ask for our recognition in practical and existential terms. *This* relationship, of course, is not symmetrical. God is the Creator, and we are not. God is also the source of our knowledge and our goodness, including our moral goodness. But that goodness, once again, is objective. It is not of human devising and is not the product of some arbitrary fiat of God's. Rather, it is because we see the marks of God's goodness not only in creation at large but also in the

access we have to objectivity in our own moral and conceptual awareness that we know of God at all—that He exists and what his nature must be.

41. As Kenneth Seeskin writes, "the only way to judge whether something deserves to be honored as a divinity is to determine whether the message we receive is *worthy* of divinity, external revelation presupposes internal." *Autonomy in Jewish Philosophy*, 13.

42. See also Psalms 45:6–8, 97:2. Compare the biblical command (Deuteronomy 17:18) that a king, once enthroned, must write out a copy of the Law, vetted by the Levites, and keep it for study throughout his reign: Political legitimacy here mirrors the legitimacy of God's rule: Both depend on justice. Cf. Psalms 93:2. For the nexus between truth and justice, see Goodman, *In Defense of Truth*, Chapter 9.

43. For the *mitzvot* as God's *testimonies*, see Deuteronomy 4:45, 6:17, 6:20, 1 Kings 2:3, 23:3, 1 Chronicles 29:19, 2 Chronicles 34:31, Nehemiah 9:34, Psalms 25:10, 119:2, and repeatedly throughout the Psalm.

44. Saadiah Gaon, on Job 34, in *The Book of Theodicy*, 360. Saadiah is glossing Elihu's demand (Job 34:18), which he translates: "*Is 'scoundrel' to be said unto the king?*" He writes: "Here Elihu makes clear that the king deserves to rule only for his justice. So it is absurd that He be a rightful king and yet be vicious."

45. Saadiah ad Job, loc. cit., *The Book of Theodicy*, 123–24, 382–401.

46. See the discussion in Goodman, *Judaism, Human Rights and Human Values*, 72–78.

47. See John Hare, *God's Call*.

48. John Hare, *Why Bother Being Good?*, 97–100.

49. Spinoza, *Ethics* 3, Introduction.

50. Hare, *Why Bother Being Good?*, 103–4.

51. Ibid, 105–6.

52. See Goodman, *God of Abraham*, 107.

53. See Angus C. Graham, *Reason and Spontaneity*, 2–3.

54. Hare, *Why Bother Being Good?*, 109.

55. Ibid, 110.

56. Ibid, 114–15.

57. Ibid, 129, and 117, citing Plato's *Ion*.

58. Ibid, 130.

59. See Goodman, *God of Abraham*, Chapter 3.

60. Hare, *Why Bother Being Good?*, 115.

61. Compare Galatians 2:9–19. Reflecting on the continuing impact of this kind of teaching, Amy-Jill Levine writes: "A substantial number of my Christian students view Jesus as opposed to Judaism rather than as a Jew himself. They see Judaism as a religion of law as opposed to to Jesus's religion of grace; they believe that Jews follow the commandments to earn a place in heaven; they suggest that Jews rejected Jesus because he proclaimed peace and love instead of violence against the Roman occupiers of Jerusalem. Comments from my Christian students typically begin, 'Why do the Jews think . . . ' as if all Jews think alike" (*The Misunderstood Jew*, 10).

Further on, she writes of the impression that by the time of Jesus,

> 'the Jews' had turned the Sabbath from a day of rest and celebration to a day of constraint. . . . The impression is symptomatic of a larger view of Judaism as a straitjacket with thousands of picky injunctions, and of Jews as fearful that if they were to violate one commandment, they would face the wrath of an angry God. Thus, all Jews at the time of Jesus had to have been hopelessly sanctimonious, obsessive, and paranoid. (31)

62. Judah Halevi, *Kuzari* 3.21.

63. Cf. Maimonides, *MT* XIV v, Kings and Wars, 12.

64. Hare, *Why Bother Being Good?*, 152.

65. See Goodman, *On Justice*, Chapter 5.

66. Exodus Rabbah 34.1.

67. Similarly, Exodus Rabbah 29.1. The Midrash has it that God's thundering voice at Sinai fanned out into all the languages of humankind and into the understanding each Israelite (even Moses, cf. Exodus 19:19) according to his capacity, much as the manna answered to the needs of each Israelite. Exodus Rabbah 5.9; and see Stephen Benin, *The Footprints of God.*

68. Xenophanes, apud Clement, *Stromat.* VII 22.2, V 109.3.

69. See Avi Sagi and Daniel Statman, *Religion and Morality.*

70. Fox, whom Twersky tends to follow on this question, holds that it is only through prophetic revelation that we human beings can discern right from wrong. See Marvin Fox, "Maimonides and Aquinas on Natural Law."

71. Yeshayahu Leibowitz propounds a similar position, declaring that "the religious Jew is he who has accepted upon himself the yoke of the commandments." Translated and cited by Harris, *Divine Command Ethics*, 37, from Leibowitz's *Yahadut, 'Am Y^ehudi, u-M^edinat Israel* (Judaism, the Jewish People, and the State of Israel), 58. But Leibowitz's often strident moralism, which typically adopts a halakhic stance, makes it hard to see any light between his halakhic and his moral views—unless the effect is to pillory the moral outlook of others as un-halakhic. For Leibowitz, then, Halakha *is* a moral authority, and the idea of God's command is a way of pulling rank on those who differ with him as to the content of moral demands. As Harris puts it, "For Leibowitz . . . human needs, interests and values have no legitimate place whatsoever in Judaism." That view, despite Leibowitz's near cult status in some circles, does not sit well with the mainstream rabbinic tradition, which holds that God cares about even a few coppers' difference in the price of a chicken for the family table.

72. Jakobovits, *Bioethics*, 119.

73. Jakobovits (*Jewish Medical Ethics*, 292 n. 5) argues that Isaac Abravanel predicates Leviticus 19:18, *Love thy neighbor as thyself*, on the sheer fact of its being God's command, since the verse concludes: *I am the Lord.* On the contrary, that phrasing, as I've argued elsewhere, is meant to underscore the moral seriousness, centrality, and objectivity of the command. But, as Harris, *Divine Command Ethics*, 110, points out, the late Chief Rabbi is overreading his source here: "Jakobovits's reading of Abravanel is unjustified. Throughout his commentary to Leviticus

Chapter 19, it is clear that Abravanel's focus is solely on the issue of the motive from which the commandments are obeyed." The issue for the Renaissance exegete here, as he seeks to explain why the Torah restates commandments already enshrined in the Decalogue, is God's intent to make it clear that Israel pursues the virtues out of deference to God—but not that these qualities would not have been virtues had God not ordained them.

74. Marvin Fox, *Interpreting Maimonides*, 202–3, 208.

75. See Kant, *Groundwork*, 439–41. Compare Kant's appeal in the opening sentence of "An Answer to the Question 'What Is Enlightenment?,'" where enlightenment is defined as an emergence from tutelage, and tutelage is understood in turn as the dependence of one's understanding on external authorities. Cf. Kant, "What Is Orientation in Thinking?" in Kant, *Critique of Practical Reason and Other Writings in Moral Philosophy*.

76. See G. de Graaff, "God and Morality," and D. Z. Phillips, "God and Ought," both in I. T. Ramsey, ed., *Christian Ethics and Contemporary Philosophy*, 33, 133.

77. See Goodman, *God of Abraham*, Chapter 1.

78. A. J. Heschel, *God in Search of Man*, 17. For the themes of *ḥesed* and covenant in the Tanakh, see Heschel, *The Prophets*, 59–60, 219–20, etc.

79. Amy-Jill Levine, *The Misunderstood Jew*, 14–15.

80. Tom Paine, *Age of Reason* (1794) Part II, Chapter 1, writes of the Bible:

> There are matters in that book, said to be done by the *express command* of God that are as shocking to humanity and to every idea we have of moral justice as anything done by Robbespierre. . . . When we read in the books ascribed to Moses, Joshua, etc. that they [the Israelites] came by stealth upon whole nations of people, who, as history itself shows, had given them no offense; *that they put all those nations to the sword; that they spared neither age nor infancy; that they utterly destroyed men, women and children; that they left not a soul to breathe*—expressions that are repeated over and over again in those books, and that, too, with exulting ferocity—are we sure that these things are facts? Are we sure that the Creator of man commissioned these things to be done? And are we sure that the books that tell us so were written by His authority? . . . The origin of every nation is buried in fabulous tradition, and that of the Jews is as much to be suspected as any other. To charge the commission of acts upon the Almighty, which, in their own nature and by every rule of moral justice, are crimes, as all assassination is, and more especially the assassination of infants, is matter of serious concern. To believe the Bible to be true, we must *unbelieve* all our belief in the moral justice of God; for wherein could crying or smiling infants offend? And to read the Bible without horror, we must undo everything that is tender, sympathizing and benevolent in the heart of man. Speaking for myself, if I had no other evidence that the Bible is fabulous than the sacrifice I must make to believe it to be true, that alone would be sufficient to determine my choice. (*Complete Writings*, 2.518–19)

Paine, we note, impugns not the Almighty but the authority of scripture. He's more than ready to believe that ancient Israelites executed what they took to be God's mandate but on other questions of historical veracity adopts a more skeptical posture:

> When Samson ran off with the gate-posts of Gaza, if he ever did so (and whether he did or not is nothing to us), or when he visited his Delilah, or caught his foxes, or did anything else, what has revelation to do with these things? If they were facts, he could tell them himself, or his secretary, if he kept one, could write them, if they were worth either telling or writing; and if they were fictions, revelation could not make them true; and whether true or not, we are neither the better nor the wiser for knowing them. When we contemplate the immensity of that Being who directs and governs the incomprehensible WHOLE, of which the utmost ken of human sight can discover but a part, we ought to feel shame at calling such paltry stories the Word of God. (2.473)

Paine here, in the manner of Voltaire, plays the sense of nature's immensity and the grandeur of the cosmos against what he finds trivial in scripture. But, again, it is not God's majesty that is called into question. On the contrary, it is presumed and put to use as the fulcrum of the argument.

81. Midrash Tanḥuma 6.10 to Deuteronomy 25:17.

82. Cf. the case of Pinḥas (Numbers 25:6), where R. Judah ben Pazzi, a notable rabbinic proceduralist among the Amora'im, makes a point of excluding such passionate outbursts from the halakhically acceptable norms. See E. E. Urbach in Baron et al., *Violence and Defense*, 104–5.

83. *M*[e]*khilta d*[e]*-R. Ishmael*, Amalek 2, ed. Lauterbach, 3.135, 137.

84. *M*[e]*khilta d*[e]*-R. Ishmael*, Amalek 3, ed. Lauterbach 3.148.

85. Harris, *Divine Command Ethics*, 137. Rashi notes (at Exodus 17:12) that Moses delegated the battle against Amalek to Joshua, as if balking at God's command—hence his arms grew heavy. Rashi details the extent of the command but seems to feel no need to justify it. Nor, as Harris notes, does Rashbam or the *K*[e]*li Yaqar* of Ephraim Sh[e]lomo ben Ḥayyim of Luntshitz.

86. Midrash Tanḥuma (6.4 to Deuteronomy 25:17) stresses that Esau, the ancestor of Amalek, was Isaac's son and Abraham's grandson.

87. Cf. Isaac Abravanel, Naḥmanides, and Ovadiah Sforno at Deuteronomy 25:16–19.

88. Rashi at Deuteronomy 25:19, echoing *M*[e]*khilta d*[e]*-R. Ishmael*, Amalek 2, ed. Lauterbach 3.160.

89. See Midrash Tanḥuma 6.10 and 6.14 to Deuteronomy 25:17.

90. The *M*[e]*khilta d*[e]*-R. Ishmael*, Amalek 2, Lauterbach 3.157, names Haman as the memory of Amalek that Israel was commanded to blot out.

91. Joseph Badad, *Minḥat Ḥinukh*, 3.425, commandment 604, cited in Harris, *Divine Command Ethics*, 144.

92. See Harris, *Divine Command Ethics*, 144.

93. *M^ekhilta d^e-R. Ishmael,* Amalek 2, Lauterbach 3.159.

94. This in his comments on Maimonides' *MT* XIV v, Kings and Wars, 5.5; the passage is quoted in Harris, *Divine Command Ethics,* 143.

95. Maimonides, *MT* XIV v, Kings and Wars, 6.1. "The moralisation," Harris writes (*Divine Command Ethics,* 146), "is not total, because the terms of peace are very demanding"; yet Rabad (Rabbi Abraham ben David of Posquieres), often a bitter critic of Maimonides', concurs with him here, although specifying that the Amalekites of the Messianic Age must accept the Noaḥidic laws—the minimal demands of civilization according to the tradition; see David Novak, *The Image of the Non-Jew in Judaism.*

96. Louis Ginzberg, *Legends of the Jews,* 6.24 n. 141, 6.25 n. 147.

97. See the *Encyclopedia of Islam* 2.917, s.v. *Fir'awn.,* citing the *tafsīr* on Qur'ān 2:46–49.

98. Cf. Avi Sagi, "The Punishment of Amalek in Jewish Tradition."

99. Samson Raphael Hirsch ad Exod. 17:14, *The Pentateuch,* 2.234.

100. Michael Harris, *Divine Command Ethics,* 141.

101. See Goodman, *God of Abraham,* 137–38.

102. Goodman, *God of Abraham,* 186–88.

103. See Ze'ev Falk, *Jewish Matrimonial Law in the Middle Ages.* Cf. Harris's trenchant discussion (p. 80) of Daniel the Tailor's moral qualms as to biblical *mamzerut,* Leviticus Rabbah 32.8, glossing Ecclesiastes 4:1. Harris, *Divine Command Ethics.*

104. See Moshe Greenberg, "The Biblical Conception of Asylum."

105. See Goodman, *God of Abraham* 117–22.

106. David Novak addresses the charge that the efficacy of reason obviates revelation with a trenchant analysis of the space allowed or denied to the distinctive modes of discourse that scripture opens up. In a society (*Gesellschaft*), he argues, revelation comes to seem irrelevant. Aristotle can situate "god-talk" in the domestic sphere, "which is beneath the *polis,*" or at the summit of the contemplative, "which is beyond the *polis.*" But many modern thinkers construe society in "technical" terms, that is, as an artifact. In effect, they "refuse any intelligible role to either the domestic or the contemplative sphere, thus denying any place to god-talk at all." Novak, *Natural Law in Judaism,* 18–19. For Novak's reading of the significance of Jethro's visit, see pp. 55–60.

107. For Lazarus's view, see *Die Ethik des Judenthums,* and Cohen's review, "Das Problem der jüdischen Sittenlehre," reprinted in Cohen's *Jüdische Schriften,* 3.1–35.

108. E. E. Urbach, *The Sages,* 1.317.

109. Hermann Cohen, *Reason and Hope,* 79.

110. Paul Tillich, "On the Idea of a Theology of Culture," an address he delivered in his first year as a Privatdozent at the University of Berlin in 1919; it was first published in *Religionsphilosophie der Kultur;* the first English translation was by William Baillee Green, in Paul Tillich, *What Is Religion?,* 155–81; for a new translation, see Tillich, *Visionary Science.*

111. See Joseph B. Soloveitchik, *Halakhic Man.*

112. As David Novak writes, "since the Emancipation and the Enlightenment, Jewish thinkers as different as Moritz Lazarus, Hermann Cohen, Aḥad Ha'Am, Leo Baeck, and Emmanuel Levinas" have sought the essence of Judaism in ethics. The earlier figures in this group were often moved, as Moses Mendelssohn was, by apologetic motives, hoping to live down in their philosophies hostile charges that Judaism was mere legalism or ritualism. But the later ones, Levinas in particular, as Novak makes clear, were theologically inhibited. See Novak, *Natural Law in Judaism*, 82–89.

113. As I argued in *In Defense of Truth* (149–50), what counts as a tautology depends on the context in which a judgment is pronounced—what assumptions are premised or withheld.

114. Paul Tillich, *Systematic Theology*, volume 3, *Life and the Spirit: History and the Kingdom of God*, 249.

115. Kenneth Seeskin, *Autonomy in Jewish Philosophy*, ix. Ze'ev Falk, similarly, argues that God does not simply impose his commandments but asks for a commitment by those who receive his covenant; Falk, *Religious Law and Ethics*, 11. Similarly, Shubert Spero, *Morality, Halakha and the Jewish Tradition*, 81–82.

116. David Hartman, *A Living Covenant*, 98.

117. See James Barr, *Biblical Faith and Natural Theology*, Gifford Lectures, 1991, University of Edinburgh.

118. The point is repeatedly made in the Ne^{c}ilah liturgy of Yom Kippur.

119. As Jeffrey Tigay comments in the JPS Deuteronomy, this compact and memorable summary of God's demands focuses on the inclination of the heart, which alone gives meaning to external observances. The passage, known as *parashat ha-yir'ah*, "the paragraph of reverence," was excerpted in the *m^{e}zuzah and t^{e}fillin* scripts found at Qumran.

120. David Weiss Halivni counts more than a hundred appeals to human motives and interests in Deuteronomy alone; *Midrash, Mishnah, and G^{e}mara*, 10–11.

121. The Torah does not distinguish these terms in the same way. See Gersion Appel, *A Philosophy of Mitzvot*, 196, note 1.

122. This is the same line that I translated in the lectures as *The rulings of the Lord are truth/ And altogether just . . .*, putting the emphasis there on the sense in context and here on Maimonides' understanding, which stresses the character of the Law as an organic and integrated system. Maimonides, like his rabbinic predecessors, affirms a distinctive halakhic conception of stare decisis, which holds (in keeping with a recognition of the genetic fallacy) that the original reasons for a halakhic rule do not affect its prescriptiveness once the rule is fixed as a principle of halakha, since it is the system as an integrated body to which one is meant to adhere.

123. For this sense of the verb in rabbinic parlance, see Sanhedrin 110a, B^{e}rakhot 19a, etc.

124. In "Eight Chapters," 6, Maimonides takes to task "modern" rabbis "infected" with *kalām* ideas, for calling some *mitzvot* rational—as if others were not. The reference is to Saadiah. See *ED* III 3.

125. The context confirms Maimonides' reading. Moses exhorted the Israelites to keep all the precepts of the Torah (Deuteronomy 32:46), and the present verse speaks of that adherence: *It is no idle thing to you, for it is your life, and by this means shall ye prolong your days on the soil that you are crossing the Jordan to inherit.*

126. M. Makkot 3.16.

127. Maimonides, *Guide* II 39 with "Eight Chapters" 3–4.

128. Maimonides, *MT* VIII, IX, Trespass in Regard to Sacred Objects, 8.8. I translate after Mendel Lewittes in the YJS.

129. Maimonides, *MT* IX VI, Substituted Offerings, 4.13 *ad fin.* Proverbs 22:22–27 goes on to spell out instances of good counsel: It cautions against abusing the helpless, mistreating the poor, alliance with the irate, and standing surety for the extravagant. These counsels push back against human inclinations toward excess; see "Eight Chapters," 3. Proverbs goes on to warn against shifting established boundary markers and urges one to observe industrious workers and the success their virtues bring (vv. 28–29).

130. See Maimonides, *Guide* III 26.

131. The root sense of *tz-r-f*, as an image of smelting and assaying, is attested at Judges 17:4, Jeremiah 6:28–30, 9:6, Zechariah 13:9, Isaiah 40:19, 48:10, Psalms 66:10, Proverbs 25:4. God's word of command itself, the Rabbis say, is called a refinement; see Psalms 18:31; 2 Samuel 22:31; cf. Psalms 119:40.

132. See Naḥmanides on the ethical import of the laws, at Genesis 26:5. And see his comments at Exodus 15:25, and Leviticus 18:6, with Tosefta Kiddushin, ad fin.

133. Naḥmanides at Leviticus 19:19; cf. at Deuteronomy 22:6.

134. See David Novak, *The Theology of Naḥmanides*, 101.

135. Numbers Rabbah 19.2–8, on Numbers 19:2, glossing Ecclesiastes 7:23.

136. See Goodman, *God of Abraham*, Chapter 5.

137. Exodus 20:13, 21:18, Numbers 35:16–18, Deuteronomy 4:42, 5:17.

138. Thus Paul urges: "Let no man, then, judge you in meat or in drink, or in respect of a holy day, or the new moon, or the sabbath days" (Colossians 2:16; cf. Romans 6:14, 7:6). At Romans 13:9, he preaches: "Thou shalt not commit adultery, thou shalt not kill, thou shalt not steal, thou shalt not bear false witness, thou shalt not covet. If there be any other commandment, it is briefly comprehended in this saying: Thou shalt love thy neighbor as thyself."

139. Saadiah, *ED* III 1.

140. In *ED* III 2, Saadiah anticipates Maimonides' underdetermination principle, arguing that the manner of worship is not specified by the principle of gratitude.

141. Cf. Maimonides, *Guide* III 29–32; Goodman, *God of Abraham*, Chapters 6–7.

142. See Goodman, "Ordinary & Extraordinary Language in Medieval Jewish & Islamic Philosophy"; "The Rational and Irrational in Jewish and Islamic Philosophy."

143. In *Natural Law in Judaism*, 70–72, David Novak explains that the Rabbis (Shabbat 53b) distinguish *mitzvot* based on nature, like the prohibition of murder, which is biblically grounded in human transcendence (*for in the image of God did He*

make man, Genesis 9:6), from those which are anchored in history, like the biblical laws against permanent enslavement of an Israelite (*for the Israelites are My slaves . . . whom I took out of the land of Egypt,* Leviticus 25:54–55). Sabbath observance is a hybrid case, binding on Jews but with its exemption from labor extended to their neighbors and employees: Historical redemption grounds its application to all Israel, but its archetype in the biblical account of creation and the light it sheds on the human image make its liberative scope and message universal.

144. See Ephraim E. Urbach's magisterial *The Sages: Their Concepts and Beliefs.*

145. See Sanhedrin 89a; *Sifre* 178; Saadiah, *ED* III 8; Maimonides, *Guide* I 63, *MT* I IV, Idolatry, 5.7; Goodman, *God of Abraham,* 183–84.

146. See Baḥya Ibn Paqudah, *Ḥovot ha-Levavot,* Introduction.

147. Naḥmanides, *Torat ha-Shem T^{e}mimah* 1.151.

148. See Exodus 35:34–35, 36:2, Deuteronomy 4:29, 6:6, etc.

149. See E. E. Urbach, *The Sages* 332–41. The classic prooftext: *Thou shalt do what is right and good in the sight of the Lord* (Deuteronomy 6:18). As Rabbi Akiva parsed it, this meant: what is good in God's sight and what is right in human eyes. See *Sifre* to Deuteronomy § 79.

150. Aristotle, *Nicomachaean Ethics* II 1.

151. Maimonides, *Guide* III 29.

152. B^{e}rakhot 33b, discussed at *Guide* I 59. Central among the epithets licensed by the Rabbis in prayer are those revealed to Moses in the exigencies of his prophetic role, at Exodus 34:6–7.

153. Cf. Rashi ad B. B^{e}rakhot 33b; R. Elḥanan and R. Eleazar Kallir at Tosafot at B. M^{e}gillah 25a.

154. See Rashi at B. M^{e}gillah 25a, B. B^{e}rakhot 33b, and B. Gittin 76a.

155. Saadiah, *ED* V 6.

156. David Novak writes: "In the case of scriptural/divine law, the rule is always prior to the principle. That is, the principle is inferred from the rule a posteriori. The principle functions more as an explanation (*ratio cognoscendi*) than a sufficient reason or ground. As such, the principle can be used to interpret the rule and even apply it. But the principle can never be the basis for dismissal of the old rule and its replacement by a new rule, even if the new rule seems to be a better means to the end that the inferred principle enunciates." Novak, *Natural Law in Judaism,* 75.

157. See Maimonides, "Eight Chapters," 3–4.

158. Cf. Roslyn Weiss, "Maimonides on *Shilluaḥ ha-Qen*"; Josef Stern, "On an Alleged Contradiction between Maimonides' *Guide of the Perplexed* and *Mishneh Torah.*"

159. See, for example Rashi, on Genesis 26:5, Proverbs 25:2.

160. See B. Kiddushin 31a, B. Bava Kamma 38a, B. Avodah Zarah 3a.

161. Naḥmanides, at Exodus 20:2, 20:8, Chavel 1.398; Notes to Maimonides' *Book of Commandments,* Negative Commandment 2.

162. Cf. Sifra to Leviticus 20:26, where one is urged not to express distaste for forbidden or restricted sensuous pleasures or appetitive gratifications but rather to say: 'I do desire such things, but my Father in heaven has forbidden them to me.'

163. "Eight Chapters," 6.

164. See Goodman, *God of Abraham*, Chapter 6.

165. Cf. Appel, *A Philosophy of Mitzvot*, 23.

166. See Maimonides, *Guide* III 31. As Novak notes, Philo, at *De Migratione Abrahami* 89–93, similarly insists that grasping the inner symbolic intent of the laws regarding Sabbaths, circumcision, or the Temple cult, say, does not obviate their observance. Novak, *Natural Law in Judaism*, 75, note.

167. For the rabbinic use of *ta'am* to mean purpose, see David Novak, *Natural Law in Judaism*, 97–98. And see Proverbs 26:16 and Job 12:20. At Job 6:6 Saadiah reads: *Will food be eaten unseasoned, without salt, or is there savor* (ta'am) *in the ooze of eggs?* (tr. Goodman, 201). The sensory facet of the word's meaning moves naturally, within scriptural usage, into a metaphoric range signifying sense and thus, as applied to the *mitzvot*, their purpose or rational basis.

168. Louis Jacobs, *The Talmudic Argument*, in Chernick, ed., *Essential Papers on the Talmud*, 52.

169. Leon Roth, *Is There a Jewish Philosophy?*, 138.

170. "Eight Chapters," 8. As Jon Levenson shows, Hebrew scripture and tradition have long linked Wisdom/Torah with Edenic life eternal. See his *Resurrection and the Restoration of Israel*, 83–92.

171. Aharon Lichtenstein, "Does Jewish Tradition Recognize an Ethic Independent of Halakha," 102–3, citing B. Eruvin 100b (We could have learned modesty from the cat, the criminality of larceny from the ant, chastity from the dove, uxoriousness from the cock). The general rabbinic principle is that ethics (*derekh eretz*) is prior to the Torah both in time and in logic (Leviticus Rabbah 9.3). Lichtenstein argues that "the existence of natural morality is clearly assumed in much that is quite central to our tradition." As Harris writes: For Lichtenstein, "natural morality sets a standard beneath which revealed imperatives could not conceivably fall." It would be untrue to the Torah itself to read its *mitzvot* in ways that would set them against moral imperatives. The *M^ekhilta* argues that bloodshed was proscribed even before the giving of the Law at Sinai: How then could Torah's requirements be less stringent? *M^ekhilta*, Mishpatim, N^ezikin, cited by Lichtenstein, "Does Jewish Tradition Recognize an Ethic Independent of Halakha," 105; quoted by Harris, *Divine Command Ethics*, 43.

172. Rabbi Eleazar ben Azariah's morally grounded halakhic teachings include the ruling that Sabbath restrictions must give way to save a life—since we are meant to *live* by the commandments, not die by them (B. Shabbat 132a)—and the well-known rule (based on the exegesis of Leviticus 16:30) that the Day of Atonement does not purge us of sins against our fellows until we have first appeased them (M. Yoma 8.9). He also propounded the key hermeneutical principle that "The Torah speaks in accordance with human language," a general guideline for halakhic exegesis but also a central prooftext of Maimonides' in resolving biblical anthropomorphisms. As David Novak notes, Eleazar ben Azariah's precept that Yom Kippur does not atone for transgressions against our fellow human beings until accounts have been settled with them has long been bruited as a prooftext in the reduction of Judaism to

ethics, relegating God to a supporting role in the human ethical drama. But as Novak rightly insists, citing M. Avot 2.12, Naḥmanides' Notes on Maimonides' *Book of the Commandments* (Positive Commandment 5) and Joseph Albo's *Sefer ha-ᶜIqqarim* 3.27, our ethical obligations to our fellow humans are part of the divine mandate, governed by God's covenant: "the ultimate end of any commandment is 'for the sake of God,' irrespective of who its immediate object is." *Natural Law in Judaism*, 90. God does not need our allegiance, but his goodness grounds every value that the *mitzvot* command us to pursue. The relationship parallels the case with causality: Just as God's ultimate causality is not rendered otiose by the operation of proximate causes and is not obviated by their discovery, so God's permanent partnership in the covenant does not negate the worth of the creatures whose interests that covenant protects, but neither is God's sponsorship obviated by the respect for his work which that covenant mandates. On the contrary, the sanctity and dignity, worth and very being, of all those creatures reflect and give determinate expression to God's infinite reality and goodness.

173. See Jon Levenson's discussion of Psalms 36, 92, and 133, in *Resurrection and the Restoration of Israel*, 86–91.

174. Harris, *Divine Command Ethics*, 151.

175. Maimonides, *Guide* I 2.

176. See M. Bava Kamma 8.6, discussed in Goodman, *Judaism, Human Rights and Human Values*, 58–59.

177. Quoted in Sagi and Statman, "Divine Command Morality and Jewish Tradition," 46.

178. But cf. Harris, *Divine Command Ethics*, 112–13.

179. Sagi and Statman, "Divine Command Morality and Jewish Tradition," 47; cf. Harris, *Divine Command Ethics*, 113–15.

180. See S. Safrai, *The Literature of the Sages*, 50; see the discussion in Goodman, *God of Abraham*, 133.

181. Ḥazon Ish, *'Al 'Inyanei Emunah, Bitaḥon, Vᵉ-'Od, 22, quoted in Harris, Divine Command Ethics, 117.*

182. Samson Raphael Hirsch, at Leviticus 18:4 (3.479); cf. *Ḥoreb*, 219.

183. See Sagi and Statman, "Divine Command Morality and Jewish Tradition," 50–51. The authors compare Shapira's view to Patterson Brown's in "God and the Good."

184. Sagi and Statman, *Religion and Morality*, 19, quoting Calvin from Idziac.

185. Plato, *Republic* 379.

186. Rudolf Otto, *The Idea of the Holy*, 99–101.

187. Otto, *The Idea of the Holy*, 101.

188. Ghazālī, *Al-Munqidh min al-Ḍalāl*, 24–25. The translation here is my own.

189. Ghazālī, *Mizān al-'Amal*, 77–79; *Iḥyā' 'Ulūm al-Dīn* III 2, 1514, 1519–20.

190. Cf. Maimonides in *Ma'amar Tᵉḥiyyat ha-Metim* (Treatise on the Resurrection of the Dead), where the Rambam calls resurrection "a bastion" of the faith but not the ultimate goal; edited with modern Hebrew translation in J. Kafih, *R. Moshe ben Maimon: Iggerot*, 69–101; translated by Hillel Fradkin, in Ralph Lerner, *Maimo-*

nides' Empire of Light, 154–77, and by Abraham Halkin, with notes by David Hartman, in *Crisis and Leadership*, 211–45.

191. For the persistence of hygienic imagery in Ghazālī's account, see Mohamed Ahmed Sherif, *Ghazālī's Theory of Virtue*, 33–35; for the otherworldly orientation of Ghazālī's ethical norms, Muhammad Abul Quasem, *The Ethics of al-Ghazālī*, 83–87. For Ghazālī's overlaying of Aristotelian virtue theory with Sufi pietism, see Goodman, *Islamic Humanism*, 112–21.

192. See Qur'ān 2:142, 213, 6:39, 87, 10:25, 16:121, 24:46.

193. Ghazālī, *Iḥyā'* III 2, 1455–56, *Mizān al-ʿAmal*, 79.

194. George Hourani offers a philosophical appraisal of Muʿtazilite moral objectivism in its mature form in *Islamic Rationalism: The Ethics of ʿAbd al-Jabbār*. Born not far from Hamadhan in 935, the year of Ashʿarī's death, ʿAbd al-Jabbār reversed the latter's course, leaving Ashʿarism for the Muʿtazila. Although a Sunni himself, after studies in Baghdad, he was patronized by the Shiʿite Buwayhids of Rayy (near present-day Tehran), where he served as chief Qāḍī. Deposed after a change of regime and stripped of the wealth he had gained in office, he remained in Rayy until his death in 1024/5. The rediscovery in 1951–52 of fourteen of the twenty volumes of his writings in a mosque library of Sana, long a Shiʿite stronghold, opened a broad window onto Muʿtazilite moral theology in its heyday. That epoch was also the era, as Hourani notes, of the Sincere Brethren of Basra and of the indefatigable essayist and philosophical memoirist Abū Ḥayyān al-Tawḥīdī.

195. See W. Montgomery Watt, *The Formative Period of Islamic Thought*.

196. Ghazālī, *Iḥyā, Tawḥīd*.

197. See Goodman, "Did Ghazālī Deny Causality?"

198. Eric Ormsby, *Theodicy in Islamic Thought*, 138; Ormsby's work traces the debate down to modern times.

199. The work is translated into Spanish by the master hand of Miguel Asín Palacios as *El Justo Medio in la Creencia*.

200. Richard M. Frank, *Al-Ghazālī and the Ashʿarite School*, 73.

201. Ibid., 33.

202. Ibid., 33–34. Miguel Asín Palacios noted parallels to Pascal's wager in Ghazālī; see A.-J. Wensinck, *La Pensée de Ghazzālī*, 73–77, citing Asín's *Los Precedentes Musulmanes del Pari de Pascal* (Santander, 1920) and translating the key passage from the *Iḥyā'* in which Satan's notion that one should take the cash and let the credit go is refuted by the disproportion between worldly finitude and eternal bliss or damnation—and doubt itself is banished by the same disproportion.

203. "Impressionistic proofs," as Frank renders the expression; see Ghazālī, *Fī Iljām al-ʿAwāmm ʿan ʿIlm al-Kalām*, 82.

204. Ghazālī, *Fī Iljām al-ʿAwāmm ʿan ʿIlm al-Kalām*, 50–84; Frank, *Al-Ghazālī and the Ashʿarite School*, 80–82; cf. Maimonides, *Guide*, Introduction, and *Treatise on Resurrection*.

205. Ghazālī, *Fī Iljām al-ʿAwāmm ʿan ʿIlm al-Kalām*, 87–88; see Frank, *Al-Ghazālī and the Ashʿarite School*, 81. A *ḥadīth qudsī* or sacred saying, that is, a divine revelation reported by Muḥammad but not recorded in the Qur'ān, echoes

1 Corinthians 2:9: "But it is written: Eye hath not seen nor ear heard, neither hath it entered into the heart of man what God hath prepared for them that love him." In its original context, Isaiah implores God to replicate his historic intervention on the stage of history, "to tear open the heavens and descend, so that the mountains quake before Thee . . . Never had it been heard or told, no eye had seen, besides Thee, O God, what He doeth for those who wait for Him" (Isaiah 64:1–3). The trope is taken up by Paul, with the sprung syntax of Isaiah's revelatory experience smoothed somewhat in the Greek. In the New Testament and in the *ḥadīth*, the theophany is no longer a memory or a hope but a promise. Taken that way it lends support to Ghazālī's reasoning that the ultimate principle that must orient our practical decisions is beyond our reach.

206. See Maimonides, *Guide* I 2.

207. B. Niddah 16b; cf. *Maimonides' Responsa*, ed. A. Friedman, § 345, 309–10.

208. See, e.g., Anselm of Canterbury, *Cur Deus Homo*—Why God Became a Man, esp. Book 1, chapters 5, 12, 19–21, 23–25. The chapter headings: "That man's redemption could not have been brought about by any other than a human person," "Whether it is fitting for God to forgive a sin out of mercy, without any restitution of what is owing to him," "That mankind cannot be saved without recompense for sin," "That recompense should be proportional to the magnitude of the sin, and that a human being cannot, of himself, make this recompense," "How heavy is the weight of sin," "What it was that man stole from God when he sinned—something he cannot give back," "That so long as a human being does not give back to God what he owes, he may not be blessedly happy, and his incapacity is unexcusable," "That it follows by necessity that mankind is saved by Christ." Translated here after Janet Fairweather, in Anselm of Canterbury, *The Major Works*.

209. Hare finds even the Ten Commandments particularistic, insofar as they address one people: "This is why Kant thought the Jews did not have a moral relation to God; he thought their claim to a special relation with God disqualified them from setting up a universal church." Christianity too, may be particularistic, Hare confesses: "there is particularism not merely in God's covenant with Abraham and the covenant with David, but also in his covenant with particular people he chooses through election to graft as Christians onto the vine." *The Moral Gap*, 152–53. Kantian universalism, as mooted here, would obviate *any* historical connection between God and humanity, leaving pure reason alone to discover God and divine his desires or rules or laws, without help from experience—an outcome that good Kantians should recognize as crippling. In response to Kant's anti-Jewish charges, we might say that history does play a role in the awakening of human awareness, and thus, indeed, in humankind's awareness of God—that is, in God's self-revelation. The idea of God's absolute transcendence and infinite perfection will, of course dawn gradually and in stages on an individual or any human group, as Maimonides is at pains to make clear. But, beyond that, one should ask just what it would mean for Israel to "set up" a universal "church"—and how it would look in the eyes of Israel's friends and detractors, and the people of Israel themselves, for her to try to impose God's law, as she understands it, on the nations of the world. That kind

of universalism is imperialism and triumphalism. With all that can be said of the nexus between God and history, one point is clear: The people of Israel have been remarkably free of such pretensions.

210. See Goodman, *God of Abraham*, 250–56.

211. Maimonides, *Guide* III 22. The point is Aristotelian: One needs the development of character and insight if one is even to chart a good course morally, let alone hew to it.

212. Thus Resh Lakish teaches that Satan, the Angel of Death and the Evil Inclination are one and the same—B. Bava Batra 16a.

213. Hare, *The Moral Gap*, 10.

214. Ibid., 11.

215. Bentham, *Works*, ed. Bowring, 8.389; see the discussion in Goodman, *On Justice*, 34–35.

Works Cited

Abul Quasem, Muhammad. *The Ethics of al-Ghazālī: A Composite Ethics in Islam* (Petaling Jaya, Selangor: Privately printed, 1975).

Adams, Marilyn McCord. "The Structure of Ockham's Moral Theory." *Franciscan Studies* 46 (1986): 1–35.

Altmann, Alexander. *Moses Mendelssohn: A Biographical Study* (Birmingham: University of Alabama Press, 1973).

Anderson, Francis, David Freedman, and William Albright, eds. *Anchor Bible: Amos* (New York: Doubleday, 1989).

Anselm of Canterbury. *The Major Works,* edited by Brian Davies and G. R. Evans (Oxford: Oxford University Press, 1998).

Appel, Gersion. *A Philosophy of Mitzvot: The Religious-Ethical Concepts of Judaism, Their Roots in Biblical Law and the Oral Tradition* (New York: Ktav, 1975).

Aristotle. *Complete Works,* the Revised Oxford translation, edited by Jonathan Barnes (Princeton: Princeton University Press, 1985). 2 volumes.

Austin, C. R., and R. V. Short. *Human Sexuality* (Cambridge: Cambridge University Press, 1980).

———. *Reproductive Fitness* (Cambridge: Cambridge University Press, 1985).

Avot d^{e}-R. Nathan (in Talmud, Minor Tractates), edited by Isidore Epstein, translated by Jacob Israelstam (London: Soncino, 1988).

Baḥya Ibn Paqudah. *Kitāb al-Hidāya ilā Farā'iḍ al-Qulūb,* edited by A. S. Yahuda (Leiden: Brill, 1912, 1942); known in Hebrew as *Sefer Ḥovot ha-L^{e}vavot,* the Arabic text is translated as *The Book of Direction to the Duties of the Heart,* by Menahem Mansoor (London: Routledge, 1973).

Baron, Salo. *A Social and Religious History of the Jews,* second edition (Philadelphia: Jewish Publication Society, 1952). 18 volumes.

Baron, Salo W., George Wise, and L. E. Goodman, editors. *Violence and Defense in the Jewish Experience* (Philadelphia: Jewish Publication Society, 1977).

Barr, James. *Biblical Faith and Natural Theology* (New York: Oxford University Press, 1993).

Beckstrom, John H. *Sociobiology and the Law: The Biology of Altruism in the Courtroom of the Future* (Urbana: University of Illinois Press, 1985).

Benin, Stephen. *The Footprints of God: Divine Accommodation in Jewish and Christian Thought* (Albany: SUNY Press, 1993).

Bentham, Jeremy. *Works,* edited by John Bowring (London: Simpkin, Marshall, 1843).

Bickel, Alexander. *The Morality of Consent* (New Haven: Yale University Press, 1975).

Blauser, Yitzḥaq. *P^{e}ri Yitzḥaq* (Jerusalem, 1974).

Brown, Patterson. "God and the Good." *Religious Studies* 2 (1967): 269–76.

Buss, David. *The Adapted Mind: Evolutionary Psychology and the Generation of Culture* (New York: Oxford University Press, 1995).

Cassirer, Ernst. "Hermann Cohen." *Social Research* 10 (1943): 219–32.

Charles, R. H. *A Critical and Exegetical Commentary on the Book of Daniel* (Oxford: Oxford University Press, 1929).

Chasman, Yehudah Loeb. *Or Yaḥel: Ma'amarei Musar Da^{c}at v^{e}-Yir'at ha-Shem* (Jerusalem, 1960).

Chernick, Michael, editor. *Essential Papers on the Talmud* (New York: New York University Press, 1994).

Cicero. *De Finibus Bonorum et Malorum,* translated by H. Rackham (Cambridge, Mass.: Harvard University Press, 1931).

Cohen, Hermann. *Jüdische Schriften* (Berlin, 1924). 3 volumes.

———. "Das Problem der jüdischen Sittenlehre." *Monatsschrift für die Geschichte und Wissenschaft des Judenthums* 43 (1899): 385–400, 433–49.

———. *Reason and Hope: Selections from the Jewish Writings of Hermann Cohen,* translated by Eva Jospe (New York: Norton, 1971).

———. *Religion of Reason out of the Sources of Judaism,* translated by Simon Kaplan (New York: Ungar, 1972; first published posthumously in 1919).

Cook, Michael. *Commanding Right and Forbidding Wrong in Islamic Thought* (Cambridge: Cambridge University Press, 2000).

Cornford, F. M. *From Religion to Philosophy: A Study in the Origins of Western Speculation* (New York: Harper, 1957).

Daniel, David, editor. *Tyndale's Old Testament* (New Haven: Yale University Press, 1992).

Darwin, Charles. *The Descent of Man, and Selection in Relation to Sex,* vols. 21–22, in *The Works of Charles Darwin,* edited by Paul H. Barrett and R. B. Freeman (London: Pickering, 1989).

Dessler, Eliyahu Eliezer. *Mikhtav Mei-Eliyahu* (B^{e}nai B^{e}rak: Sifte Ḥakhamim, 2004; first published by a group of his students, 1955); translated by Aryeh Carmell as *Strive for Truth* (New York: Feldheim, 1999).

Dodds, E. R. *The Greeks and the Irrational.* The Sather Lectures of 1949 (Berkeley: University of California Press, 1964).

Ehrenfeld, Shmuel. *Ḥatan Sofer* (New York, 1947; first published, 1874).
Falk, Ze'ev. *Jewish Matrimonial Law in the Middle Ages* (Oxford: Oxford University Press, 1966).
———. *Religious Law and Ethics: Studies in Biblical and Rabbinic Theonomy* (Jerusalem: Mesharim, 1991).
Fox, Marvin. *Interpreting Maimonides: Studies in Methodology, Metaphysics and Moral Philosophy* (Chicago: University of Chicago Press, 1990).
———. "Maimonides and Aquinas on Natural Law." *Dine Israel* 3 (1972): 5–27.
Frank, Richard M. *Al-Ghazālī and the Ashʿarite School* (Durham: Duke University Press, 1994).
Garver, Eugene. *Aristotle's* Rhetoric*: An Art of Character* (Chicago: University of Chicago Press, 1994).
———. *For the Sake of Argument: Practical Reasoning, Character, and the Ethics of Belief* (Chicago: University of Chicago Press, 2004).
Gauthier, David. *Morals by Agreement* (Oxford: Oxford University Press, 1986).
Ghazālī, Abū Ḥāmid. *Iḥyā' ʿUlūm al-Dīn* (Reviving the Religious Sciences) (Cairo: Lajnat Nashr al-Thaqāfat al-Islāmiyya, 1937–38).
———. *Fī Iljām al-ʿAwāmm ʿan ʿIlm al-Kalām* (On Keeping the Masses from Study of *Kalām*), edited by M. al-Baghdadi (Beirut: Dar al-Kitāb al-Arabī, 1985).
———. *Kitāb al-Iqtiṣād fī 'l-Iʿtiqād*, translated as *El Justo Medio in la Creencia: Compendio de Teologia Dogmatica de Algazel*, by Miguel Asín Palacios (Madrid: Instituto de Valencia de D. Javan, 1929).
———. *Mizān al-ʿAmal* (The Scale of Action) (Cairo: Maṭbaʿat Kurdistan al-ʿIlmiyya, 1910).
———. *Al-Munqidh min al-Ḍalāl* (Deliverance from Error), edited by Farid Jabre (Beirut: UNESCO, 1959).
Ginzberg, Louis. *Legends of the Jews*, translated by Henrietta Szold (Philadelphia: Jewish Publication Society, 1966; first published in English, 1909). 7 volumes.
Goldberg, Steven. *The Inevitability of Patriarchy* (New York: Morrow, 1973).
———. *Why Men Rule: A Theory of Male Dominance* (Chicago: Open Court, 1993).
Goldman, Alan. *Moral Knowledge* (London: Routledge, 1990).
Goodman, Lenn. "Did Ghazālī Deny Causality?" *Studia Islamica* 47 (1978): 83–120.
———. "God and the Good Life: Maimonides' Virtue Ethics and the Idea of Perfection," in *Die Trias des Maimonides: Jüdische, Arabische, und Antike Wissenkultur*, edited by George Tamer (Berlin: De Gruyter, 2005), 123–35.
———. *God of Abraham* (New York: Oxford University Press, 1996).
———. *In Defense of Truth: A Pluralistic Account* (Amherst, N.Y.: Humanity Press, 2001).
———. *Islamic Humanism* (New York: Oxford University Press, 2003).
———. *Judaism, Human Rights and Human Values* (New York: Oxford University Press, 1998).
———. "Matter and Form as Attributes of God in Maimonides' Philosophy," in *A Straight Path: Studies in Honor of Arthur Hyman*, edited by R. Link-Salinger et al. (Washington, D.C.: Catholic University of America Press, 1987), 86–97.

———."Naked in the Public Square," forthcoming.

———. *On Justice: An Essay in Jewish Philosophy* (New Haven: Yale University Press, 1991; updated edition, Littman Library of Jewish Civilization, 2008).

———. "Ordinary and Extraordinary Language in Medieval Jewish and Islamic Philosophy," *Manuscrito* 11 (1988): 57–83.

———. "The Rational and Irrational in Jewish and Islamic Philosophy," in *Rationality in Question: On Eastern and Western Views of Rationality*, edited by S. Biderman and B. Scharfstein (Leiden: Brill, 1989), 93–118.

———. "Respect for Nature in the Jewish Tradition," in *Judaism and Ecology: Created World and Revealed Word*, edited by Hava Tirosh-Samuelson (Cambridge, Mass.: Harvard University Press, 2002) 227–59.

———. "Some Moral Minima," in *Universality of Political Principles. . . . .*, edited by Stephen Elkin and Stephen Simon (*forthcoming*).

———. "What Does Spinoza Contribute to Jewish Philosophy?" in *Jewish Themes in Spinoza's Philosophy*, edited by L. E. Goodman and H. Ravven (Albany: SUNY Press, 2002), 17–89.

Goodman, Lenn, and Madeleine Goodman. "'Particularly Amongst the Sunburnt Nations'—The Persistence of Sexual Stereotypes of Race in Bio-Science." *International Journal of Group Tensions* 19 (1989): 221–43, 265–84.

Graham, Angus C. *Reason and Spontaneity* (London: Curzon, 1985).

Grayling, A. C. *The Meaning of Things: Applying Philosophy to Life* (London: Weidenfeld and Nicolson, 2001).

Greenberg, Moshe. "The Biblical Conception of Asylum." *Journal of Biblical Literature* 78.2 (1959); reprinted in *Studies in the Bible and Jewish Thought* (Philadelphia: Jewish Publication Society, 1995), 43–50.

Ḥafetz Ḥayyim. *Ahavat Ḥesed* (Warsaw, 1888).

———. *Ḥovat ha-Sh^{e}mirah* (Warsaw, 1920).

Judah Halevi. *Kitāb al-Radd wa 'l-Dalīl fī 'l-Dīn al-Dhalīl* (The Book of Rebuttal and Evidence in Behalf of the Abased Religion, Known as the *Kuzari*, ca. 1130—1140), edited by David H. Baneth (Jerusalem: Hebrew University Press, 1977); translated by Hartwig Hirschfeld under the title *Kuzari* (New York: Schocken, 1964; first English edition, 1905).

Halivni, David Weiss. *Midrash, Mishnah, and Gemara: The Jewish Predilection for Justified Law* (Cambridge, Mass.: Harvard University Press, 1986).

Hare, John. *God's Call: Moral Realism, God's Commands, and Human Autonomy* (Grand Rapids, Mich.: Eerdmans, 2001).

———. *The Moral Gap: Kantian Ethics, Human Limits, and God's Assistance* (Oxford: Oxford University Press, 1997).

———. *Why Bother Being Good? The Place of God in the Moral Life* (Downers Grove, IL: InterVarsity Press, 2002).

Harris, Michael J. *Divine Command Ethics: Jewish and Christian Perspectives* (London: Routledge and Curzon, 2003).

Hartman, David. *A Living Covenant: The Innovative Spirit in Traditional Judaism* (New York: Free Press, 1985).

Ḥatam Sofer. *Otzer Ḥayyim* (Tel Aviv: Makhon ha-Ḥatam Sofer, 1971).
Ḥazon Ish. *'Al 'Inyanei Emunah, Bitaḥon, ve-'Od* (On Matters of Faith, Trust, and Other Matters) (Jerusalem: Makhon Pitḥei M[e]gadim, 1996).
Helm, Paul, editor. *Divine Commands and Morality* (Oxford: Oxford University Press, 1981).
Hertz, Joseph H., editor. *The Pentateuch* (London: Soncino, 1937, 1952).
———,translator with commentary. *Sayings of the Fathers* [= M. Avot] (New York: Behrman House, 1945).
Heschel, Abraham Joshua. *God in Search of Man: A Philosophy of Judaism* (New York: Farrar, Strauss and Cudahy, 1955).
———. *The Prophets* (Philadelphia: Jewish Publication Society, 1962).
Hirsch, Samson Raphael. *Horeb: A Philosophy of Jewish Laws and Observances*, translated by Isidor Grunfeld (London: Soncino, 1962).
———. *The Pentateuch*, translated by Isaac Levy (Gateshead: Judaica Press, 1982).
Hobbes, Thomas. *De Cive or the Citizen* (1642) translated by the author, edited by Sterling Lamprecht (New York: Appleton-Century-Crofts, 1949).
———. *Leviathan: or the Matter, Forme, and Power of a Commonwealth, Ecclesiastical and Civil* (1651) edited by Michael Oakeshott (Oxford: Blackwell, 1960).
Hourani, George. *Islamic Rationalism: The Ethics of 'Abd al-Jabbār* (Oxford: Oxford University Press, 1971).
Hujwīrī, Alī b. ʿUthmān. *Kashf al-Maḥjūb* (The Mystery Unveiled), translated by Reynold A. Nicholson as *The Oldest Persian Treatise on Ṣufiism* (London: Luzac, 1967).
Hume, David. *Enquiries Concerning Human Understanding and Concerning the Principles of Morals* (1772/1777), edited L. A. Selby Bigge (second edition, 1902); third edition revised by P. H. Niddich (Oxford: Oxford University Press, 1975, 1982).
———. *A Treatise of Human Nature* (1739), edited by L. A. Selby-Bigge (Oxford: Oxford University Press, 1888, 1968).
Ikhwān al-Ṣafā'. *The Case of the Animals vs. Man before the King of the Jinn*, translated by L. E. Goodman (Boston: Twayne, 1978). (A new critical edition and translation are in preparation by L. E. Goodman and Richard McGregor, to be published by Oxford University Press.)
Jacobs, Louis. *The Talmudic Argument: A Study in Talmudic Reasoning and Methodology* (New York: Cambridge University Press, 1984).
Jakobovits, Immanuel. *Bioethics* (New York: Sanhedrin, 1979).
———. *Jewish Medical Ethics: A Comparative and Historical Study of the Jewish Religious Attitude to Medicine and its Practice*, edited by Fred Rosner and J. David Bleich (New York: Sanhedrin, 1967).
Jastrow, Morris. "*Ro'eh* and *Ḥozeh* in the Old Testament." *Journal of Biblical Literature* 28 (1909): 42–56.
Jonah ben Abraham Gerondi. *Sha'arei Teshuvah, The Gates of Repentance*, edited and translated by Shraga Silverstein (New York: Feldheim, 2003).
Kant, Immanuel. *Groundwork of the Metaphysic of Morals* (1786), translated by H. J. Paton (New York: Harper and Row, 1964).

———. *The Metaphysics of Morals* (1797), translated by Mary Gregor (Cambridge: Cambridge University Press, 1991).

———. *Political Writings*, edited by Hans Reiss, translated by H. B. Nisbet (Cambridge: Cambridge University Press, 1971; includes "An Answer to the Question 'What Is Enlightenment?')

———. *Critique of Practical Reason and Other Writings in Moral Philosophy*, edited and translated by Lewis White Beck (Chicago: University of Chicago Press, 1949; includes "What Is Orientation in Thinking?").

Karo, Joseph. *Shulḥan Arukh*, with standard commentaries (New York: Hotzaat Me'orot, 1995).

Kaufman, Gordon. *God the Problem* (Cambridge, Mass.: Harvard University Press, 1972).

Keith, A. *A New Theory of Human Evolution* (London: Watts, 1948).

Kellner, Menachem. *Must a Jew Believe Anything?* (London: Littman Library, 1999).

Klein, Ernest. *A Comprehensive Etymological Dictionary of the Hebrew Language* (New York: Collier Macmillan, 1987).

Korsgaard, Christine. *The Sources of Normativity* (Cambridge: Cambridge University Press, 1996).

Kulka, Tomás. *Art and Kitsch* (University Park: Pennsylvania State University Press, 1996).

Lee, Vernon (Violet Paget), and C. Anstruther-Thomson, editors. *Beauty and Ugliness and Other Studies in Psychological Aesthetics* (London: John Lane, 1912).

Leibowitz, Nehama. *Studies in Devarim*, translated by Aryeh Newman (Jerusalem: World Zionist Organization, 1980).

Leibowitz, Yeshayahu. *Yahadut, ʿAm Yehudi, u-Medinat Israel* (Judaism, the Jewish People, and the State of Israel) (Tel Aviv: Schocken, 1979).

Lerner, Ralph. *Maimonides' Empire of Light* (Chicago: University of Chicago Press, 2000).

Levine, Amy-Jill. *The Misunderstood Jew: The Church and the Scandal of the Jewish Jesus* (San Francisco: Harper Collins, 2006).

Levenson, Jon. *Resurrection and the Restoration of Israel: The Ultimate Victory of the God of Life* (New Haven: Yale University Press, 2006)

Lichtenstein, Aharon. "Does Jewish Tradition Recognize an Ethic Independent of Halakha," in *Contemporary Jewish Ethics*, edited by Menachem Kellner (New York: Hebrew Publishing Company, 1978).

Lotze, Hermann. *Mikrokosmos* (1856–64); translated by Elizabeth Hamilton and E. E. Constance Jones as *Microcosmus: An Essay Concerning Man and His Relation to the World* (Edinburgh: T. & T. Clark, 1885).

Lucretius. *De Rerum Natura* (ca. 55 B.C.E.), edited and translated by Cyril Bailey (Oxford: Oxford University Press, 1963).

Mackie, J. L. *Ethics: Inventing Right and Wrong* (London: Penguin, 1977).

Maimonides. *Book of the Commandments*, translated by Charles Chavel (London: Soncino, 1967). 2 volumes.

———. *Crisis and Leadership: Epistles of Maimonides*, translated by Abraham Halkin (Philadelphia: Jewish Publication Society, 1985).

———. *Dalālat al-Ḥā'irīn* (*Guide to the Perplexed*), 3 vols., edited and translated into French by Salamon Munk (Paris, 1856–66; reprinted, Osnabrück: Zeller, 1964).

———. *Eight Chapters,* edited and translated by Joseph I. Gorfinkle (New York: Columbia University Press, 1912; reprinted, New York: AMS, 1966).

———. *Maimonides' Responsa,* edited by A. Friedman (Jerusalem: Mekize Nirdamim, 1934).

———. *Mishneh Torah,* edited by Zvi Preisler (Jerusalem: Ketuvim, 1993); translated in the Yale Judaica Series by various hands as *The Code of Maimonides.*

———. *R. Moshe ben Maimon: Iggerot,* Letters, edited by J. Kafih (Jerusalem: Mossad Harav Kook, 5754).

Mandelkern, Solomon. *Veteris Testamenti Concordantiae* (Leipzig: Veit, 1896).

Mann, William E. "Modality, Morality and God." *Noûs* 23 (1989): 83–99.

McFayden, John Edgar. *A Guide to the Understanding of the Old Testament* (New York: Doran, 1927).

Mendelssohn, Moses. *Nacherinnerung zur "Antwort" Lavaters,* in *Gesammelte Schriften* (Leipzig: Brockhaus, 1843).

———. *Phaedon: Or the Death of Socrates* (New York: Arno, 1973).

Mekhilta de-Rabbi Ishmael, edited and translated by Jacob Z. Lauterbach (Philadelphia: Jewish Publication Society, 1935).

Midrash Tanḥuma, 3 volumes, edited by Solomon Buber (Jerusalem: Eshkol, 1990); translated by John T. Townsend (Hoboken: Ktav, 1989, 1997, 2003).

Murphy, Mark C. "Divine Command, Divine Will and Moral Obligation." *Faith and Philosophy* 15 (1998): 3–27.

Murray, James A. H., editor. *The Oxford English Dictionary* (Oxford: Oxford University Press, 1971; the original ten-volume edition was completed in 1921).

Novak, David. *The Image of the Non-Jew in Judaism: An Historical and Constructive Study of the Noahide Laws* (Toronto: Mellen, 1983).

———. *Natural Law in Judaism* (Cambridge: Cambridge University Press, 1998).

———. *The Theology of Nahmanides Systematically Presented* (Atlanta: Scholars Press, 1992).

Obermann, Heiko. *The Harvest of Medieval Theology: Gabriel Biel and Late Medieval* Nominalism (Durham, N.C.: Labyrinth Press, 1983; first edition, 1963).

Ormsby, Eric. *Theodicy in Islamic Thought: The Dispute over al-Ghazālī's "Best of All Possible Worlds"* (Princeton: Princeton University Press, 1984).

Otto, Rudolf. *The Idea of the Holy: An Inquiry into the Non-rational Factor in the Idea of the Divine and Its Relation to the Rational,* translated by John W. Harvey (London: Oxford University Press, 1969; first German edition, 1917).

Outka, Gene, and John P. Reeder, editors. *Religion and Morality* (Garden City, N.Y.: Anchor, 1973).

Paine, Tom. *Complete Writings,* edited by Philip S. Foner (New York: Citadel, 1969).

Philo. *De Specialibus Legibus,* translated by F. H. Colson (London: Heinemann, 1939; repr. 1960).

Pirkei d^{e}-R. Eliezer, edited by Gerald Friedlander (New York: Hermon Press, 1965).

Plaut, W. Gunter, ed. *The Torah: A Modern Commentary* (New York: Union of American Hebrew Congregations, 1981; first edition, 1962).

Pope, Marvin. *The Anchor Bible: Job* (Garden City, NY: Doubleday, 1980).

Quinn, Philip L. *Divine Commands and Moral Requirements* (Oxford: Oxford University Press, 1978).

Rachels, James. "God and Human Attitudes." *Religious Studies* 7 (1971): 325–37.

Rader, Melvin. *A Modern Book of Aesthetics* (New York: Holt, Rhinehart & Winston, 1961).

Rakover, Nahum. *Law and the Noahides: Law as a Universal Value* (Jerusalem: Library of Jewish Law, 1998).

Ramsey, I. T., editor. *Christian Ethics and Contemporary Philosophy* (London: S.C.M. Press, 1966).

Rashi, *Ḥamishah Ḥumshei Torah: ᶜim Perush Rashi* (Pentateuch with Rashi's Commentary), edited with English translation by Abraham Ben-Isaiah, Morris Charner, Harry Meyer Orlinsky, Benjamin Sharfman (Brooklyn: S.S. & R. Publishing Company, 1977).

Rawls, John. *Political Liberalism* (New York: Columbia University Press, 2005).

Rooney, Paul. *Divine Command Morality* (Aldershot: Avebury, 1996).

Roth, Leon. *Is There a Jewish Philosophy?* (London: Littman Library of Jewish Civilization, 1999).

Saadiah Gaon. *The Book of Theodicy: Translation and Commentary on the Book of Job*, translated by L. E. Goodman (Yale University Press, 1988).

———. *Kitāb al-Mukhtār fī 'l-Āmānāt wa 'l-Iʿtiqādāt* (= *Sefer ha-Nivḥar ba Emunot ve-Deʿot*, The Book of Critically Chosen Beliefs and Convictions, commonly known as the *Emunot vᵉ-Deʿot*), edited by J. Kafih (Jerusalem: Yeshiva University Press, 1970); translated as *The Book of Beliefs and Opinions*, by Samuel Rosenblatt (New Haven: Yale University Press, 1948).

Safrai, S. *The Literature of the Sages* (Assen: Van Gorcum, 1987).

Sagi, Avi. "The Punishment of Amalek in Jewish Tradition: Coping with the Moral Problem." *Harvard Theological Review* 87 (1994): 323–46.

Sagi, Avi, and Daniel Statman. "Divine Command Morality and Jewish Tradition." *Journal of Religious Ethics* 23 (1995): 39–67.

———. *Religion and Morality* (Amsterdam: Rodopi, 1995).

Sarna, Nahum. *The JPS Commentary: Genesis* (Philadelphia: Jewish Publication Society, 1989).

Seeskin, Kenneth. *Autonomy in Jewish Philosophy* (Cambridge: Cambridge University Press, 2001).

Sherif, Mohamed Ahmed. *Ghazālī's Theory of Virtue* (Albany: SUNY Press, 1975).

Shilo, Shmuel. "Lifnim Mishurat Hadin." *Israel Law Review* 13 (1978): 359–90.

Soloveitchik, Joseph B. *Halakhic Man* (Philadelphia: Jewish Publication Society, 1983); first published in Hebrew, *Talpiot* 3–4, 1944.

Spero, Shubert. *Morality, Halakha and the Jewish Tradition* (New York: Ktav/Yeshiva University, 1983).

Spinoza, Baruch. *Opera*, including *Ethica ordine Geometrico Demonstrata* (1677), edited by Carl Gebhardt (Heidelberg: Winter, 1972; first edition, 1925), 4 volumes; *Complete Works*, translated by Samuel Shirley (Indianapolis: Hackett, 2002).

Stern, Josef. "On an Alleged Contradiction Between Maimonides' *Guide of the Perplexed* and *Mishneh Torah*" (in Hebrew), in *Sh^enaton Ha-Mishpat 'Ivri* [Annual of the Institute for Research in Jewish Law] (Jerusalem: Hebrew University, 1989), 283–98; revised and translated in *Problems and Parables of Law: Maimonides and Nahmanides on Reasons for the Commandments* (Albany: SUNY Press, 1998) 49–66.

Susskind, Alexander. *Y^esod ve-Shoresh ha-'Avodah* (The Root and Foundation of Worship), edited by H. Fishel (Jerusalem: Beit Miskhar v^e-Hotza'at S^efarim, 1977).

Tacitus. *Complete Works*, translated by Moses Hadas (New York: Random House, 1942).

Tichener, Edward B. *Lectures on the Experimental Psychology of the Thought-Processes* (New York: Macmillan, 1909).

Tigay, Jeffrey. *The JPS Commentary: Deuteronomy* (Philadelphia: Jewish Publication Society, 1996).

Tiger, Lionel. *Men in Groups* (New York: Vintage Books, 1970).

Tiger, Lionel, and Robin Fox. *The Imperial Animal* (New York: Holt, Rhinehart and Winston, 1971).

Tillich, Paul. *Religionsphilosophie der Kultur* (Berlin: Reuther und Reichard, 1919).

———. *Systematic Theology* (Chicago: University of Chicago Press, 1963).

———. *Visionary Science*, translated by Victor Nuovo (Detroit: Wayne State University Press, 1987).

———. *What Is Religion?* edited by James Luther Adams (New York: Harper and Row, 1969).

Urbach, Ephraim. *The Sages: Their Concepts and Beliefs*, translated by Israel Abrahams (Jerusalem: Hebrew University Press, 1975). 2 volumes.

Vischer, Robert. *Über das optische Formgefühl* (Leipzig: Credner, 1873).

Watt, W. Montgomery. *The Formative Period of Islamic Thought* (Edinburgh: Edinburgh University Press, 1973).

Weiss, Roslyn. "Maimonides on *Shilluaḥ ha-Qen*" (Maimonides on the Release of the Mother Bird). *JQR* 79 (1989): 345–66.

Wensinck, A.-J. *La Pensée de Ghazzālī* (Paris: Maisonneuve, 1940).

Wertheimer, Alan. *Exploitation* (Princeton: Princeton University Press, 1996).

Wilbur, Richard. *Collected Poems 1943–2004* (Orlando: Harcourt, 2004).

Wilson, E. O. *Sociobiology: The New Synthesis* (Cambridge: Harvard University Press, 1975).

Worringer, Wilhelm. *Abstraktion und Einfühlung* (Munich: Piper, 1921); *Abstraction and Empathy*, translated by Michael Bullock (London: Routledge, 1953).

Zank, Michael. *The Idea of Atonement in the Philosophy of Hermann Cohen* (Providence: Brown Judaic Studies, 2000).

———. *Reconciling Judaism and Cultural Consciousness: The Idea of Versöhnung in Hermann Cohen's Philosophy of Religion* (Ann Arbor, Mich.: University Microfilms, 1994).

Zaturenski, Moshe Zalman. *'Eqev Anavah: b^{e}-Birur Halakhot Ga'avah ve-'Anavah* (Vilna, 1902; repr. Jerusalem, 1974).

General Index

stasis, 104
weighed in the balance, 34, 40–41, 57, 76
Deontology, 8, 36, 43, 52, 88
Desecration, 58, 69, 118, 173n. 73
Despair, 180n. 15
Destructiveness, 38, 64, 79, 104–05, 111, 120, 148, 181n. 23
Dialogue and diversity, in Judaism, 133–34
Dignity, 10–21, 26, 29, 32–35, 39, 42, 46–48, 56–57, 59, 69, 73, 76–77, 85, 90–91, 93, 100, 102, 119–20, 135, 137, 183n. 33, 204n. 172
the body, 12, 21, 29
civility, 52
lying, 187n. 56
Disadvantage, 16–17, 28, 96
Disobedience, 74–75
Divine right of kings, 9, 74, 94
Dogma, 35, 38, 53–54, 72–74, 107, 110, 134, 141, 146, 148
Duns Scotus, 100, 152

Eakins, Thomas, 21
Education, 153
Ego, 4–5, 11, 15, 31, 35, 59, 73, 82, 118, 148
mastery of, 10, 65, 154, 174n. 74
Ehrenfeld, Shmuel (Ḥatan Sofer), 173n. 67
Eleazar ben Azariah, 135, 203, 204
Election, 45, 142, 206n. 209
Elenchus, 88–89
Eliezer ben Hyrcanus, 16–17
Empathy, 3–5, 11, 167n. 1
Ephraim of Luntshitz, 198
Epicureans, 5, 33, 48, 55, 107, 109, 151, 194n. 34
Esther, 57
Equality (*See also* Dignity), 11–13, 26, 46, 77
Essentialism, 7, 81, 130, 144
Ethos, 27–29, 34, 40, 57, 66, 103–4, 115–16, 123–30, 138, 155, 168n. 17, 170n. 40
Eudaimonism, 88
Evidence, 6, 40–41, 145, 183n. 33, 197n. 80
Evolution, 5, 7, 9, 66, 67, 74, 78, 99, 134, 168–69
Expedience, 22, 74, 87
Exploitation, 46, 152, 155, 176n. 88, 181n. 28

Fanaticism, 36–37, 54, 56–57
Faith, 35, 63, 76, 103, 118, 121, 127–28, 139–44, 172n. 59, 175n. 86, 179n. 14, 180n. 19
Falk, Ze'ev, 199n. 103, 200n. 115
al-Fārābī, 145
Fear, 5, 11–12, 38, 76, 187n. 59, 193n. 29, 196n. 61
of freedom, 141–43
Fielding, Henry, 79
Formalism, 37, 90–91, 100
Fox, Marvin, 108, 119, 132, 139
Frank, Richard, 144–45
Freedom, 55–56, 73, 118, 149, 177n. 107, 182–83n. 33
Augustine, 86
Baḥya, 33
Kant, 29–30, 48, 153
Lucretius, 55
Paul, 103
Nietzsche, 55–56, 148
Rawls, 21
Romantic, 91, 107
Frost, Robert, 23

Gamaliel II, 131
Gamaliel III, 117
Gandhi, M., 155, 182n. 28
Gates, 176n. 89
Generosity, 16, 28, 37, 45, 49, 60, 66–68, 94–99, 106, 118, 126, 178n. 111
Genocide, 22, 36, 41, 44, 111
Gershom of Mainz (Me'or ha-Golah), 185n. 45
al-Ghazālī, 10, 141–145
Ginzburg, Asher (Aḥad Ha-ʿAm), 180n. 15, 200n. 112
Ginzburg, Louis, 114
God
glory, 33, 38, 66, 93–94
justice, 37, 44, 48–54, 93–96, 104, 110, 135–142, 185n. 49, 186n. 50, 188n. 61, 195n. 44, 197n. 80
mercy, 130, 141

Index Locorum

New Testament

Qur'ān

Classical Rabbinic Sources

Tosafot

Midrash

Philosophers, Poets, and Theologians